A THOUSAND SHADES OF GREEN

A THOUSAND SHADES OF GREEN

SUSTAINABLE STRATEGIES FOR COMPETITIVE ADVANTAGE

Pieter Winsemius
and
Ulrich Guntram

Routledge
Taylor & Francis Group

LONDON AND NEW YORK

First published 2002 by Earthscan

2 Park Square, Milton Park, Abingdon, Oxon OX14 4RN
711 Third Avenue, New York, NY 10017, USA

Routledge is an imprint of the Taylor & Francis Group, an informa business

First issued in paperback 2016

ISBN: 978-1-85383-846-0 (hbk)
ISBN: 978-1-138-99828-5 (pbk)

Typesetting by PCS Mapping & DTP, Gateshead, UK
Cover design by Danny Gillespie
Cover illustration: *A Thousand Shades of Green*, Hannah Winsemius

A catalogue record for this book is available from the British Library

Library of Congress Cataloging-in-Publication Data

Winsemius, Pieter.
A thousand shades of green : sustainable strategies for competitive advantage / Pieter Winsemius and Ulrich Guntram.
p. cm.
Includes bibliographical references and index.

1. Industrial management–Environmental aspects. 2. Environmental management. I. .Guntram, Ulrich, 1954- II. Title.

HD30.255.W56 2002
658.4'08–dc21

2002004805

CONTENTS

PART II INTEGRATED RESPONSE

PART III PROACTIVE RESPONSE

LIST OF ILLUSTRATIONS

FIGURES

TABLES

BOXES

ABOUT THE AUTHORS

Pieter Winsemius is a former scientist, politican and environmentalist and senior partner with McKinsey & Company. As The Netherlands' Minister of the Environment from 1982 to 1986, he developed the framework for the renowned Dutch Green Plan, which builds on the self-responsibility of business. Upon returning to McKinsey, he assumed joint leadership (with Ulrich Guntram) of its global Environmental Practice, where he worked on sustainability issues with a variety of leading corporations and government organizations.

From 1988 to 1998 he also served as chairman of the Dutch Society for Nature Conservation which, with nearly 1 million members, is one of the largest non-governmental organizations in the world.

Mr Winsemius is the author of numerous publications on environmental management and policy-making, including *Guests in Our Own Home* (1990) and, with Jim MacNeill and Taizo Yakushiji, *Beyond Interdependence* (1991). He is a board member of the World Resources Institute, a trustee of the Shell Foundation and, at the time of writing, serves on the environmental advisory councils of Dow Chemicals, Unilever and the Association of the Dutch Chemical Industry, among others. On behalf of the Sustainable Challenge Foundation he is a professor of the management of sustainable development at Tilburg University in The Netherlands.

Ulrich Guntram is chief operating officer of AXA Art Insurance, the competence centre for AXA's worldwide art insurance activities. Since joining the AXA group in 1996 he has held several board positions within the German subsidiary AXA Colonia. In early 2000, Dr Guntram was mandated by AXA's management board to lead a pan-European initiative for building financial portals on the internet and create a new company, AXA European e-Services, based in Paris.

Before moving into financial services, Dr Guntram was managing director of a medium-sized company conducting empirical research in marketing and sociology. Prior to this he spent ten years with McKinsey & Company as a management consultant in Düsseldorf, New York and Stuttgart. As a McKinsey partner he co-founded, with Pieter Winsemius, its Environmental Practice and was co-leader of the European Information Technology and Systems practice.

ACRONYMS AND ABBREVIATIONS

3E	effectiveness, efficiency and equity
3P	Pollution Prevention Pays
ABC	aspirations based change
CAP	community advisory panel
CDM	clean development mechanism
CEO	chief executive officer
CFC	chlorofluorocarbon
CFO	chief financial officer
CO_2	carbon dioxide
DCF	discounted cash flow
DFD	design for disassembly
DFE	design for environment
DFR	design for recycling
DFRE	design for reusability
DSD	Duales System Deutschland
EAB	external advisory board
EAP	environmental action plan
EDF	Environmental Defense Fund (US)
EHS	environment, health and safety
EMP	environmental management programme
EMS	environmental management system
EOA	environmental options assessment
EPA	Environmental Protection Agency (US)
ET	emissions trading
GHG	greenhouse gas
GMO	genetically modified organism
ICOLP	Industry Cooperative for Ozone Layer Protection
ICT	information and communications technology
IIMD	International Institute for Management Development
IRDP	Integrated Rural Development Programme
IUCN	World Conservation Union
IVA	Royal Swedish Academy of Engineering Services
JI	joint implementation
kWh	kilowatt hours
LCA	life cycle analysis

NGO	non-governmental organization
nimby	not in my back yard
NPV	net present value
NO_x	nitrous oxide
OECD	Organisation for Economic Co-operation and Development
PFC	perfluorocarbon
PLC	policy life cycle
PR	public relations
PVC	polyvinyl chloride
R&D	research and development
RCL	Real Change Leaders
SERA	safety, environment and regulatory affairs
SMART	Save Money And Reduce Toxins
SO_2	sulphur dioxide
SO_x	sulphur oxide
STE	strategy–technology–environment
TCF	totally chlorine-free
TQM	total quality management
UN	United Nations
UNCED	United Nations Commission for Environment and Development
UNEP	United Nations Environment Programme
VOC	volatile organic compound
WBCSD	World Business Council for Sustainable Development
WMO	World Meteorological Organization
WOW	Wipe Out Waste
WRAP	Waste Reduction Always Pays
WWF	World Wide Fund for Nature

INTRODUCTION

This book is directed at today's business leaders. Thirty or forty years ago, its subject matter – excellence in environmental management – would, at best, have meant little or nothing to their predecessors; at worst, it would have been laughed at. Today, top managers who scoff at 'soft' environmental issues are as rare as flat-earthers.

The nature of the environmental debate as we know it in the West began to take shape during the last quarter of the 20th century, when our societies were rudely awakened to the reality of the damaging impact of human activities on our environment. Air and water pollution were the issues that produced the loudest wake-up calls. Frightening images of burning rivers, choking smog, oil-drenched birds and poisoned fish – often thrust into the consciousness of an apparently indifferent public by the new activists – were the catalysts for greater environmental awareness.

But, of course, such environmental problems were not new. The devastation wrought by humans on their natural surroundings has a long history, especially since the inception of urban, industrial society. It was only in the 1970s, however, that current environmental attitudes began to take hold. In other words, the environmental activists of the time confronted societies that had changed; societies that, however grudgingly, were receptive to the new perspective.

'What does it mean for the environment?' is now a standard question in most decision-making processes. From political leaders to product developers, farmers to miners, business leaders to scientists, petroleum engineers to civil engineers, from the International Olympic Committee to the city hall and, of course, from food consumers to car consumers, most of us have to some degree incorporated a concern for the environment into our actions and behaviours.

Over the years, however, the environmental arena has evolved. The issues have changed. What had traditionally been thought of as local problems of, for example, water and air pollution have become regional – as in the case of 'acid rain' – or global, as in ozone depletion and global warming. Seas, more than rivers or lakes, are now increasingly subject to eutrophication (over-fertilization due to excessive inflow of phosphates and nitrates). Uncontrolled and highly complex chemical reactions involving man-made substances, such as sulphur dioxide (SO_2), nitrous oxide (NO_x) and ammonia, now contribute to the acidification of our air, soil, water and even buildings. These multi-substance/multi-media issues have become more important than much more manageable single-substance/single-media issues, such as mercury in water. Local threats to specific biospheres have evolved into threats to entire habitats, as exemplified by the rapid disappearance of rainforests. Most importantly, some of these new environmental impacts cause damage that is not only widespread but also irreversible. Whereas previously we could take comfort in the thought that, given proper attention, the environment would recover, this no longer is true. Our activities increasingly have the potential to exceed the carrying capacity of specific ecosystems and perhaps even upset the global equilibrium, and thus ultimately threaten our very existence.

The growth in environmental awareness and understanding has brought with it a greater appreciation of the complexity and wide-ranging nature of the issues – particularly in light of scientific, technological and economic developments – and of the costly and time-consuming processes of tackling them. One result of this is that heated disputes can arise about the nature and dimensions of a particular problem, such as greenhouse gases or genetically modified foods. Also, of course, the international nature of many issues has increased the importance of multilateral cooperation, which is reinforced by corporations' concerns that they could be disadvantaged by regulations that might not affect their foreign competitors. In fact, this worry about 'unlevel playing fields' is one factor that has increasingly drawn business into the environmental arena.

Governments have begun to realize that legislative and regulatory tools cannot always deliver environmental policy objectives: other means, often involving market mechanisms and cooperation with the targeted sectors and other governments, need to be explored. Consumers and business customers, better informed and frequently prompted by the actions of environmental non-governmental organizations (NGOs) and the media, have begun to exercise their market muscle.[1] They are doing this either positively, for instance by purchasing 'green' products, or negatively, by boycotting perceived environmental offenders for their behaviour both at home and abroad.

Finally, the deepening permeation of environmental awareness in people's everyday lives has meant that many, particularly younger people, have started to assess every component of their behaviour, including the organizations they work for, at least partly in terms of the environmental yardstick.

This book is aimed at helping business leaders to understand and better manage their companies in this context, which is undergoing constant development and requires ongoing attention and evolving, creative and flexible management responses. It is one of our basic convictions that the environment has, from a management perspective, evolved from being an operational-cost issue – related to meeting regulatory requirements – to an issue of central strategic concern. In other words, environmental management is increasingly offering companies opportunities for differentiating themselves from the competition and thus, ultimately, of providing their shareholders with more value.

We have chosen to represent this new context graphically using the concept of a 'differentiation space', a concept that we use throughout our discussion (Figure I.1). The space is represented by a box, the dimensions of which are determined by pressures exerted on the company because of evolving regulation and market expectations (vertical axis), and by the time the company has available to respond to these pressures (horizontal axis). It is clear to us that the space is expanding in both dimensions: companies are under greater pressure to respond, and have to look further ahead to scan the environmental horizon to search for opportunities and threats to their competitive position. However, this expanding space also means that companies have greater freedom to develop proper strategic responses. In other words, the differentiation opportunities are growing.

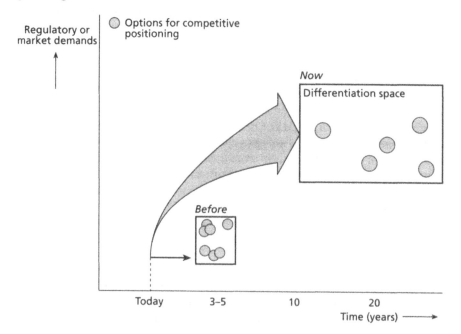

Figure I.1 *Differentiation space*

On the regulatory front, governments are not just implementing more stringent policies; they are also increasingly coming to the conclusion that traditional regulatory tools are inadequate given the complexity of the problems, their sometimes incomplete knowledge, the long timeframe and the number of players involved. Too often, these tools don't, in our shorthand, meet the '3E' criteria: they are not effective (ie they don't meet the objectives), they are not efficient (ie they are not lowest-cost) and they are not equitable (ie their burden is not shared equally among their target group – that is, the companies or the sector targeted by the policy).

Governments are therefore turning to approaches that involve more cooperation with the target groups, in search, whenever possible, of win–win solutions – ie solutions that provide companies with the opportunity for strategic differentiation (and hence economic benefit), while also contributing to solving the environmental issues faced by government. They are also more open to innovative economic mechanisms such as taxes and tradable permits, whereby one company buys so-called 'emission rights' from another to achieve its government-set environmental targets. And, while making environmental regulations more stringent, governments are also broadening their scope – for example, rather than simply curbing a company's emissions, they might make it responsible for its products throughout their life cycles, even after their sale.

On the market front, as has already been mentioned briefly, being good environmental corporate citizens is becoming more and more important for companies. This matters, in the first instance, with regard to meeting consumers' growing demands for environmentally friendly products. This encompasses all phases of a product's life – conception, testing, distribution, consumption and disposal. This reality is reflected in the words of Unilever's Business Group President, Antony Burgmans,[2] who said that his company's brands:

> *are intended to meet the emotional as well as the physical needs of consumers. There is no question that a significant proportion of consumers would not purchase any product if they believed that in doing so they would be contributing to a global environmental problem.*[3]

But it is also becoming clear that companies have a powerful interest in being good environmental corporate citizens in order to elicit the loyalty and pride of their employees, or 'coworkers' to use a term more in harmony with our times. Indeed, increased environmental awareness coupled with tightening labour market conditions means that actual or potential coworkers increasingly expect their employer to aspire to an environmental record beyond the minimum level established by regulation – a record of which they can, as coworkers, be proud. In a nutshell, excellent environmental management is not just fundamental to attracting and retaining customers: it is also the key to attracting and retaining talent.

As we'll see, the range of company responses to this challenge has, to date, been extremely wide. In general, however, managers still tend to be hesitant and reactive in their approach to environmental issues. Most often, environmental responsibilities are not incorporated into normal business practices. The environment is perceived as being somehow separate or abstracted from the real substance of a company's business. Indeed, improved environmental performance is frequently seen as something that is gained at the expense of business performance. The result of this is that companies frequently stumble into damage-control mode when confronted with unexpected NGO, consumer or government action. The damage incurred in the marketplace and in the eyes of the businesses' employees is also typical: neither customers nor coworkers want much to do with them. The echoes of the public outcry following the *Exxon Valdez* accident in Alaska, or Union Carbide's disaster in Bhopal, can still be heard.

This stumbling is not unavoidable. Companies have only themselves to blame for this sort of unpleasant surprise, or 'broadsiding'. Usually, it is the result of seeing the environment as being separate from the company's core business. As we'll see, this not only increases the chances of being broadsided by external actions, but also causes the companies to miss out on important new opportunities offered by the differentiation space. Ultimately, of course, such a less-than-perfect approach to the environmental challenge can lead to an erosion of shareholder value. It is, at best, inadequate; at worst, it can threaten the survival of a business. What companies need is a consistent and well-thought-out environmental strategy: an ad hoc strategy is no strategy at all.

But there is no single, correct environmental strategy applicable to all companies: there are 'a thousand shades of green'. The different ways in which companies respond to the expanding differentiation space depend on a variety of factors. We do not claim to present a magic pill or panacea, nor do we want to suggest that the best endgame to pursue is always the 'greenest' or most progressive. We are convinced, however, that companies must examine their own circumstances (markets, technologies, customers, country presence, etc), understand the choices they face, be wise to the approach of their competitors, have a clear view of their own abilities, and then clearly define their own environmental strategy.

The environmental challenge is, in essence, one of change management. We have written this book in the hope of helping business leaders to understand the challenge at hand, decide what kind of change is most appropriate to their company, and implement the change that is deemed necessary. We feel that, in a surprisingly large number of instances, this process will lead companies to the realization that achieving environmental management excellence is one of the keys to market success and to attracting and retaining quality coworkers, and thus, ultimately, to increasing shareholder value.

***

This book is divided into three parts. Part I is dedicated to an all-embracing discussion of the nature of the environmental management challenge. Chapter 1 examines what lies behind this challenge: why societies have changed and become more receptive to environmental issues, and how companies have responded. Chapter 2 discusses the first steps companies might take to define their 'environmental endgame' and what their environmental management goals should be. Chapter 3 offers an overview of the other main players in the environmental arena, an understanding of which is a prerequisite for excellent environmental management. Chapter 4 details the range of value-creation options available to management in the environmental area, and provides a tool to help managers assess the best options for their selected endgame. Chapter 5 discusses the final steps that managers need to take before embarking on environmental change programmes – that is, validating the endgame, assessing change preparedness and preparing for change.

Parts II and III focus on two of the strategic approaches to environmental management that go beyond a simple, functional response to regulatory and market demands. We call these 'integrated' and 'proactive' responses. Although these reflect an evolution or development in the way companies respond – the proactive strategy being the most advanced – we don't mean to imply that they are always necessarily the most appropriate choices for a company. We do, nevertheless, believe that most companies will ultimately opt for one of these two more advanced strategic approaches, and for this reason Parts II and III are dedicated to their implementation.

Part II, which deals with the integrated approach, is divided into two chapters. Chapter 6 focuses on the implementation of the strategy. Its centrepiece is the environmental management programme, the purpose of which is the full incorporation of environmental issues into business strategy. Chapter 7, in turn, is dedicated to a discussion of partnerships with other players in the environmental arena – a fundamental component of the integrated strategy.

Part III covers the implementation of a proactive strategy, which is undoubtedly the most challenging environmental management response. Chapter 8 discusses how companies can build the inspired corporate communities needed for such an approach. Lastly, Chapter 9 concentrates on another essential ingredient in a successful proactive strategy: trust. The discussion explores how top management, by renegotiating the terms of its coworkers' personal contracts, can create the level of trust needed to ensure the success of its chosen proactive strategy.

***

Throughout the book we refer readers to other relevant literature, in case they are interested in delving more deeply into specific areas. We have also included a number of boxes with discrete material elaborating on points in the text. We do not, of course, pretend to have been exhaustive in providing answers to all questions. The environmental arena is still evolving and the contours of many solutions – and many problems, for that matter – are only vaguely discernible at this time. Since we can all gain from others' experience in the highly challenging and rewarding field of managing environmental issues, we invite readers' comments and suggestions for updating and upgrading the text.

Working on business and the environment has provided us with a source of great professional and personal satisfaction. This book would not have been possible, however, without the inspiration and support of our clients and fellow partners at McKinsey & Company.

We would like to express our special thanks to and respect for our junior colleagues who, as founding members of McKinsey's Environment Practice, volunteered to help chart this relatively unknown territory – sometimes at the cost of considerable personal sacrifices. Their creativity and dedication were a source of energy and pride. Over an eight-year period they included Ron Bloemers, Hans Grünfeld, Jan Karel Mak, Berit Mastenbroek, Ian Simm, Frédérique Six and Mark Weintraub from Amsterdam; Peter Bruun from Copenhagen; Brad Whitehead from Cleveland, Ohio; Ralph Lehmann from Düsseldorf; Massimo Fioruzzi from Milan; Patrick Morin from Paris; Keith Alexander and Andreas Merkl from San Francisco; Walter Hahn from Stuttgart; Mika Kawachi from Tokyo; Christine Service from Toronto and London; and Georg Wiebecke from Zürich.

We'd also like to express our thanks to our former colleagues Josh Dowse, Michael Jung, Mickey Huibregtsen and Jan Karel Mak for their thought-provoking and valuable input to the manuscript. Jim Adams played a very special role through his superb editing of the manuscript. Lastly, Marieke Groeneveld, Angela Zsiray and Denise de Jong provided the support and stability that were essential for completing this task.

PART I

THE CHALLENGE

1

THE ENVIRONMENTAL MANAGEMENT CHALLENGE

Thirty years ago the very idea of a 'Minister of the Environment' was unknown in most countries. Ten years ago, the prospect of environmental activists walking the corridors of world power would have seemed impossible to many. However, today both are a reality, and the former is taken for granted. Non-governmental organizations (NGOs) such as Greenpeace and the World Wide Fund for Nature (WWF) have become household names with huge global followings. Media companies like CNN, together with specialized television channels such as Discovery and National Geographic, give ample coverage to environmental mishaps and successes. Most importantly, 'normal' people, who don't necessarily consider themselves activists, are changing their ways; they separate their household waste, seek out environmentally friendly products and even vote for green political parties. The environment has become part of everyday life in many societies.

What lies behind such changes? What was it that allowed attitudes, actions and even lifestyles promoted by small groups to enter mainstream consciousness? More concretely, why did so many wake up to the threat that their modern, industrial societies posed to the environment, and begin to take actions to thwart it?

We feel that knowing the answers to such questions is an important step in meeting the environmental management challenge faced by corporations. The failure of many well-intentioned, and often very ambitious, environmental management initiatives can be attributed to companies misreading the environmental needs and expectations of their stakeholders – whether internal (coworkers) or external (shareholders and host communities) – as well as of external parties such as consumers, governments or NGOs.

Monsanto's much-discussed and unfortunate introduction of genetically modified soy beans into the European market is a case in point. The action led to furious consumer and, subsequently, political reactions, which eventually had repercussions for the company's

North American and Asian markets. A decade earlier, the German packaging industry was also unpleasantly surprised by its government's introduction of a take-back obligation. This resulted in serious consequences for companies' competitive positions and the establishment of a notoriously inefficient packaging recovery system.

A better grasp of such varied, evolving needs and expectations is also of special importance in an increasingly globalized economy. Companies operating on the international stage need to have a good understanding of environmental needs and aspirations at home and abroad. This is a complex matter, since not all societies share the same attitude – not to mention the fact that stakeholders in one country often have expectations about a business's environmental management in another. There are many such examples, such as Shell's activities in Nigeria, that could be added to the Monsanto case above. In sum, an understanding of stakeholder needs is necessary to grasp the dimensions of the differentiation space, both nationally and internationally.

In this chapter we first examine changing stakeholder needs, and then look at how corporations have so far responded to changes in environmental attitudes.

CHANGING STAKEHOLDER NEEDS

In our view, the familiar 'hierarchy of needs' concept of Abraham Maslow, the US psychologist, provides a useful framework for understanding our evolving environmental needs.[1] Maslow argued that people have a hierarchy of needs that they satisfy sequentially. He suggested that in an ideal world, each individual would progress from the satisfaction of very basic needs to ever-higher ones. At the bottom of the 'staircase', the first priorities in life are food, clothing and shelter. When these are satisfied, our priorities on the second level are safety and security; family and neighbourhood play a major role in this respect. Next, on the third step, follows the need to 'belong' to a relevant group – a job, a religion or a sports team can all contribute to this. On the fourth step, we want to gain the respect of our peers and seniors, and eventually of ourselves. We want to be recognized as excelling at something, whether at school, in sports, in arts or in work. Having established this stable platform at Maslow's fourth step, we are now ready for the ultimate climb towards the fifth level of self-actualization, when we are in harmony with ourselves – ie we are everything we want to be.

Although Maslow's approach is often criticized for being too deterministic, most psychologists agree that people's needs are organized in this kind of hierarchical manner.[2] For our purposes, it is important that the hierarchy of needs seems to apply to the average individual. Similarly, the evolving needs can also be seen to be generally reflected in the behaviour of more or less homogenous groups of individuals, from clubs to corporations to nation-states. This is particularly the case in institutions that embody democratic representation to some degree or other – that is, situations in which the group members' needs can be reflected in the concerns and objectives of the group and its leaders.

We therefore believe that, in broad terms, Maslow's individual framework can be adapted to describe the needs of a collective. It is also clear that among the wide variety of needs applicable to each stage – for example, material, social or psychological – one set of needs, whether individual or collective, is related to the environment. There thus exists what one might call an 'environmental hierarchy of needs'. An understanding of this hierarchy of stakeholder needs provides a particularly useful foundation for corporate leadership in determining environmental management.

The environmental hierarchy of needs

In building an environmental hierarchy of human needs that accompanies the evolution of our general needs, we have found it appropriate to make a distinction between three different aspects of the environment. The environment is, first of all, something we as individuals and as societies have an impact upon – we use its resources and discharge our waste into it, for example. Secondly, the environment is a source of threats to human life. Sometimes these threats arise independently in nature – for instance, in the case of diseases and natural calamities – and sometimes they are, as in the case of global warming, a result of our own behaviour. The third aspect relates to the environment as something that we value for non-economic reasons, for example, as a source of recreation, aesthetic pleasure or inspiration. These three aspects are present in each of the steps of the environmental hierarchy of needs, to which we now turn.[3]

1 Food, clothing and shelter

Our most basic needs are physiological: full stomachs and warmth. Agriculture, flora, animals, minerals and forests all contribute in different ways to meeting these needs. Access to such resources and an adequate physical environment are therefore essential. Satisfying such needs involves environmental management to ensure resource sustainability – eg measures, which are often formalized in traditional taboos and customs, to avoid over-hunting or over-cultivation.[4] In many hunter-gathering and simple agricultural communities this is frequently the case, and the impact of such societies on the environment is minimal: they can, as it were, live off the land and the water.

However, in a number of poor areas of the world today – where millions still struggle to meet these basic physiological needs – this is often not the case. Deforestation, desertification, erosion of marginal agricultural land and recurring delta flooding all provide evidence of the limits of environmental capacity under conditions of sustained population pressure.

People also take measures to protect themselves against the threats presented by the environment. Frequently, instructions or commands relating to various sanitary practices are part and parcel of prevailing religions, promoted by religious leaders and laid down in the canon – for example, the Koran and the Old Testament contain explicit rules for personal hygiene and food consumption. Communities also take initiatives to control animal plagues in order to prevent the spread of contagious diseases. In many parts they raise their buildings on poles or knolls to limit the threat of floods.

An appreciation of the beauty of nature – often a part of religious tradition – is also common. From the elegant animal cave paintings of our distant ancestors and the artful pottery of the Ancient Greeks and Etruscans to the decorative woodwork of today's hunter-gatherer societies, there is ample evidence that, even in difficult material situations, humans have celebrated their physical surroundings.

2 Safety and security

Once our basic needs are met, we focus on safety and security. The impact on the environment at this point is essentially associated with population growth and concentration and, eventually, with industrialization. The development of cities and industry is accompanied by the positive and negative consequences of our 'harvesting' of the environment. The greater scale and specialization of human activities, which take place in more diverse and less coherent societies, often lead to a localized over-burdening of the physical environment – for example, oxygen shortage in surface waters or air pollution – or to the depletion of jointly-exploited resources, as in the case of over-fishing. Indeed, the risk of the depletion or destruction of resources that are jointly exploited but not owned or controlled – the so-called 'tragedy of the commons' – becomes very real at this stage.

Although it is an engine for growth, the environment also becomes the source of threats associated with the concentration of people, namely disease and poor sanitation. Contagious diseases that result from over-crowding, inadequate personal hygiene, poor nutrition and contaminated water spread like wildfire: tuberculosis and cholera are examples. Animal plagues that result from polluted and stagnant waters can threaten the very existence of entire human populations (eg the bubonic plague) or inflict severe physical damage. One example of this in parts of West Africa is river blindness, which is caused by an excessive number of infected blackflies (a type of aphid).

Societies can respond to such threats. In a variety of guises, environmental management focuses on the prevention of contagious diseases through, for example, better housing, safe drinking water, sanitary facilities and sewage systems. Other threats to human health and safety that are directly associated with specific economic activities, such as industry and mining, are also regulated.

People at this secondary stage also begin to value the quality of their living environment as a source of inspiration and recreation. Various art forms, ranging from painting to music, glorify nature in a way that perhaps reflects nostalgia for a (sometimes romanticized) rural existence. Government schemes are undertaken alongside private initiatives in housing, nature conservation and the construction of urban and regional green spaces for recreational purposes.

3 Quality surroundings

When environmental and other safety needs are satisfied, people are free to move up to the third step in the hierarchy of needs. In Maslow's terms this is the need to belong to a relevant community, which implies acceptance and affection. From an environmental perspective, this is expressed in a desire for better-quality surroundings. Ironically, the same processes of industrialization that lifted most of the population to this higher aspiration level also tend to undermine the development of such communities, as they often pose indirect threats to human health. The spreading of toxic substances in water or air, for instance, does not necessarily cause death directly, but can lower people's resistance to deadly disease and famine.

The greater scale of economic activities leads to a shift in the nature of the issues. Whereas previously these were primarily local, they have now become regional or even international, and thus more difficult to tackle; river-basin pollution and acidification in Europe are examples. Moreover, economic expansion and greater wealth give rise to new spatial issues, ranging from the loss of habitat to traffic jams and urban sprawl.

This is the hierarchical step reached by many countries in the West in the last quarter of the 20th century. The debate surrounding environmental management has been thrown wide open. Scientific findings play an important role in alerting the public and, after some delay, political decision-makers.

The greater value that we attach to the quality of our physical environment is reflected in our growing support for NGOs. International institutions such as WWF or Birdlife International, as well as more aggressive groups such as Greenpeace and Friends of the Earth, attract greater levels of support. National organizations like the

National Trust (UK), the Audubon Society and the Sierra Club (US) and Natuurmonumenten (The Netherlands) have also gained prominence. Playing an increasingly active role, these NGOs add to the increasing pressure on politicians to protect the environment.

Government regulation to counteract threats in the sphere of public health tends to be sector-focused: improving the quality of water, air and (later) soil, controlling noise nuisance and managing solid-waste streams are examples. In a sense, the primary goal is to clean up the mess created by the errors, ignorance and negligence associated with industrialization.

The growing awareness of the damaging environmental impacts of unbridled growth leads to increased questioning of the absolute primacy of economic imperatives. The clear spatial division of competing societal functions becomes a central objective: land-use planning and zoning are hotly disputed issues. Nature conservation efforts are broadened to encompass systems of national and international significance.

As we'll see in our corporate response discussion below (see p11), increased external pressure forces corporations to place the environment on their agendas. Following an initial reactive response, companies gain experience and become more comfortable with their new environmental responsibilities, and approach them in a more functional manner.

4 Quality ecosystems

On Maslow's fourth step, the emphasis shifts to the satisfaction of the need for approval, recognition and, eventually, self-respect. The environmental counterpart is an enhanced need to create one's own environment, as well as the realization that resolving environmental issues requires everyone to assume much higher levels of self-responsibility.

The continued viability of ecosystems becomes a principal objective. As organisms are weakened by the excessive presence of foreign substances, and natural habitats are diminished or unbalanced by human activities, entire regions or bodies of water become unable to sustain the life-support systems necessary to the survival of various species. Although direct threats to human health and safety are reduced, we become concerned about the long-term impact of our combined activities. We recognize that we are part of our ecosystems and, moreover, that we have a direct ethical responsibility for the environmental legacy that we will leave for future generations.

People also strive for greater individual wellbeing. As a result, the quality of our rural and urban environment is assessed according to new measures – for example, inner-city renewal plans and suburban housing developments are judged on the basis of their impacts on the identity, beauty and quality of life offered by given areas. The subjectivity of such assessments, of course, further complicates and politicizes the decision-making process.

Since we want to limit the threats we pose to our environment and simultaneously protect the diversity and beauty of our physical surroundings, our ambition is to ensure healthy ecosystems. We begin to understand, for instance, that we can't conserve nature or protect an endangered species simply by fencing off an area: external factors like acid rain in forests and lakes, chemical substances in surface water, or lower groundwater levels due to agriculture activities, demand joint action by many parties. The catchword, therefore, is integration: society has to find new answers in which the desire for economic growth (on the part of, for instance, industry and agriculture) is integrated with the need for environmental protection.

Policy development also gains an international dimension. People recognize that environmental problems and solutions cross community boundaries: they have become environmentally interdependent. Policy-makers, urged on by scientists and NGOs, call for greater international action to address joint environmental problems. Industries and other environmental policy target groups, faced with rapidly escalating environmental costs, increasingly demand level playing fields. Governments, companies and environmental organizations cautiously form tentative alliances with their counterparts in other countries. International initiatives remain vulnerable, however, to national priorities – to interests 'back home'.

Most importantly, during this phase different players in the environmental arena begin to recognize that they all have to join hands and work together. It becomes evident that so-called internal integration – ie increased cooperation between government agencies with environmental responsibilities, or between NGOs and corporations – is no longer adequate. Instead, all the major players in the environmental arena – government agencies, NGOs and corporations – must cooperate with each other. In other words, external integration becomes crucial: new joint approaches are needed to find 3E (effectiveness, efficiency and equity) solutions.[5]

Increasingly, individuals stop thinking solely in terms of their own impacts on the environment, and improved environmental quality becomes an objective in its own right. Companies realize that the environmental challenge might offer business opportunities: some consumers develop a willingness to pay a premium for green products or services. Nature conservation becomes less defensive and turns to nature development instead. When top managers as well as coworkers strive for increased (self-) respect, it becomes personally and collectively rewarding to assume a position of environmental leadership.

5 Sustainability

At the top of the hierarchy, all the needs culminate in a desire for harmony: all stakeholders – current and future – derive what they want to derive from 'their' community, while the institution as a whole is 'at peace' with its surroundings. Environmental threats are well managed, environmental impacts are minimized and the environment is an integral part of the emotional and creative experience of life.

Ever since the 1987 publication of the report of the World Commission on Environment and Development (otherwise known as the Brundtland Commission), the word 'sustainability' has been used to describe this stage. Defined generally as 'meeting the needs of the present without compromising the ability of future generations to meet their own needs', sustainability represents the environmental component of Maslow's need for self-actualization.[6]

True sustainability, as defined above, might never be realized, but, as is the case with many ideal objectives, by pursuing it we will at least come close to it, even if we do not quite reach it. During our pursuit, however, it is important to realize that if we want to follow the road to sustainability, all needs – environmental as well as economic and social – must be met simultaneously.

In Maslow's terms, no individual can be too far ahead along a single dimension, while lagging on the others, and the same applies to society at large. In other words, it will be possible to achieve the desired long-term balance between humans and the environment only when the needs of the world population as a whole are met. If this doesn't happen, human behaviour arising from the pursuit of immediate and urgent needs might result in unsustainable pressures: over-fertilization, deforestation, the exhaustion of scarce mineral and biological resources, and excessive emissions of greenhouse gases.

At an individual level, the internalization of the environment – ie the acceptance of the environmental challenge as an integral part of one's responsibilities, and the translation of this acceptance into everyday behaviour – is a very demanding proposition. It requires a fundamental understanding of environmental developments and of resulting long-term societal needs. To create harmony between thoughts and actions, individuals must think in terms of structural solutions. Like travellers planning a trip, they must know the nature of their ultimate destination and the approximate means of getting there.

The challenge is even greater for large groups of diverse people, such as multinational corporations, which encompass individuals with widely differing needs and hence often lack homogeneity of purpose. Yet, despite the scope of the environmental challenge, an increasing number of corporations have chosen to pursue the ambitious sustainability objective. Setting their aspirations high, they hope to inspire pride and loyalty in coworkers and customers which, in turn, is ultimately reflected in increased shareholder value.

The changes required to reach the highest plateau in the environmental hierarchy of needs will be substantial, and it will be many years before most of the world's population will be able to attain it. Only then will the environmental challenge have been truly addressed, and only then will we be able to enjoy the condition of sustainability, in which humans are in harmony with their global environment.[7]

EVOLVING CORPORATE RESPONSES

The new environmental attitudes now widespread in the West – and increasingly widespread in the more advanced developing countries – reflect the fact that most of these countries have succeeded in stepping up to the third level of the environmental hierarchy of needs. As societies and individuals move up through the hierarchy, all institutions – from governments and businesses to sporting clubs – are affected sooner or later. This is not only because they exist within society and must respond to the changes going on around them, but also because their own members will increasingly exert pressure for change.

Among society's numerous institutions, business organizations – in contrast, for example, to educational or religious institutions – have typically been on the front line of debates occasioned by changes in attitudes towards the environment. This stands to reason, since most environmental concerns are sparked by the impact of economic development on the environment, a process that, historically, has primarily involved the extraction and transformation of natural resources and the production of waste. As major economic players, businesses are thus destined to play a central role in the environmental arena.

Four corporate responses

When we examine how corporations have responded to the environmental developments over the past two to three decades, we can distinguish four responses (Figure 1.1).

1 Reactive

Corporate responses to environmental scandals and consequent regulation are typically reluctant, technical and compliance-oriented. New environmental restrictions are seen as constraints on their operations and as obstacles to the development of shareholder value. In essence, the reactive response runs thus: 'We think this is all

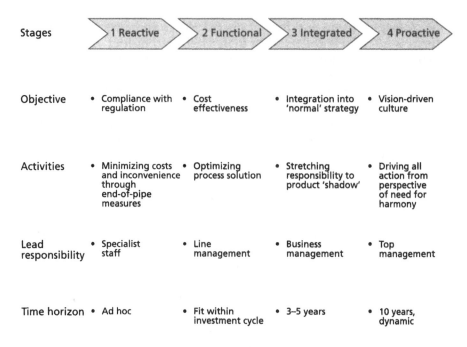

Stages	1 Reactive	2 Functional	3 Integrated	4 Proactive
Objective	• Compliance with regulation	• Cost effectiveness	• Integration into 'normal' strategy	• Vision-driven culture
Activities	• Minimizing costs and inconvenience through end-of-pipe measures	• Optimizing process solution	• Stretching responsibility to product 'shadow'	• Driving all action from perspective of need for harmony
Lead responsibility	• Specialist staff	• Line management	• Business management	• Top management
Time horizon	• Ad hoc	• Fit within investment cycle	• 3–5 years	• 10 years, dynamic

Figure 1.1 *Development stages in corporate response*

greatly exaggerated: the measures are overkill and the issues are not scientifically proven. But if the government tells us to do it and all our competitors are forced to do the same, we will be loyal citizens and we'll do it.' Such corporations see environmental planning as an ad hoc process of 'staying out of trouble' by keeping regulators and consumers happy, while minimizing the costs and inconvenience of doing so.

Staff specialists are generally given responsibility for making sure that operations comply with standards and procedures. This usually involves the implementation of 'end-of-pipe' solutions – eg add-on features to existing facilities, such as filters on river outlets, scrubbers (apparatus for purifying gases or vapours) in smokestacks, or catalytic converters in car exhaust systems. This minimal reaction is due not only to management reluctance, but also to the fact that corporate or divisional staff departments – usually consisting of engineers and scientists – often lack the support, resources and credibility required to address the root causes of environmental risk or waste generation, or to enable their company to pursue environmental business opportunities.

While responding minimally, many companies, individually or collectively, also dedicate significant resources to aggressive lobbying and/or legal campaigns against increased regulation. Such actions are particularly common in the US, where companies are not so accustomed to non-market conflict situations. Thus, when threatened by NGO or government action, they often resort to the courts before considering other approaches.

Commenting on his company's early reactive response, Frank P Popoff, Chief Executive Officer (CEO) and Chairman of Dow Chemical, observed:

> *When the chemical industry found itself in the centre of an environmental outcry in the 1950s, its initial response – ours too – was to deny everything: 'What do you mean, we are jeopardizing the planet?' This response was not very satisfactory because we kept shouting at – and talking past – each other.*
>
> *Soon we realized that even though we could reject some of the more egregious claims, we needed to address the rational arguments. We then moved to the data stage, where we got tied up in meaningless debates: 'My data are better than yours.' It was a slight improvement over the first stage – at least we were communicating with one another – but it failed to satisfy people. They either challenged the data or said, 'You don't understand. We don't want data, we want improvements – and improvements that address our concerns, not yours.'*[8]

2 Functional

As companies gain experience and become more comfortable with new environmental realities and their new responsibilities, they gradually shift to a more positive attitude: 'Okay, if we have to do it, let's be smart about it: let's do it cost-effectively.' This is doubly sensible, since most of the easy-to-implement measures will have been carried out – the 'low-hanging fruit' has been picked – and the cost of the next generation of regulations escalates rapidly.

Governments, too, start to recognize the limitations of initial end-of-pipe solutions. Thus, their somewhat confrontational approaches tend to soften, and they become more open to proposals from industry about process-integrated solutions that yield the same or better environmental improvement, but at a much lower cost. Significantly, they also modify their regulatory approaches. Rather than relying on the prescription of means (such as 'best technical means'), they specify targets (such as emission-level deadlines).

Given the greater financial stakes, line management now assumes responsibility – within the boundaries of the current business – for developing solutions that meet governmental criteria as efficiently as possible. Standardized environmental management systems (EMSs), for instance, bring best practices to the shop floor.[9] Although some solutions may require process redesigns that are integrated into multi-year investment plans, most are of a more functional nature. Within line organizations, the focus tends to be on optimizing the existing production configuration.

One might say, however, that these changes are not fundamental. The response is still primarily technocratic and limited. It is often conducted in tandem with more sophisticated lobbying efforts to 'defeat' new regulation. In other words, companies do not join the authorities or the NGOs in thinking about possible win–win solutions. Their interaction with outside parties is at arm's length: 'You do your job – ie shaping policy or raising awareness – and we'll do ours – ie implementation.'

On the other hand, things are not always so black and white, and the divisions aren't always so clear-cut. For instance, some individuals become increasingly conscious of the need for good-quality ecosystems (the fourth step of the environmental hierarchy of needs). In practice, this means they are more and more ready to build bridges to the other players, based on their understanding of and respect for their imperatives. However, these people are still in the minority, and are slightly ahead of their time.

One example of such a person is Peter van Duursen, President of Shell Netherlands, who noted:

> *It is essential that government and industry develop a common strategy in which the long term objectives should be the politicians' discretion, but not after having had an intense dialogue with industry. A constructive attitude towards those authorities, who subsequently will be developing the necessary, new, and mostly more stringent legislation should be adopted. Primarily to prove the position of industry as a key participant in finding solutions to the issues raised.*[10]

3 Integrated

As attitudes towards the environment start to encompass a broader conception of ecosystems (the fourth hierarchical step), the various players in the environmental arena realize that in order to arrive at 3E solutions to environmental problems, they have to cooperate. Thus, governments and NGOs begin to reach out to industry. The solutions have to be good for the environment and, at the very least, better for business than simple compliance with the regulations. Changing societal needs are also reflected in the expansion of the differentiation space along the market axis: consumer choices begin to exert an influence on corporate behaviour.

In a 1988 speech, Chevron Chairman George Keller said that 'compliance means that the moral initiative lies elsewhere – outside of industry'.[11] The time had come, he added, for industry to move forwards. As businesses make this transition from functional to integrated responses, industry leaders begin to look beyond the boundaries of their current business to find more fundamental answers to environmental questions. Such leaders earn the right to participate with other parties in the development of the most appropriate solutions. They incorporate environmental considerations in their business strategies, and establish partnerships – not just with other private enterprises but also with government agencies and even NGOs. Most importantly, as they strive to be respected as good corporate citizens, they increasingly accept environmental responsibility for their activities.

DuPont's Chairman and CEO, Edgar S Woolard, put the case for an integrated response thus:

> *No other industry has carried a greater burden of environmental regulation than the chemical industry. Yet the chemical industry remains one of the most competitive industries in the United States – a leading exporter with a positive balance of trade... Environmentally innovative companies have gotten that way through the thorough integration of environmental innovation with operations. The most successful companies are those that no longer see environmental compliance as a problem to be handled by isolated specialists within the company. Rather, they factor environmental opportunity into every business plan as a means of gaining competitive advantage.*
>
> *These companies have made the transition from the regulation-driven corporate environmental programmes of the 1970s and 1980s to the corporate-leader-driven challenges of the 1990s. They are now moving into the customer-and-market-driven integrated approach that will characterize corporate environmental progress in the 21st century. At DuPont, we trace this evolution from our old policy of 'meet all laws and regulations' to a more recent one of 'meet the public's expectations' to our current policy of 'the goal is zero' for all waste emissions.*[12]

Interestingly, Woolard found that it was actually easier to motivate the 80 top managers to commit to zero emissions than it had been, five years earlier, to motivate them to commit to an 80 per cent reduction in waste.[13] Apparently, the combination of experience with ambitious and extreme targets inspired the commitment.

Government policy instruments also reflect the change towards a more integrated approach. Regulations emphasize self-responsibility for assessing (potential) environmental impacts: environmental impact assessments and strict testing requirements for chemical substances prior to their commercialization are examples. As they move away from direct regulation, new policy measures make increasing use of economic instruments such as levies, taxes and deposits. The thinking becomes even broader as consideration is given to tradable emissions rights, for example, which are aimed at making measures more efficient and/or integrating environmental costs into market prices.

Business managers increasingly acquire responsibility for integrating the environment into the strategies and operations of their units. The policy horizons also begin to stretch: measures are taken with a view to environmental benefits 10 to 20 years down the road. Further, having learnt lessons from previous environmental experiences – when process or product waste came back to haunt the erstwhile producers, in highly expensive soil clean-up efforts, for instance – they adopt 'cradle-to-grave' approaches, whereby they accept responsibility for their product even after it has been sold. They also establish new partnerships with suppliers, customers and especially competitors to pursue joint goals, such as waste collection and recycling, green product labelling or contractual agreements (covenants) with governments.

Eventually, these companies broaden their view of their environmental impact to include the 'ecological shadow' cast by their activities.[14] This extends the perception of environmental impact to encompass a company's purchases and transportation on the upstream side of its value-delivery system. Moreover, these companies come to realize that incremental improvements, which sufficed in the past, are no longer appropriate. They recognize that major technological and/or organizational changes are required to meet the regulatory and market demands.[15] The growing pressure from customers and, particularly, coworkers exercising their power in product and labour markets causes the differentiation space to expand rapidly. As a result, these companies adapt their business strategies and, when necessary, seek to exploit business opportunities arising from environmental developments.

4 Proactive

Although there are clear signs that companies are beginning to toy with this approach, proactive environmental management is still mostly a projection; we expect it to become an increasingly common corporate response as stakeholders push more and more for sustainable solutions.

As detailed in Part III, the proactive response requires deep organizational change. It involves the transformation of the business culture into one driven by an environmental vision, in which all management actions are directed by a quest for shareholder value through harmony with the environment. The path to sustainability can be scary, since the very nature of the business might be challenged. Maybe the service or product – say, cars or detergents (as we know them today) – is inherently incompatible with sustainability if the global atmosphere or waters are not able to carry the burden.

The quest for sustainability will become increasingly significant in the light of current environmental reality and public awareness of the global environmental challenge. Threats to global ecological security are not hard to find. Indeed, they are increasingly real: in addition to the generally acknowledged destabilization of the atmosphere caused by ozone depletion and global climate change, there is now a growing preoccupation with the possible destabilization of the oceans, which would have huge implications for virtually all aspects of life. The alarm signals are evident, ranging from changing currents to excessive algae growth, and from the breakdown of immune systems in certain species to the rapidly increasing frequency of and damage caused by hurricanes.[16] If the current levels of world population and development can generate such effects, imagine the impact as both factors increase in the future. Ultimately, sustainability is not simply a privilege, a reward for having reached the top of the hierarchy: it is also a matter of planetary survival.

In response, both governments and the public expect business – particularly large multinationals – to assume a significant share of responsibility by virtue of their impacts on the environment and the resources they command. National governments lack the international clout to go it alone. For their part, multilateral institutions such as the United Nations and the World Bank, although they are making progress, are not up to the task of designing and implementing the 3E policies needed for dealing with these complex issues. Governments thus increasingly need to ask business to assume a position of co-leadership.

At the same time, customers and coworkers – both potential and actual – increasingly demand that the corporations they have dealings with embark on proactive environmental management. Top managers will become more and more aware of this challenge, and will respond by more openly linking their concerns as environmentally-aware citizens with their business responsibilities. As Frank Popoff said: 'To win the hearts and minds of people in all countries, we know we must be "up-front" and "out in front" on the great environmental issues ahead. And above all else, we must continue to demonstrate not just compliance, but leadership beyond compliance.'[17]

Businesses will also become increasingly conscious of their competitive self-interest in sustainability: the differentiation space will become compelling. Further, a truly proactive response that allows a company to exist in harmony with the long-term needs of sustainability would ultimately free up resources and the intellects, allowing them to focus on other priorities.

Thus, companies with this mindset will no longer set up 'crash' programmes to deal with immediate problems such as upcoming regulation or competitive action, as is typical of the reactive response. Nor will they be satisfied with the excellent implementation skills of a perfected functional response. Even the refocusing of an organization to achieve a medium-term winning formula, motivating its business managers to pursue best practice objectives through a carefully planned and executed action programme, is insufficient. Rather, they will build corporate attitudes and values that stimulate all individuals throughout the organization to bring their everyday behaviour into line with the corporate environment-driven vision. It is this long-term vision that drives the medium-term strategy, which in turn serves as the basis for practical short-term action plans.

Robert B Shapiro, Chairman and CEO of Monsanto, gave this example of a proactive approach:

> *Monsanto makes nylon fibre, much of which goes into carpeting. Each year, nearly 2 million tons of old carpeting go into landfills, where they constitute about 1 per cent of the entire US municipal solid-waste load. Nobody really wants to own carpet; they just want to walk on it. What would happen if Monsanto or the carpet manufacturer owned that carpet and promised to come in and remove it when it required replacing? What would the economics of that look like? One of our customers is exploring that possibility today. It might be that if we got the carpet back, we could afford to put more cost into it in the first place in ways that would make it easier for us to recycle. Maybe then it wouldn't end up in a landfill.*
>
> *We're starting to look at all our products and ask, What is it people really need to buy? Do they need the stuff or just its function? What would be the economic impact of our selling a carpet service instead of a carpet?*[18]

Current status

Between 1992 and 2000, McKinsey & Company conducted in-depth, multilevel surveys of 16 major corporations in a wide variety of sectors in countries belonging to the Organisation for Economic Co-operation and Development (OECD), in an effort to assess where their environmental management stood.[19]

The surveys reveal that half of the companies have a functional approach to their environmental management.[20] Those surveyed cite 'complying with regulations' and 'preventing incidents' as their key environmental concerns, while factors such as 'enhancing a positive corporate image', 'integrating environment into business strategy' and 'realizing new market opportunities' are rated much lower. Maintaining a traditional, production-oriented approach to environ-

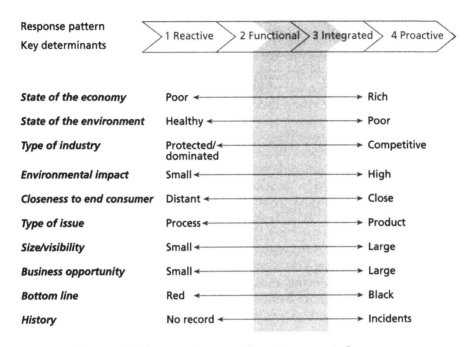

Figure 1.2 *Determinants of environmental response*

mental issues, they focus on incident prevention and regulatory compliance. Considering 'the environment' as a cost factor only, they worry primarily about achieving the most efficient solutions. Their top management is therefore only marginally involved, if at all, in the environmental arena.

Nevertheless, seven of the surveyed companies pursued an integrated approach, and one company could even be said to have a proactive one. The question is: Why did these companies move on from the functional approach? The surveys do not answer this directly, but reveal ten different factors that are positively correlated with the likelihood that a company will make the transition from a functional approach to an integrated one (Figure 1.2).

At the top of the list of factors that correlate strongly with more evolved environmental responses are the state of the economy and the environment within a given region. If a region is affluent, the environment is given a high priority. If the environment is under heavy pressure from population and economic activity, it also tends to be the focus of more attention. These factors explain why many leading environmental corporations are based on the West and East Coasts of the US and in Northwestern continental Europe (Germany, Scandinavia, The Netherlands and Switzerland).

The third determinant is sector-specific: it appears that the more openly competitive an industry, the more evolved its environmental response. Sectors that are specially protected tend to have more reactive management approaches. For instance, state-owned or government-sponsored sectors, such as utilities, or ones that are politically sensitive (as sources of employment in poor regions, or because of national considerations, as in the case of the defence and high-tech sectors) are often more reactive; apparently, if push comes to shove, they have greater access to friends in high places and thus avoid having to do more than the minimum. Similarly, corporations in monopolistic or oligopolistic industries often are quite effective in keeping their differentiation space small. They discourage competitors from launching new market-driven initiatives by using market discipline and aggressive lobbying to stymie new regulations. In many countries, the car industry and the energy sector qualify on both these counts.

The next three determinants often go hand in hand. When trying to increase the priority that a population gives to the environment, it is important for politicians and environmental activists alike to focus people's attention, and hence regulatory and market forces, on understandable 'targets'. Thus, the higher the current environmental impact of a sector, the more advanced its response. Similarly, the closer a sector is to the end-consumer, the more evolved its approach tends to be. Also, the more the industry is product- rather than process-intensive, the more likely it is to have an integrated response.

All of these last three factors are especially important when accompanied by a fourth: company size and visibility. Examples of companies combining impact with visibility include mammoth multinationals in the (petro-) chemical industry. Those combining closeness to the consumer with visibility include food businesses (eg producers of branded goods, fast-food chains and supermarkets). The coatings segment of the chemical industry offers examples of large companies that have more evolved approaches because of their product-orientation (eg the elimination of cadmium and lead from paint, and the introduction of water-based paints), in contrast to other more process-oriented segments, like basic chemicals.

The last two determinants are again sector- and/or company-specific. Financial performance almost always has a significant influence: when the bottom line is red, resistance to the costly environmental measures associated with an evolved response is high. The US and Southern European car industries provide vivid illustrations of this. As a rule, companies are not successful because they are green: they are green because they are successful.

Finally, a further determining factor may be applicable: involvement in environmental incidents tends to push a company or sector into the forefront of environmental policy sensitivity. Novartis' attitude reflects its component company Sandoz's pollution of the Rhine, and Shell's attitude reflects the fall-out from its attempt to dump the Brent Spar oil production platform.

In summary, the surveys confirm that regulatory and public pressure have greatly influenced the position and the shape of the differentiation space. Minimum regulatory requirements tend to be demanding in countries that are rich and heavily polluted, and in sectors that are characterized by open competition and solid economic returns, high environmental impact and closeness to the end-consumer. The differentiation space open to companies in such countries, however, is also relatively large. If they can develop strategies that better satisfy regulatory or market demands, and in addition have a greater value to their stakeholders, they can significantly strengthen their competitive position.

***

Defining the appropriate environmental management approach for a company is not necessarily complicated. Nevertheless, company environmental staff and consultants frequently point to the difficulty of persuading top management to assess the issue. Many business leaders still appear to be satisfied with the functional approach, sometimes combined with the added effort of spending half a day every year on 'the state of the environment' and presenting an annual corporate environmental report.

It is our conviction that the price of such an attitude can be high, in terms of both real and opportunity costs. Environmental questions have clearly taken on strategic significance in most industries, and should be accorded appropriate attention. In essence, what this means is that companies should acquire a good understanding of the dimensions of their own particular differentiation space – that is, the regulatory and market pressures they can be expected to face over time. This assessment process provides them with an outline of the differentiation possibilities they might face and, ultimately, an idea of what their environmental management objectives are – their 'endgame', to use an analogy from chess.

The appropriate strategy might require a functional, integrated or a proactive response. Whatever the case, it is important that top managers examine their company's particular differentiation space before consciously deciding on a particular course for their environmental management strategy. This assessment process is the subject of Chapter 2.

2

TOWARDS AN ENVIRONMENTAL MANAGEMENT ENDGAME

No company is an island. Each operates in a societal context and is obliged sooner or later, as our previous discussion has shown, to adapt to changes and demands occurring both outside the company and inside its walls, among its coworkers. It is our objective in this chapter to help companies assess this context and the manner in which they are likely to evolve in the future, as a basis for the definition of their environmental management strategy.

The approach we propose is that a company should take two steps towards defining its environmental endgame. First, scan the environmental horizon to determine an initial mental model of its particular differentiation space; and, second, select its preferred endgame within that space (Figure 2.1).

SCANNING THE ENVIRONMENTAL HORIZON

'The most certain prediction for the future is that something will happen that we now have predicted.' The words of Bernie Goldstein of Rutgers University capture a truth about forecasting.[1] Though many of the specifics of the environmental horizon present a major forecasting problem, ultimately one development is predictable. As elaborated in our discussion of the environmental hierarchy of needs, we feel that the momentum of people's environmental demands, particularly in the West, will – barring serious economic or political setbacks – move in the direction of a quest for sustainability. Pressures in favour of sustainability will be more and more constant. When contemplating a new environmental management strategy business leaders should take this into account, whatever the particular approach they choose.

Actually, many business leaders worldwide do recognize this – at least in theory. In interviews and surveys, an overwhelming majority

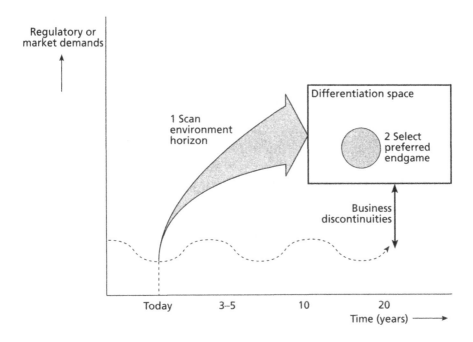

Figure 2.1 *Defining the environmental endgame*

characterize the environmental challenge as one of the central issues of the 21st century. Publications, for instance, by the International Chamber of Commerce[2] and the World Business Council for Sustainable Development (WBCSD)[3] as well as respected members of the business community also provide significant evidence of this awareness.[4] Roberto Guizueta, CEO of Coca-Cola, noted for instance that:

> *While we were once perceived as simply providing services, selling products and employing people, business now shares in much of the responsibility for our global quality of life. Successful companies will handle this heightened sense of responsibility quite naturally, if not always immediately. I say this not because successful business leaders are altruistic at heart. I can assure you many are not. I say it because they will demand that their companies will remain intensely focused on the needs of their customers and consumers.[5]*

Still, even in the most environmentally advanced companies, top management's time horizon tends to be short.[6] Managers are often blindsided by a development they underestimated or ignored and, when eventually convinced of the need to act, embark on crash programmes to meet the new regulatory or market demands. The notion of sustainable development thus would appear a fairly distant consideration in their everyday behaviour. What such managers need, in the first instance, is a better sense of what lies on their horizon and how these developments might affect the corporate differentiation space. In practice, three substeps can be distinguished in this process: determine the themes (if any) that are likely to affect their company's environmental horizon; scope the corporate 'environmental profile', that is, gain a clear sense of the current impact that the company has on the environment; and, finally, develop a mental model of the company's relevant differentiation space.

Scanning for environmental themes

While always bearing in mind the underlying growing pressure for sustainability, top management should first focus on the environment at a more detailed level – that is, on those themes that have the greatest impact on their company. In most cases, they'll find that a combination of in-house and external environmental experts can usually quite quickly produce a first overview.[7]

A useful tool in this forecasting process is what we call 'triple-focus scanning'. The idea is straightforward and can be represented simply as a cube. Environmental developments can be looked at from three different perspectives: namely, environmental themes (eg ozone depletion, soil pollution or packaging waste); countries/ regions; and industries (Figure 2.2).

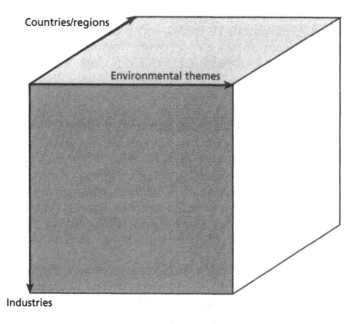

Figure 2.2 *Triple-focus methodology*

Each dimension of the cube has its own experts and means of communication. Specialized scientific institutions, environmental agencies, multilateral organizations and, occasionally, suppliers of products or services use a finely meshed system of topical publications and conferences to share and refine insights with respect to environmental themes. Expertise regarding the power game in the environmental arena in a specific country or region resides with, for instance, governments, NGOs, industry associations and market leaders. Information regarding the developments within an industry sector can be gained from the global or regional market leaders and industry associations, but also (a much-underestimated source) from technical consultants and various sector departments within government. Once again, sector publications and industry forums provide quite sophisticated channels of communication.

The above three dimensions clearly are interdependent. Each has its own dynamic and also exerts its own influence on the others. For instance, when environmental scientists gain new insights on a theme such as ozone depletion, national policies and industry approaches are adapted accordingly. Similarly, when automobile manufacturers develop a super-efficient engine, this will have an impact on opinions about global warming and national energy policies, for instance. These inter-relationships are evident. What is problematic, however, is that many signals on future environmental developments are weak and diffuse.

Using a small team to gather – drawing on interviews and other sources – and analyse insights from each of the three dimensions, the triple-focus methodology allows inputs to be checked against each other. In itself, such information often seems too feeble to allow for any meaningful conclusions – overly tentative, insufficiently fact-based or even self-serving. However, when critically analysed and weighted (eg according to its depth of insight and its role in the policy-making process), it can be amalgamated to provide a solid basis for medium- and longer-term business planning. In this way, the inevitable redundancies resulting from looking at the same subject from three different perspectives are not actually a negative by-product but a core element of the methodology. Much like the X-ray scanning equipment that is used to pinpoint brain tumours, the triple-focus methodology allows a project team to translate weak and confusing signals into powerful information with respect to the endgame demands of each of the main players and the business discontinuities that might result.

As far as the environmental themes dimension is concerned, we would further propose, in an effort to facilitate this scanning process, that the diverse and complex group of issues be first broken down into their three essential categories, as follows.

	Eutrophication	Disruption	Dispersion of toxics	Disposal of waste
Effect	• Certain species favoured over others, affecting flora and fauna	• Noise, smell, vibration and visually offensive buildings • Magnetic fields	• Deposits of heavy metals and other toxic substances affecting people, flora and fauna	• Increasing amounts of waste to dispose of, causing – diffusion of environmental toxins – reduction of green spaces – squandering of natural resources
Cause/ source	• Emissions of nitrogen and phosphorous compounds – industrial combustion – sewage – agriculture	• Industrial plant, mining, livestock • High voltage transmission lines (magnetic fields)	• Stable chemical compounds of low degradability – pesticides – cleansing agents • Heavy metals from surface processing, ore mining and processing, and waste depots	• Household, business and industrial waste
Solution	• Improved balance between emissions and the environment's capacity to absorb nitrogen and phosphorous compounds • Reduced nitrogen emissions – reduced energy use – low-nitrogen fuels – improved combustion technology and sewage treatment	• Improved filtering, noise suppression and screening • Design influenced by, and in accord with, the needs of the environment	• Reduced emissions of stable compounds	• Recycling • Improved combustion processes • Reduced material flows

	Acidification	Global warming	Ozone depletion
Effect	• Higher concentrations – damage to plants, animals, people and inanimate objects • Low concentrations – altered living conditions, diminished biological diversity	• Increasing global average temperature – rise in sea-level – altered conditions	• Higher doses of UV radiation – damage to skin and eyes – damage to animals and plants
Cause/ source	• Acidifying gases – sulphur dioxide: combustion of fossil fuels – nitrogen oxides: motor vehicles, combustion – ammonia: livestock	• Greenhouse gases and emission sources – carbon dioxide: combustion of fossil fuels – CFCs: coolants, dry cleaning compounds – methane: landfills, livestock – nitrogen oxides: motor vehicles, agriculture	• CFCs: coolants, dry cleaning compounds, degreasing agents, aerosol propellants • Halogens in fire extinguishers • Nitrogen oxides from airplanes
Solution	• Short term – liming – filtering emissions • Long-term – reduced energy use – low-sulphur and low-nitrogen fuels – improved combustion technology	• Reduced energy use • Renewable energy sources • Improved combustion technology • Phasing out CFCs	• Phasing out CFCs and similar substances

Source: Royal Swedish Academy of Engineering Sciences (IVA); McKinsey & Company; World Wide Fund for Nature (WWF)

Figure 2.3 *Major pollution themes*

1 **Depletion** themes are those primarily related to the finiteness of natural resources. Increasingly the source of concern in the minds of many environmentalists and policy-makers, but hardly appreciated outside these circles, this category encompasses the depletion of minerals, fresh water, soil (through degradation) and biological resources (eg through over-fishing).
2 **Pollution** themes essentially refer to the quality of resources. In most industrialized countries, a short 'hit-list' of seven issues – ranging from eutrophication to ozone depletion – covers the generally recognized targets of environmental policy; these are detailed in Figure 2.3.
3 **Expulsion** themes concern the diminishing variety of natural resources. Most attention in this category is focused on the decrease in biodiversity (ie number of animal or plant species).[8]

Naturally, the list of environmental themes is constantly evolving, as certain issues become resolved and others, previously unknown or non-existent, become the focus of concern; ozone depletion and global climate change are, for example, relatively new in this way.

Scoping the environmental profile

All products of human economic activity pass through a life cycle, from the initial resource usage, through product shaping, to product usage, and ending with either disposal (eg dumping or incinerating) or reuse/recycling. In the latter instance, the product (in case of reuse) or the substances (in case of recycling) may go on to participate in another cycle. This amounts to an extended vision of the traditional business system, and is appropriate for companies that are assessing their environmental impact.

In its most basic form, the cycle can be visualized as an integrated chain (Figure 2.4). Such chains are composed of at most six links. Generally, however, companies are involved in a single link only. Still, through their pull over suppliers and their push towards customers, they cast an environmental shadow on activities elsewhere in the chain.

This integrated chain provides the context for the development of a company's environmental profile, which expresses the overall impact of a company – or a business unit, production configuration, process or a product – by recording performance in terms of each relevant environmental theme.

The approach to the environmental profile we recommend is fairly straightforward, and generally requires no major new studies. The direct impact of a company's activities with reference to each theme can often be simply measured – eg emissions, waste streams, energy consumption. The 'extended shadow', or indirect impacts along the rest of the chain – for example, impacts associated with the inputs used by the company in its processes and the outputs it produces –

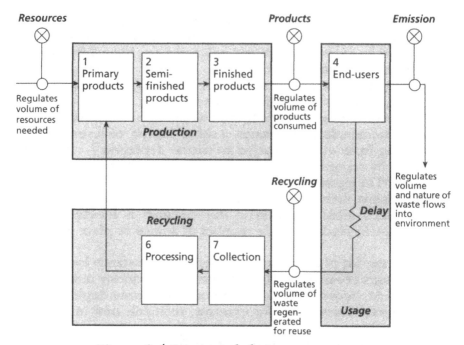

Figure 2.4 *Integrated chain management*

must also be taken into account. As these impacts tend to be difficult to measure, companies must frequently settle for estimates.

It is important that a company's impact with regard to each environmental theme is quantified using a common unit of measurement. Thus, for example, the relevant unit for evaluating the impact on global warming would be 'tons CO_2 (carbon dioxide)-equivalent'. A total impact of 'x' tons of CO_2-equivalent could reflect a combination of 'y' tons of CO_2 emitted plus 'z' tons of chlorofluorocarbons (CFCs). The latter volume can be expressed in terms of the amount of CO_2 that would have the equivalent impact on global warming. Also, to gain a perspective on the relevance of a specific impact and the associated likelihood of a company becoming a prime target or beneficiary of changing regulatory or market demands, the impact regarding each theme should be expressed in relative terms: for instance, as a percentage of the total impact produced by a specific country or industry.

An example of the sort of environmental profile that results from this procedure, in this case for a public utility, is shown in Figure 2.5.[9] Although the profile can be calculated in great detail, often drawing on extensive environmental analyses that have already been performed by staff specialists or by technical consultants, the level of detail shown in this example generally suffices for general scanning purposes.

The protrusions in the profile highlight the main themes that should be the focus of top management's attention. Indeed, experi-

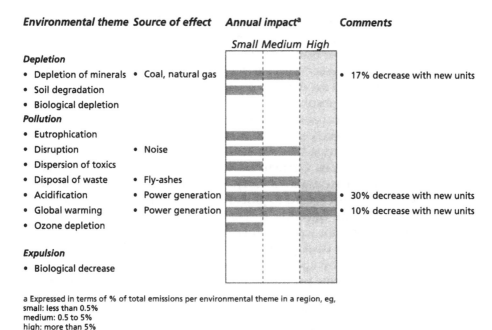

a Expressed in terms of % of total emissions per environmental theme in a region, eg,
small: less than 0.5%
medium: 0.5 to 5%
high: more than 5%

Figure 2.5 *Environmental profile illustration: public utility*

ence shows the environmental impact is generally dominated by just
a few themes. For this reason we do not recommend aggregating the
assessments into a single index. Although such aggregation has
obvious appeal, it inevitably requires a subjective weighting system,
usually drawn up by experts. Such weighting thus adds a 'black box'
element that invites general management to delegate this – to them –
incomprehensible task to functional staff. This is not desirable:
managers should be made truly responsible, even if this involves
doing some in-depth homework.

Developing a model for the differentiation space

Having identified the themes that are most relevant to the company,
management can then turn its attention to anticipating how these
are likely to evolve in the future. The question, in essence, is: to what
extent will the evolution of the various themes affecting the company
lead to regulatory and market pressures on environmental management, and perhaps open up differentiation opportunities?
Management thus must scope the contours of the corporate differentiation space by addressing the question: to what extent does the
combination of potential regulatory or market demands on the one
hand, and their anticipated timing on the other, allow the company
to differentiate itself in a positive manner from the competition and
hence provide shareholders with value?

To begin with, a sense of the urgency of each of the themes – and thus of the timing of regulatory or market pressure – can be gained by assessing the available carrying capacity of the environment with regard to the particular theme. This capacity is defined as the extra burden that can be imposed on the ecosystem without overloading it – that is, before reaching its absolute carrying capacity. In a sustainable world, of course, carrying capacities would never be surpassed.

In some cases, such as the eutrophication of specific lakes, or the acidification of regions like the so-called 'Black Triangle' – the area where the former East German border meets Poland and the Czech Republic – the environment's carrying capacity has evidently already been exceeded. With regard to global warming, on the other hand, the jury is still out. The question is: Do we still have time to recover, or will the impact on, for instance, oceanic currents result in irreversible damage and even a disruption of global equilibrium? This issue is at the top of the political agenda and should attract corresponding attention from corporations producing greenhouse gases. The situation for other issues, such as the impact of genetically modified organisms (GMOs) on local and global ecosystems, is not as clear and companies need to assess them, both globally and locally.[10]

A growing number of published sources detail methods to gain a better perspective of how the various environmental themes might evolve in the future.[11] Allen Hammond of the World Resources Institute, for instance, constructs three possible worlds that might await us in the 21st century.[12] In the same vein, the WBCSD built on the expertise of Shell International – a recognized leader in the field – and other major multinationals to develop three scenarios for the future.[13] It should be pointed out, however, that much of the attention is focused on global developments, so that the understanding of global carrying capacities is often more advanced than that of local capacity. Fortunately, a company's own staff is likely to be the best source of information on local carrying capacities, so this situation is soluble. This is one of many instances we'll come across that stress the importance of coworkers in the process of delineating a company's differentiation space.

'Heat seeking exercises' is the name we give to the process of drawing on the accessible external and in-house expertise. Typically, senior executives participate in a half- or full-day workshop with environmental experts. The latter must possess an acute sense of the interactions between the main players in the relevant policy-making arena, which will allow them to make educated guesses about possible developments in the demands and positioning of policy-makers and lobbyists and – if possible – of competitors, customers and suppliers.

Essentially, two workshop set-ups are possible. Management can present an overview of the existing market situation and the company's competitive position, together with a strategic plan. The environmental experts can then develop a critical test of the conceivable extent of the environmental challenge. Alternatively, the environmental experts can take the lead. Having been briefed on the corporate strategy, they can prepare and subsequently present their ideas and concerns by sketching the contours of the possible differentiation space.[14] In an iterative process, the business experts react and scope the potential impact on their competitive arena as well as the readiness of the corporation to respond.

In either case, the end-product of the workshop should be an overview of the issues that might seriously affect the business: that is, that might cause a 'business discontinuity'. In compiling this list, one basic rule should be followed: if there is doubt about the relevance of an issue, it should be included. It is better to be comprehensive and safe than specific and sorry.

It is also important to note that the search for potential business discontinuities during a heat-seeking workshop does not have to be precise nor definitive. Instead, it should provide a first overview of the business challenge at hand. Top management also does not have to be concerned about all the environmental issues; rather, it should concentrate on those that allow a significant scope for a discretionary response.

Clearly, the outcome will vary greatly according to sector-type and geography. Some industries are faced with environmental themes, almost all of which demand solutions involving sustainability. Insiders and outsiders involved with the car industry, for instance, recognize that the converging trends of increasing urbanization and mobility pose immense challenges. As John F Smith, Jr, Chairman and CEO of the General Motors Corporation, points out:

> *Infrastructure and land-use issues will take centre-stage, along with the need for transportation that is fast, effective, and environmentally compatible.... Certainly, no car company will be able to thrive in the future being solely dependent on the internal combustion engine.*[15]

John Smith's counterpart at the Ford Motor Company, Bill Ford, Jr, is even more specific:

> *Our goal has to be nothing less than an emission-free vehicle that is built in clean plants, which contribute to the environment. And it can happen within my lifetime – hopefully, within my working lifetime.*[16]

The current challenge to the car industry is the satisfaction of sustainability criteria with regard to emission controls, energy efficiency, recycling, alternative fuels and road congestion. However, some would argue that, ultimately, the car is inherently incompatible with sustainability. If true, this would raise the question as to whether the industry can reshape itself to face this challenge (or opportunity), or whether other industries are better positioned to do so.

The food industry is another that increasingly has to confront the need for sustainable solutions. These are the words of Iain Anderson, Unilever's Strategy and Technology Director:

> *Unless we find ways to maintain the Earth's productive capacity, food security, continuous supplies and stable prices will come under increasing heat.... We believe we have a responsibility to start finding solutions now. We see Unilever playing a pivotal role, bringing upstream and downstream partners together with others outside the food chain, to help generate the momentum needed to create sustainable food production around the world for the long term. Using our global reach, our scientific base and our local expertise we want to provide the framework for a worldwide knowledge network that can help transform the rate of progress towards sustainable food production.*[17]

Even though every company and sector faces a specific situation, we have found that it makes the business discontinuity forecasting effort easier if the environmental themes are broken down according to the scope of the regulatory and/or market demands and their timing, as shown below.

• **Scope and timing known.** The market and regulatory implications of some environmental themes are evident. Noise abatement, waste management, acidification, eutrophication and ozone depletion, for example, have already attracted regulatory attention. The solutions are also fairly well known: for example, the technology to be applied, behavioral change to be pursued, or reduction or total abolition of the use of a substance or practice.

  Still, the necessary actions might give rise to serious business discontinuities among geographic regions and sectors, and individual companies within these sectors. For example, in the late 1980s Germany adopted a far-reaching take-back obligation in response to the problem of the collection and recycling of packaging waste. Its very costly implementation most probably put the German companies affected at a significant disadvantage vis-à-vis their competitors in neighbouring countries, where regulation was different or less stringent. Competitive distortions also arose in a number of European countries when the plastics industry successfully lobbied for milder treatment than that meted out to the cardboard, metals and glass sectors.

- **Scope and/or timing uncertain.** These themes, many of which are global in nature, are recognized to be relevant, but their magnitude, not to speak of the nature of possible solutions, is unclear. They include issues ranging from global warming to endocrine disruptors[18] (presumably caused by the uncontrolled dispersion of chemical micro-substances and possibly affecting male fertility), all the way to the shortage of fresh water supplies[19] or the loss of biodiversity (caused, among others reasons, by large-scale and uncontrolled deforestation).

  Given what is currently known about these issues and the extent of environmental damage involved, it is reasonable to assume that they will be the subject of increasing market and regulatory pressures. These will be fueled by the continued growth of the world's population and the rapid economic expansion in newly-industrialized nations. But since the developed countries will most probably have to assume the lead in coming up with solutions, large multinational companies will almost inevitably be among the primary targets for new policies and consumer pressure. One can therefore expect a rapid expansion of the differentiation space for companies affected by these themes, and hence a significant opportunity for competitive differentiation as these issues are addressed in the years to come.

- **Scope and/or timing unknown.** These are themes that are being tentatively raised by some experts – most often scientists or environmentalists – while others feel that there is a need for more proof before their relevance is recognized. These issues include: indoor air, the quality of which often does not meet outdoor air standards; the environmental impact of genetic engineering – one question being: How can society prevent 'bad science' from turning a potential blessing into an environmental disaster?; the need to promote biodiversity (as opposed to preventing its loss); and the possible destabilization of the oceans.[20]

  These issues rank in the category of 'could be's'. Although neither the problem nor solution is clear, top management would be wise to take a first look at their potential impact on business activities. In fact, managers would be well-advised to set up some sort of monitoring system to keep track of developments – for example, by forming an environmental advisory board of external experts. We return to the possible role of such a board in Chapter 6.

On the assumption that the first group of issues is already attracting sufficient management attention and action, the scanning focus should be placed on the second group, while the more remote third group should be monitored. We have found it useful to plot the possible discontinuities of the last two types in a 2x2 matrix, taking the most extreme responses – for instance, 'new' versus 'old' technology, and market-driven versus regulation-driven changes in demand – to stretch the mind. By way of illustration, car makers could think about hydrogen fuel cells versus battery-powered engines, or conceivably even about the very use of cars versus public transportation or electronic communication. The current oil giants could envisage a future without fossil fuels, and paper companies a paperless society.

A supporting task force is then asked to 'fill out' the four squares of the matrix with a description of the competitive arena that would arise in say, 2020, if a specific scenario were to occur. This would entail answering questions like: How large would the market be? What would be the key success factors and which companies would be the winners? What would the role of the regulators be, and how significant would the barriers to entry or exit be? Top management should add its own colour to each of these scenarios and, as a group, assess their likelihood. Eventually, management should add a first estimate of the time dimension – ie assess when the discontinuity, whether occasioned by regulators or the market, is likely to come about. Throughout this process, knowledge of and intuition with regard to government, NGOs, customers and competitors will contribute to a better forecasting of the market and regulatory pressures, which will determine the dimensions of a company's differentiation space.[21]

SELECTING THE PREFERRED ENDGAME

On the basis of the above exercises, top managers should be in a position to produce a blueprint of the endgame they envisage for their company within the boundaries of its differentiation space. Again, the 2x2 matrix has proved to be a powerful device for inducing top management, with the support of its task forces, to generate options for the long-term development of the corporation, by envisioning the company in each of the squares and eventually selecting a preferred position. Based on this broad assessment, it must make a go/no-go decision. That is, it should decide on whether it should pursue a functional, integrated or even proactive response.

If management feels that the business discontinuities are minor, an extrapolation of regulatory and market demands cuts through the differentiation space. In that case the corporate endgame can be realized through a continuation of its current, functional approach. As argued by our colleagues Walley and Whitehead,[22] functional environmental measures often suffice when the potential value impact of a specific issue is low or when regulation or practical

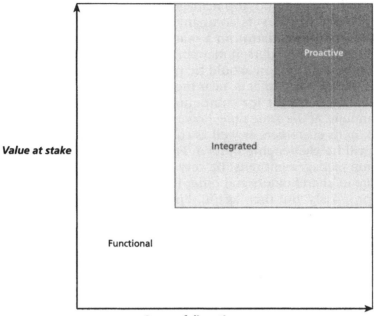

Figure 2.6 *Sorting environmental issues*

considerations leave little margin for managerial manoeuvre (Figure 2.6). Given the number of such issues and the magnitude of the necessary investments, flawless execution can in itself lead to a significant improvement in a company's competitive position. In most major companies, line management with the support of environment, health and safety (EHS) staff can, and does, ably handle these tasks. In this scenario the active involvement of top management usually can be limited to high-level discussions with national and multilateral policy-makers, where the continuous optimization of already-existing regulations may offer companies opportunities for significant economic yield.

If the potential value at stake due to business discontinuities is considerable and if the strategic freedom to act is great, a new preferred endgame must be defined within the contours of the differentiation space. Again, a company does not have to be a green front-runner. Given its portfolio of other strategic challenges outside the environmental arena, top management could be well advised to adopt a follower position, aiming, for instance, at an endgame in the middle or even the lower right-hand portion of the differentiation space. Still, as extrapolation of the current response mode probably will not bisect this endgame objective, the company will have to revise its strategy and opt for an integrated tack in order to adequately address the business discontinuity.

If, on the other hand, top management recognizes that a business discontinuity provides its company with a unique opportunity for competitive differentiation in a manner that can satisfy all internal and external stakeholders, it may consider a proactive response. Most likely, the endgame now would be positioned at the forefront of the differentiation space; that is, near the top-left corner. It thus would be trying to raise the bar for competitors by increasing their business discontinuity. At the same time, however, it also increases the demands placed on its customers as well as coworkers; the behavioural change effort will be challenging indeed. Frequently surrounded by scepticism, top management must be very convinced of its endgame vision to excite its shareholders and other funding sources with the wisdom of its proposals. But then again, this is what business is all about. A business discontinuity is nothing but a gap in the market that good entrepreneurs see and others don't!

The importance of good entrepreneurship is also reflected in the need for good intuition. Although much of the process of producing an endgame blueprint, as we've seen, is based on applying rational or fact-based tools in an effort to decipher what the future might have to offer, an intuitive sense of this future is also an important component. Intuitive managers may not know exactly where they are going, but they usually know pretty well where they should not go.

Thus Bill Stavropoulos, CEO of Dow Chemical, summarized it for most of his peers: 'We can visualize our destination. The road to sustainability leads to a safer, healthier, more prosperous life for all of us. We know how to get there. Together, let's get moving.'[23]

***

Having produced a blueprint for its endgame, the company's management must, as the next step, test the opportunities for a differentiating medium-term strategy. Clearly the initial blueprint is rough and may require considerable refinement and re-examination; it may later undergo the key process of validation. Its main role at this point, however, is to assist top management in deciding how it should respond to the challenge of change. In this 'backcasting' exercise, top management, with the support of its internal and external environmental experts, must make a first integrated assessment of the pros and cons of various options on the path to its endgame.

We examine the value-creation measures that can contribute to a medium-term strategy in Chapter 4. Before we do that, however, let us look at the context in which the management decisions we are examining will be taken. An understanding of this context, and particularly of two critical players in the environmental arena – namely, government and NGOs – is an important ingredient in corporate environmental management decisions.

3

UNDERSTANDING THE ENVIRONMENTAL ARENA: GOVERNMENT AND NGOS

Strategy is about people: understanding them and, whenever possible, getting the best out of them; finding common ground and working together. Top managers know this, and increasingly ground their strategies in systematic, fact-based approaches – for example, in marketing research and management development. The environmental arena is new to them, however. It is inhabited by players with whom they are not familiar.[1] When defining the details of their environmental strategies, managers can therefore benefit immensely from understanding government policy-makers and NGOs, both of which are vitally important influences in defining environmental policy and thus the dimensions and development of the corporate differentiation space.[2]

THE POLICY-MAKING PROCESS

The prospect of getting involved in the policy-making process understandably has limited appeal for most managers. They lack strategic support from their staff departments, since these tend to be technically-oriented. The experience of the corporations and of their managers is sometimes scarred by earlier clashes with government agencies or NGOs. They also doubt whether they can be effective in the policy formulation process: there are a huge number of environmental issues and, from an outside perspective, the whole process seems to be bewildering and to involve an inordinate amount of mud-slinging.

Still, analysis of policy-making experience worldwide suggests things are not as complicated as many senior executives fear. Whether the ultimate solution is found through government-driven regulation, through market forces or through proactive self-regulation by industry, each environmental issue goes through four distinct phases

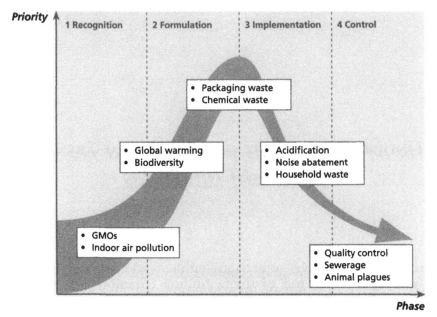

Note: Examples refer to current state in industrialized countries

Figure 3.1 *Policy life cycle*

(Figure 3.1). The corresponding policy life cycle (PLC) offers an excellent framework for understanding the process itself, and hence for becoming more effective as a player in predicting probable developments, or even influencing the dimensions of the differentiation space.[3]

Because of its similarity to the well-known product life cycle concept, most senior managers have little difficulty grasping the essence of the PLC framework. Instead of a product, the cycle involves four stages in the resolution of a particular environmental problem. The variable on the vertical axis is not value added, however, as it would be in a product life cycle diagram. Instead, the critical measure, which characterizes each PLC phase, is the societal priority that is attached to a specific issue at a given time.[4]

Phase 1: Recognition

The first signals that a problem might exist typically originate in scientific discovery and trend analysis. Much of the modern environmental debate, for example, was initiated in 1962 by Rachel Carson's *Silent Spring*, and the 1972 publication of the Club of Rome's *The Limits to Growth*.[5] Both documents drew on new scientific insights and methods to a powerful effect: the Club of Rome's Meadows and Forrester were the first to apply dynamic modelling techniques to world population and resource issues, while Rachel Carson turned the spotlight on the phenomenon of pesticide accumulation and longevity in living organisms.

Today, scientific discovery often directly drives government decision-making. For example, the breakthrough National Environmental Policy Plan of The Netherlands (1989) – the first attempt at comprehensive environmental policy-making – drew heavily on a scientific report by the National Institute for Public Health and the Environment. The 1992 United Nations Commission for Environment and Development (UNCED) agreement and the subsequent 1997 Kyoto Protocol on global warming were, in turn, significantly influenced by the scientific findings of the Intergovernmental Panel on Climate Change, which was set up by the United Nations Environment Programme (UNEP) and the World Meteorological Organization (WMO). Earlier satellite measurements of the atmosphere's ozone layer had created alarm and subsequent action in response to ozone depletion.

During this first stage of the PLC, scientists and/or environmentalists lead the process. In the beginning, opinions usually differ greatly as to the nature and extent of the problem, as well as to its causes and effects. Since empirical knowledge is incomplete, policy-makers focus on the reduction of uncertainty, whereas industry – if at all involved – tends to advocate the need for further research.

The transition to the second PLC phase takes place when government authorities – or, in the admittedly rare event of self-regulation, companies – conclude that the problem must be solved, generally because of a trigger event, such as new scientific findings or – quite often – a major incident. Typical issues that are still in the recognition phase include the ecosystem impact of GMOs and indoor air pollution – ie those issues that we earlier labelled 'could be's' and that give rise to business discontinuities of unknown scope and timing.

Phase 2: Policy formulation

This phase tends to be characterized by fierce debate about the most appropriate measures and the equitable distribution of their cost. Media attention and market pressures are often intense, and crisis management skills are called into play. Policy-makers emphasize effectiveness rather than efficiency. Their motto is 'find a solution that works, whatever the costs, and get the legislators (or the partner companies in the case of self-regulation) to accept it'. Environmentalists tend to criticize proposals as being too little, too late. On the other side of the table, business often plays a delaying game, suggesting, for instance, the need for still further research or a high-level steering group to re-examine the available material and the best possible solutions.

Significantly, companies and their industry associations tend, in terms of the 3E framework, to focus on the equity of the potential policies rather than on their effectiveness or efficiency. This produces pressure for international harmonization of regulation and equal burden sharing, which have become central concepts in environmental policy-making. Nobody likes a free rider: the market should not reward low production costs based on poor environmental performance.

Industry has actually taken many initiatives aimed at levelling the international playing field, though in an increasingly global business world and with mounting North–South tensions this is becoming more and more complicated. Developing countries often bristle at the prospect of slowing down their growth for the sake of environmental safeguards that have been profitably ignored by the industrialized world for so long and are suddenly thrust on them. Corporate lobbies target national governments and, increasingly, multilateral forums such as the European Commission: think of the out-and-out effort of US industry to prevent a Kyoto agreement on greenhouse gas emissions, and the tendency of European industry to adopt policies only if the US and Japan do the same.

Typical issues that are now in the policy formulation phase include climate change and biodiversity – ie those issues that give rise to the business discontinuities of uncertain scope and timing, as discussed earlier. Clearly, the strategic freedom that still tends to exist for corporations, especially in the early stages of Phase 2, may call for the involvement of top management in formulating a strategic response.

Phase 3: Implementation

The actual implementation of policy measures is often costly and may have a major impact on companies. Nonetheless, once the solution has been determined, political and managerial attention tends to die away. Furthermore, as the focus shifts towards operational management, more emphasis is placed on enforcing and particularly on streamlining regulations and procedures for efficiency – what is known as 're-regulation'. This, in turn, often involves the devolution of responsibilities to lower levels of government (states, municipalities) or, within companies, to operational and/or functional management.

Packaging and chemical waste disposal, in most industrialized countries, are still near this peak of the PLC. Acidification (acid rain), noise abatement and household waste disposal have progressed further down the curve and now belong to the category of issues that give rise to business discontinuities with a scope and magnitude that are fairly well known. As we pointed out in Chapter 2, flawless implementation of environmental measures can lead to a significant improvement of a company's competitive position. Apart from influencing the reshaping of the differentiation space – eg in the case of re-regulation or the formation of partnerships for realizing a most efficient solution – the role of top management tends to be limited, however.

Phase 4: Control

The final phase begins when the initially targeted improvement in environmental quality has been realized and the problem reduced to acceptable proportions. Policy-makers now must ensure that the problem remains under control. As the policy is internalized throughout society, regulations can often be simplified and sometimes even abolished (deregulation). Similarly, within companies, measures can possibly be relaxed or forgotten about as long as they constitute an ingrained part of a corporate culture. Ongoing vigilance, however, remains necessary. Examples of issues that have reached this phase in the industrialized countries include old stalwarts like the quality control of food and drinking water, sewerage systems and the control of animal plagues, but also more recent ones such as smokestack soot emissions.

Every so often, an issue that is thought to be under control resurfaces. Government must then take new, targeted measures. Instances where this is necessary can be the result of the disregard for earlier measures (as in the case of mad cow disease), unforeseen consequences of existing policies (as in the acid rain problems aggravated by the raising of the smokestacks to limit the foul smell of sulphur emissions), or the inadequacies of those policies (the hygiene of saunas proved to be unsatisfactory when, over time, their average temperature was raised, to the delight of both humans and bacteria). New government action might involve tightening existing approaches (such as in the sauna example), but it also may require terminating the PLC and beginning anew in an effort to address the newly-defined environmental issue from scratch.

THE CHANGING RESPONSES OF
KEY ENVIRONMENTAL PLAYERS

The above evolution of policy development has significant implications for the behaviour of all players in the environmental arena. Since the characteristics of each phase of the cycle vary, the requirements for success at each phase also differ; unsurprisingly, this has led to a certain specialization on the part of the various players (Figure 3.2).

Traditionally, most companies have concentrated their activities on the highly operational implementation phase, while industry

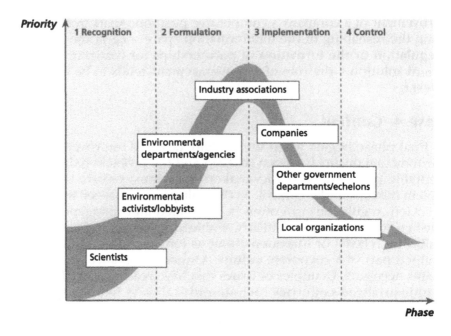

Figure 3.2 *Range of cultures*

associations have been particularly active at the end of the formulation phase and early on in the implementation phase. Government
policy-makers, on the other hand, have tended to specialize in policy
formulation (Phase 2) activities, while other government institutions
have developed a strong culture directed at implementation (Phase
3) and control (Phase 4). Some, such as departments of industry,
energy, transportation and agriculture, are involved in the policy-
making process, but are driven by their traditional, specific
imperatives. Others, such as enforcement agencies, and often also
lower echelons of government, concentrate on implementation and
control.

Environmental scientists, for their part, tend to be strongly
focused on issue recognition (Phase 1), whereas environmental
activists and lobbyists are particularly skilled at accelerating the
transition from Phase 1 to the end of Phase 2 – the PLC's peak – when
policy has already been formulated and implementation is about to
begin. Local grassroots organizations, in turn, tend to place their
priority on the control phase.

As might be expected, such different priorities are also reflected
in evident cultural differences and a lack of understanding. Surveys
of top managers reveal that they find government policy inconsis-
tent, corporate lobbies ineffective and corporate communication
with the public insufficient. The gaps between industry and environmental scientists, activists and lobbyists are even wider. They might

be said to speak different languages. Many of the early bitter battles between these parties – particularly when businesses were taking a reactive response to environmental issues – left deep wounds, some of which have not entirely healed. It also doesn't help that some NGO and business leaders are grandmasters of insensitive rhetoric, thereby strengthening the caricatured images of each other. Although much progress has been made, it still often comes as a surprise to both sides when 'normal' discourse proves entirely possible.

What is important for business strategy, we feel, is that the contours of the differentiation space are determined during the transition from Phase 1 to Phase 2 of the PLC. This is exactly the period when NGOs and government agencies are at their best and private companies are at their most uncomfortable. The result: at a crucial stage in the process, business is relatively inactive and lacks insight into the other parties' imperatives. This problem effectively constitutes one of the main barriers to change within industry, but it also limits corporate influence on the process of shaping the differentiation space.

As a result, business is forced into a defensive posture. By participating too late in the process, it frequently finds itself concentrating on damage control, which almost inevitably creates an antagonistic relationship with the other players. Win–win solutions are difficult to bring to the table. As latecomers, business-people also miss opportunities to proactively develop technologies, shape market demands or form alliances. To get ahead of competitors and build sustainable advantages, an active involvement in policy formulation (Phase 2) is usually required.

Such an approach not only implies significant opportunity costs to business, but is also unfavourable to the environment. Earlier in our discussion of the environmental hierarchy of needs, we noted that in step 4 (quality ecosystems) there is a growing realization – by corporations, policy-makers and environmental activists – of the need to develop 3E solutions for environmental problems. This increasingly implies cooperating with former rivals and the assumption of responsibility by industry early on in the process.

This fundamental change augurs well for the cooperative solution of many unresolved environmental problems over the next 10 to 15 years. As a basis for corporate action, it is important that companies have an understanding of the other parties as well as of the process. Let's look at the environmental NGOs and government policy-makers in turn.

Environmental NGOs

Most large companies today accept the validity of the concept of a societal 'license to operate'. They take their neighbours much more seriously. They no longer vehemently deny environmental incidents or ascribe them to chance or fate. They even react more proactively and constructively to the public's growing risk awareness, even if it makes the siting of new industrial facilities, landfills and incinerators, for example, extremely difficult.

Much of this was learnt the hard way, with environmental NGOs serving as the (frequently despised) taskmasters.[6] These organizations have perfected their skill at moving issues from the recognition to the policy formulation phase of the PLC.[7] With the help of the media, the publicity impact of catastrophic accidents is no longer limited to neighbouring communities, but quickly spreads throughout society at large, and increasingly worldwide via the internet. One result of this is that corrective measures are often felt throughout the industry and in other parts of economy and society: the Exxon Valdez oil spill led to a US design mandate for double-hulled tankers, while Sandoz's contamination of the Rhine led to a drastic tightening of environmental liability legislation in Germany.

NGOs have also been a significant force in extending the public's environmental awareness far beyond the immediate risks presented to life and safety. Consumer pressure has turned up the heat on individual companies for a wide range of reasons, varying from shortcomings in product design (eg McDonald's 'clamshell' packaging), to sourcing practices (eg Burger King's alleged use of 'rain forest beef') and the dumping of oil platforms, much to Shell's chagrin.[8]

Over the last 15 years, the NGOs, originally scattered and with chaotic operations, have become more professionally organized and politically astute.[9] Their constituencies have grown, in some cases spectacularly: the combined membership of the six largest environmental NGOs in The Netherlands, for instance, has risen from just over 0.5 million to over 2.5 million, covering a sizeable proportion of roughly 6 million Dutch households. In their capacity as voters, NGO members and sympathisers exert considerable pressure on party programmes and political decision-making; and green parties have garnered a considerable share of the vote in national elections in countries such as Germany, France and Belgium.

Still, many business-people over-estimate the capabilities of NGOs. In fact, corporations and their representatives have far greater financial and personnel resources than NGOs, though their public support and legitimacy in the policy system is weaker. These differences have typically led industry to favour reliance on scientific analyses and technologically-driven policies; environmentalists, in turn, are more sceptical of these alternatives and inclined instead to favour immediate, drastic measures such as the (partial) closure of 'valves' in a company or industry's integrated chain.[10]

Moreover, members of the business community often find it difficult to fully grasp the intricacies of interaction between NGOs. Although the specifics vary from country to country, in the West we

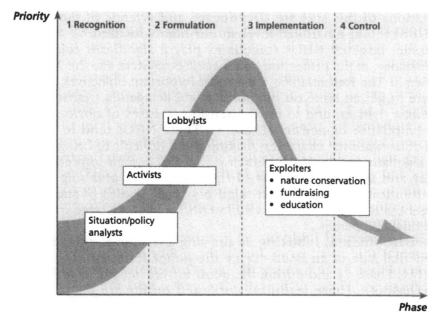

Figure 3.3 *NGO focus*

can generally distinguish four types of organization, each with their own strengths and vulnerabilities. Using the PLC framework, these organizations can be said to be 'specialized' in the following manner (see also Figure 3.3).

- **Environmental situation and policy analysis**, ie scanning the horizon for new developments, and developing thinking about and awareness of (potential) issues and solutions, and the overall degradation of nature and the environment. Organizations such as the Worldwatch Institute (US) and, in international nature conservation, the World Conservation Union (IUCN) excel at ringing the environmental alarm bell when necessary. Institutions like the World Resources Institute (US), the Wuppertal Institute (Germany), the Institute for Environment and Development and the Royal Institute of International Affairs (both UK) have traditionally focused on PLC Phase 1. Many of these think-tanks work in close cooperation with university groups and semi-governmental research institutions. Further, they have recently shifted their emphasis to include the instrumentation of solutions, such as the application of economic instruments, and increasingly take joint policy initiatives with industry leaders.
- **Environmental activism**, ie raising awareness of 'new' issues, primarily by drawing public attention through media-grabbing actions. On the international scene, the most prominent organi-

zations of this sort are Greenpeace and Friends of the Earth. However, at a national level and/or highly focused on a single issue, targeted NGOs sometimes play a significant role – for instance, in the protection of a specific ecosystem like the Wadden Sea in The Netherlands. Their most important objectives usually are to get an issue on the political/public agenda (transition of Phase 1 to 2), and to draw attention to cases of obvious non-compliance or neglect (Phase 3). These NGOs tend to have a confrontational character, making them difficult to bring to the negotiating table. Much of their power lies in their unpredictability and swiftness. In view of the necessity of grabbing media attention, combined with relatively small bodies of staff, they generally target publicly visible entities such as large multinational companies.

- **Environmental lobbying**, ie drawing attention to the environmental side of an issue during the policy formulation process (PLC Phase 2) and during the quest for greater policy efficiency (Phase 3). These technically-oriented outfits are usually well networked and highly adept at political and media footwork. Given their considerable know-how, they also tend to serve as sources of information for the media and increasingly the public at large. They do this in many ways: for example, through their published materials and omnipresence in public gatherings. As yet, these organizations tend to be nationally or even regionally focused. This makes them vulnerable and sometimes ineffective in international policy-making forums such as the European Union or the United Nations (UN), where, because of their complex federal structures, they lack the agility and the concentrated mass to have political clout.

- **Environmental anchoring**. The first three NGO categories might be classified as 'explorers' – ie they test out new frontiers; they also generally have their roots in the public health side of environmentalism. Those who follow in their footsteps – the 'settlers'– have their origins in nature conservation, where their grassroots local activities make them uniquely suitable for stimulating value change within their constituency, and hence for anchoring behavioural changes. These NGOs are mainly active well into the PLC Phases 3 and 4 – eg nature conservation (also in developing countries), fund raising, education and the broadening of the public support base (through membership and publications). However, their often large memberships, public respectability and strong network connections in the political, scientific and business worlds are increasingly making them effective participants in selected issues in Phases 1 and 2. This NGO group embraces a kaleidoscope of organizations, including large multinational NGOs (eg WWF and Birdlife International), strong national NGOs with international reach (eg US-based The Nature Conservancy and Conservation International), national NGOs (the Sierra Club and the Audubon Society (US), the National Trust (UK) and Natuurmonumenten (The Netherlands)), and a multitude of sometimes highly specialized and/or local organizations.

Reflecting their different origins, their belief-driven volunteer cadre and their – compared to government and industry – relatively limited financial and personnel resources, the narrow focus of these NGOs is virtually a condition for their survival. Although they therefore often have significant expertise in their chosen range of activities, the limitations of the NGO framework as a whole are serious. The handover of the baton of responsibility from one organization to the next as an issue progresses through its PLC is also frequently far from perfect. Very few NGOs are effective at the top of the PLC peak, and especially in the implementation phase when policies are 'finalized' and subsequently optimized. In fact, leading environmentalists or activist NGOs who set up (semi-) commercial consultancies to support private businesses increasingly fill the resulting gap.

In addition to the vulnerability of its vertical chain, the horizontal dimension of the NGO network is almost non-existent. Despite the good work of institutions such as the IUCN, international cooperation among like-minded organizations is weak. This is particularly significant for multinational companies, since it makes it difficult for them to find suitable partners within the NGO community that are able to add value worldwide throughout major parts of the PLC.

Government policy-making

In our earlier discussion of the fourth, quality ecosystems, step of the environmental hierarchy of needs, we noted that its characteristics included an increasing awareness of the complexity of environmental regulation, of the need for cooperation among the different parties to find 3E solutions, and of the necessity for international cooperation.

These characteristics can increasingly be found in much Western and multilateral environmental policy-making today. The regulatory framework is becoming more complex, is frequently very tight, and involves local, regional, national and multinational entities. Some of these have mandates related to very specific issues, like biodiversity or ocean pollution.

Under such circumstances, the outcome at this policy-formulation stage of the PLC is commonly very hard to predict. Examples abound of environmental regulations that ended up being far more sweeping and drastic than anyone could have predicted at their inception less than 15 years ago. The 1987 Montreal Protocol ban on

CFCs, for instance, forced many producers to undertake product and process redesign efforts of massive proportions. In another example, the German packaging take-back obligation, in effect since 1991, assigned environmental responsibility for the entire distribution chain to the major producers of packaging materials; the resulting infrastructure costs were huge. Similarly, the 1990 US Clean Air Act, intended to reduce sulphur dioxide emissions causing acid rain, involved compliance costs for the electric utility and petrochemical industries upwards of $10 billion per year. Southern California air quality regulations will severely limit the use of most gasoline-powered internal combustion engines over the next 20 years and may force the relocation of large industrial plants from the Los Angeles Basin.

But as we look ahead, such regulatory initiatives may prove to be mere finger exercises prior to the grand concert. Governments are preparing the implementation of their obligations arising from the Kyoto Protocol. New approaches, emphasizing a much greater reliance on market-based mechanisms[11] such as emissions trading or joint implementation, and on 'green taxation',[12] will be developed as the policy-makers increasingly realize that their task is more formidable than ever before. One can also expect that so-called 'perverse' subsidies which, especially in agriculture, hamper sustainable development will be questioned and often abolished.[13]

Business leaders engaged in responding to the environmental challenge need to be familiar with the underlying mechanics of policy-making in order to focus their efforts. This includes knowing who the relevant players on the regulatory scene are, what instruments they apply and how rapidly they might change course. The access to the regulatory scene is complicated by the continuously shifting division of tasks between multilateral and national institutions, and the simultaneous decentralization to regional and municipal authorities. Still, experience shows that it is generally possible to distinguish four development stages in environmental policy-making as it affects industry (Figure 3.4).

1   **Ad hoc policy.** During the first phase of environmental policy-making, the official response to external challenges is characterized by an ad hoc handling of urgent tasks. In reacting to the most immediate needs and crises, and dealing with highly sceptical counterparts in other government departments and in industry, policy-making departments lack appropriate resources, experience, organization and credibility.

   A major share of resources is spent on developing tools (such as regulations), people networks and infrastructure. The policy-makers' planning horizon is usually shorter than one year; their objective can best be characterized as 'survival'. Importantly, their

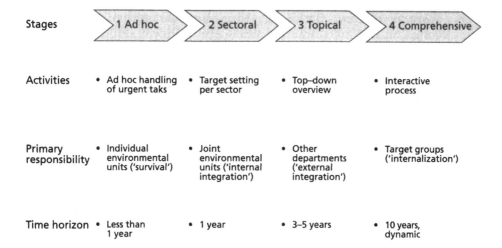

Stages	1 Ad hoc	2 Sectoral	3 Topical	4 Comprehensive
Activities	• Ad hoc handling of urgent taks	• Target setting per sector	• Top–down overview	• Interactive process
Primary responsibility	• Individual environmental units ('survival')	• Joint environmental units ('internal integration')	• Other departments ('external integration')	• Target groups ('internalization')
Time horizon	• Less than 1 year	• 1 year	• 3–5 years	• 10 years, dynamic

Figure 3.4 *Development stages in environmental policy planning*

instrumentation is fairly crude and relies almost entirely on direct regulation, such as end-of-pipe requirements for substance-specific emission levels – eg emissions of mercury into water or SO_2 into the air. Top–down enforcement, virtually without exception, is far from perfect, giving rise to significant abusive practices, especially in the area of chemical waste.

2 **Sectoral policy.** The transition to the second stage of environmental policy-making is made when the basis is sufficiently sound for target setting by specific environmental sector, like air, water, noise or soil. Work programmes focus on near-term regulations, implementation and enforcement objectives. In most countries, the associated responsibilities are divided between various echelons of government (national, regional, municipal). Thus a major focus of attention during this phase is internal integration, ie the alignment of all government units with direct environmental responsibility. Although the sectoral plans often provide a medium-term perspective, for practical purposes the planning horizon is generally one year.

The transition from stage 1 to stage 2 frequently coincides with an environment department being accorded full ministerial status: in the more advanced countries this occurred in the early 1980s. However, the policy instruments, now enforced by increasingly effective specialized units, are still based on a command-and-control approach. Nevertheless, the first successful experiments point in the direction of a greater use of indirect regulations, using economic (dis-)incentives and emission-related standards (eg concentration limits of hazardous substances in a river).

3 **Topical policy.** Based on the improved organization and cohesion of environmental units, the policy-making focus now changes to external integration – that is, integrating environmental objectives into the strategy of other government departments, eg industry, energy, transportation and agriculture, each with its own sector-specific goals. This requires 'translating' such goals into terms that are workable in these departments and in the relevant sectors of industry – that is, the policy target groups.

The transition to integrated planning is all the more necessary because, within environmental departments or agencies, sectoral policies frequently prove inadequate in dealing with the increasingly complex environmental issues of advanced economies, which require an over-arching, multi-sector perspective. The governmental organizations are therefore refocused around central policy themes such as acidification, eutrophication or global warming. Representatives of different sectoral units work together on a programme/project basis to develop practical solutions, often using direct interaction with members of other departments and the relevant target groups.

Plans typically have a horizon of three to five years, and specify overall reduction targets to be realized during the period. The instrumentation shifts towards more indirect regulation and, by way of experiment with leading sectors, self-regulation, which involves voluntary industry standards and limits enforced without state intervention.

4 **Comprehensive policy.** The contours of a fourth stage of policy-making can be discerned today in the most environmentally advanced countries.[14] A central feature is the co-responsibility of third parties, especially the target groups, which are required to develop effective, efficient and equitable solutions to the environmental problems. Joint objectives are set on the basis of a situation analysis of the state of the environment, and the time-paths to achieve them accommodate the specific situation of each target group and its reasonable wishes and needs. Moreover, in assessing the options for actions, the strengths and weaknesses of government organization are taken into account. The resulting action plans therefore tend to be more realistic than in the earlier stages.

Although the planning horizon is much longer, say ten years, comprehensive policy-making recognizes the unpredictability of major parts of the environmental agenda and allows for dynamic adaptation as new evidence or political priorities develop. Clearly, direct regulations, although still essential tools for handling some highly sensitive issues, are less appropriate in this context. Indirect regulation and eventually self-regulation offer the advantages of a greater flexibility in the joint search for 3E solutions.[15]

Most importantly, environmental considerations are fully integrated into other areas of government policy-making. Thus the policy, market, planning and property rights failures that are currently all too common will become less frequent.[16]

Gauging the power game

In Chapter 2 we discussed the value of an initial scanning of the horizon as part of management's pre-assessment of the environmental issues that could potentially have an impact on its company. Part of this, of course, is getting a sense of how the power game will be played out in the environmental arena. It is beyond the scope of the current text to discuss this in depth. Still, we will risk mentioning what might be called simple rules of thumb that could be of use for business leaders when acting in the environmental arena.

- Always check the political hit-list. When socioeconomic issues reach the top of the agenda, even in the currently most advanced environmental settings, the knees of policy-makers as well as business-people often become surprisingly weak. Unemployment or red bottom lines, for instance, quickly focus the mind. On the other hand, when environmental issues are perceived as life-threatening, they receive absolute priority almost without exception.
- The richer the country (or region) and the greater an environmental problem, the higher it ranks on the public and political priority list and the more skilled the policy-shapers from all sides will be. Thus, Japan and California have emerged as leaders in combating air pollution; the Scandinavian countries and Germany are the farthest advanced in dealing with acidification; The Netherlands and New Jersey are most advanced in remediating soil. Representatives from these geographic areas are thus ideally suited for scanning the policy-making horizon in triple-focus interviews.
- There are wide variations in national and regional approaches. US policy-making, for example, is characterized by a fairly polarized relationship between business and government; regulation is quickly thought of as 'interference'. Similarly, the business-to-business interactions in the US tend to be more at arm's length than in Europe, where relationships can be cosier. On the other side of the globe, Japan is marked by a reliance on unwritten rules: its government negotiates voluntary compliance (often with some arm-twisting).[17]
  Regional differences, on the other hand, are more pronounced in Europe. The six founding members of the European Community have perfected the art of compromise:

frequent vetoes would have been too damaging. This is less true of more recent entrants, who joined for economic rather than idealistic reasons. At the same time, Southern Europe is marked by greater centralization and hierarchy in decision-making, as well as by a more relaxed attitude towards implementation and enforcement.

Within the European Union, even neighbouring nations with very similar policies differ in their implementation. For instance, German industries, following extensive and detailed negotiations with regulators, excel at compliance. Their Dutch counterparts, on the other hand, have developed a great skill and trust-base in reaching voluntary agreements – the so-called 'covenants' – that allow a greater implementation flexibility.[18]

- There is also a tendency for countries to act together in groups. In Europe, for instance, one can often distinguish a group of environmental leaders comprised of Germany, the Scandinavian countries, The Netherlands, Switzerland and Austria. A second group, including the United Kingdom, Belgium and France, follows at a distance of some years, whereas Southern European countries such as Italy, Spain, Portugal and Greece tend to implement environmental measures after further delay.

  This tendency is stimulated by the increasing maturity and credibility of international negotiating forums in the environmental arena. The preparations for UNCED and Kyoto, for instance, both saw the formation of a number of clearly defined coalitions or power blocks – eg European Union versus US; North versus South.[19]

- Business lobbies tend to aim at levelling the playing field, ie at the equity aspect of policy-making. Generally cooperating within the frameworks of their industry associations, corporations have traditionally tried to keep the environment out of their competitive arena. Private companies joined forces to promote international harmonization of measures and equal burden sharing – ie no free riders. As an example, the chemical industry in Canada and the US has introduced the concept of 'responsible care', which spreads the environmental cost burden among competitors. If all industry participants act in the same environmentally sound fashion, the overall competitive position is thus not distorted. In effect, these initiatives limit the dimensions of the differentiation space.

- Especially in the more advanced industries and regions, the various environmental players are becoming more and more aware of the price of confrontation. Governments turn to industry for market solutions, reflecting either a greater comfort with regard to the solution of a specific issue (ie in PLC Phase 3) or, on the contrary, a realization of their own inability to find 3E solutions alone. NGOs, in turn, are increasingly forming partnerships with major corporations instead of challenging them through public actions.

- A central theme of our discussion in Chapter 4 is that leading companies are beginning to feel they can benefit from taking environmental action. They increasingly break ranks in their core markets and consciously try to make use of their expanding differentiation space. In many cases, for instance, product design is found to create competitive advantages. On both sides of the Atlantic, petrochemical companies such as ARCO and OK Petroleum in Sweden have scored public relations coups with the introduction of more environmentally friendly car fuels. Recently, car giants such as Toyota, General Motors and DaimlerChrysler announced huge investments in the development of super-efficient engines. Although the publicly-known examples are less numerous, some technological powerhouses such as Shell and Exxon also use their competitive advantage over companies with fewer skills and/or resources by developing very advanced process designs. Such initiatives by leading companies appear frequently to catch the less advanced players off-guard.

- Understanding the timing of the probable actions of other players as a basis for the correct planning of one's own response is becoming increasingly important as the pace of change in regulatory and market demand accelerates. Top management must develop a sense of the 'trigger points', ie the event(s) that might cause an environmental issue to change status at some time in the future. To this end, the division of issues presented in Chapter 2 should be helpful. By categorizing trigger points in this way, top management can gain valuable insight into the magnitude of the challenge at hand.

***

After this small diversion to provide a clearer understanding of the other players in the environmental arena, we turn now to our examination of the various value-creation options open to business in the environmental area.

4

DEFINING THE PATH TO THE ENDGAME: MAKING VALUE CREATION CHOICES

Since corporations have the obligation to maximize shareholder value, their top management, when assessing the different options for addressing discontinuities in its business, must produce a suitably attractive value proposition. To this end, it needs to carefully assess the value creation potential of the various specific environmental initiatives that will form the content of its strategic approach, be it functional, integrated or proactive. This assessment and selection process is the subject of this chapter.

Companies that come this far already embody a new view of environmental management; one that accepts that the quest for solutions to environmental issues is an essential component of overall corporate strategy. They have left behind the days when environmental issues were dealt with on a case-by-case basis, and staff departments or task forces were asked to come up with proposals to respond to specific environmental problems or opportunities, while overall corporate objectives were worked out separately in another part of the organization. Clearly, the comprehensive approach is essential to excellent environmental management, and should be reflected in the value proposition.

The classical environment-versus-economy controversy may still surface in specific cases, but most corporate leaders now have little doubt about the importance of sustainability. Ranging from DuPont's outspoken CEO, Chad Holliday Jr ('There's no need for debate – let's get on with it.')[1] to Novo Nordisk's Mads Øvlisen ('We are beyond the point where the financial community questions whether we have to be environmentally proactive. That's how we can create value.')[2] and Shell's Mark Moody-Stuart ('In the end, if the shareholders don't think it's a good idea, you have a problem. We haven't had that problem.')[3] the message is the same: Let's do it!

Developing an actionable strategy – outlining objectives and means, allocating the resources and the time required, and assigning

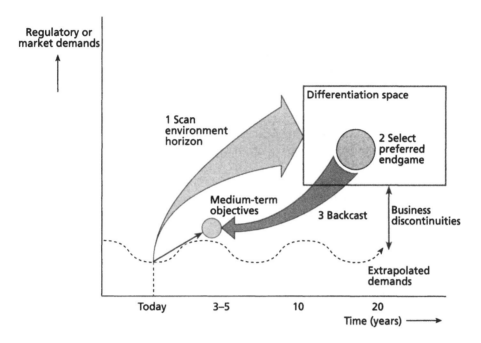

Figure 4.1 *Backcasting to medium-term strategy*

authorities and responsibilities – is like going on holiday: once you know your destination (ie the blueprint of a preferred endgame), it's much easier to select a route (ie in-between objectives) and to pack (ie the means). In general, given the uncertainties of the endgame, it also pays to determine an action plan for the first stages only (ie a medium-term strategy), to ensure a proper blend of an endgame focus with the flexibility to adapt as circumstances change or, importantly, as management and its coworkers learn.

Thus, building on the earlier horizon scanning and using the endgame blueprint as its basis, top management must 'backcast' (as opposed to forecast) a medium-term strategy (Figure 4.1).[4] In essence, this process consists of two steps that often involve a significant number of internal and external experts, working in a task force charged with generating and assessing options for action as part of an overall action programme.

GENERATING OPTIONS

Earlier, in Chapter 2, we suggested that top management should think about its business activities in terms of an integrated chain. This notion has proved to be highly effective in facilitating the efforts of taskforces to generate complete overviews of specific options for actions. Although the flow diagram shown in Figure 2.4 is clearly a simplification, in principle no more that four 'valves' are available to manage the volume flow. Early in the chain one can open or shut the inflow of raw materials used. If the same number of end products still has to reach the end consumer, one must either reduce the volume of the material used per product unit or limit the emissions of the integrated chain as a whole. Other conceivable combinations, almost without exception, also involve the manipulation of two or more valves to control the process flow.

The art of integrated chain management now involves effectively and efficiently adjusting the valves in order to match the throughput of the substance with its sustainable level of production, and to minimize 'leaks' from the system. For example, an integrated chain approach to paper and board would focus on the system by which cellulose fibre is transformed from wood to pulp and paper and then recycled, incinerated, or – if such treatment is impossible – disposed of as landfill. Using such an approach, consumption of cellulose fibre should be matched to the sustainable rate of harvesting forests.

In practice, options for action are identified on the basis of a quantified volume flow diagram. Studying the flows, it quickly becomes apparent where either the consumption of resources or the leaks from the system contribute to an unsustainable environment, or which valve needs to be turned to gain an advantage over competitors. Checklists such as that developed by Jacqueline Cramer as part of her so-called STRETCH (from 'selection of strategic environmental challenges') methodology may serve as a practical guide for systematically testing the pros and cons of manipulating each specific valve (Table 4.1).[5] A joint discussion with the most knowledgeable line and staff managers almost invariably results in a relevant overview of realistic options.

The options for action that are thus generated tend to cover a wide range of very different actions. In some cases, it may prove to be beneficial to close the leaking valve, for instance, through process improvements or emissions recovery. It may also be the case that opening the recycling valve or optimizing the resources and products valves – eg through miniaturization or substance/product substitution – is more appropriate. Based on a first rough assessment of their benefits, the long-list of available options should therefore be cut down to a short-list of the most promising options for further detailed evaluation.

Option evaluation is further facilitated by a framework – the environmental option map – which we have developed to assist managers in the task (Figure 4.2). The environmental option map's axes represent the two main criteria in the assessment of environmental actions: economic impact – ie the net effect on shareholder value; and environmental yield – ie the net benefit to the environment. The zero-point represents a 'do-nothing' approach: the

Table 4.1 *Checklist for manipulating environmental management valves*

Objective	Illustrations
Minimization of production impact	Minimization of waste, emissions and energy use Multiple use of energy, water and materials on regional scale (eg through use of waste heat from neighbouring company) Respect for biodiversity
Minimization of product impact	Reduction of toxic substances Minimization of materials consumption (eg through miniaturization, weight reduction, systems integration) Minimization of use of non-renewable resources Minimization of fossil energy consumption (eg through energy efficiency and renewable energy use)
Efficient distribution and logistics	Substitution by environmentally friendlier modes of transportation Efficiency improvement of logistics (eg high loading) Transport prevention (eg of air, liquids and water)
Intensity of use	Increased service intensity of products Shared product use (with third parties)
Durability of products	Re-use of products/components Technical upgrading Lengthening of lifetime, if sensible Improving reparability/refurbishing
Recyclability of materials	Reduction of materials diversity Materials re-use (through cascading) Design for disassembly Selectivity: safe disposal

Source: Adapted from Jaqueline Cramer/Philips Sound & Vision

environmental yield and the economic impact of an option is positioned as change for the better or worse compared with doing nothing.

Economic impact can be positive or, at least in the short term, negative. But even if it is negative this does not mean, of course, that it offers no differentiation advantages: implementing a measure might be costly to a company, but if it does so more efficiently than its competitors, it gains an advantage over them.

Furthermore, the benefits of environmental actions should not only be seen in rational terms. In particular, companies that opt for proactive strategies can garner benefits – such as goodwill within and outside the company – which though intangible are no less real. Such

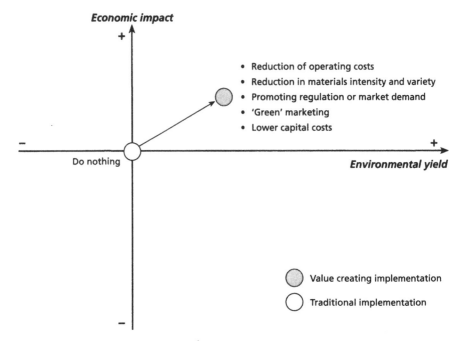

Figure 4.2 *Win–win options*

intangibles may include intellectual property, brand name or corporate image, and external networks. Critical, however, is the thrill among the internal stakeholders, notably coworkers. This X-factor can turn an 'irrational' decision into sound business, and should be built-in to the corporate option assessment exercise. As Swiss industrialist Stephan Schmidheiny, the initiator and chairman of the Business Council for Sustainable Development, said: 'Rational arguments alone will not guide people onto paths of sustainability – convincing and forceful as they may be. Only strong emotions carried by values and driven by beliefs can do the trick.'[6]

Such words are amplified by businesspeople as different as Edgar Woolard of DuPont ('I have never seen a stronger force for coalescing the organization about a common purpose than the environment. Our people were waiting to be empowered to do the right thing.')[7] and Ben Cohen, co-founder and Chairman of Ben and Jerry's Homemade ('What a strange thing we're discovering: as our business supports the community, the community supports us back').[8] Perhaps the essence of the X-factor was best summarized in the down-to-earth words of Paul O'Neill, CEO of the aluminium giant Alcoa: 'If people realize the company cares for the quality of that environment and safety, they will care for their products and services, and customers will notice.'[9]

On our environmental option map we can group the various actions into three types: win–win, beat-the-alternative and jump-ahead.[10] After looking at the options, we close the chapter with a suggestion as to how companies can assess which specific options are most appropriate for them.

Win–win options

These options – graphically illustrated in Figure 4.2 – are usually based on improved efficiency and green marketing, and exist when the scope and timing of a business discontinuity are known (ie the environmental issues are in Phases 3 and 4 of the PLC) and there is an economic incentive for companies to come up with efficient and quick solutions.

Responding to environmental pressure is, in most cases, an expensive proposition in the short term. Although reliable data are difficult to obtain, most industry sources suggest that current anti-pollution expenditures in the OECD countries average about 2 per cent of value added, with sectors such as petroleum and pulp mills reaching into the double digits. Any win–win option that can benefit the environment while reducing cost is therefore obviously welcome.

The managerial trade-off, however, is often complicated since the true costs to the environment are usually not incorporated in the assessment. We, for instance, assume that clean air is free, and we grant subsidies, designed with social objectives in mind, that distort utility prices. Not without reason, policy-makers as well as corporate leaders point to the desirability of full-cost accounting, ie internalizing the true costs of the use of natural resources and environmental pollution in the prices of products and services. Only then is the market able to make rational decisions. Helmut Maucher, Nestlé's CEO, puts it this way:

> *Lack of profitability is the most severe obstacle to efficient environmental protection. Legislation by itself will not do the trick – a company will not be able to comply with environmental standards unless it can afford to make the necessary investments. One of the basic lessons we all should have learned from the collapse of the Communist countries is that only market-oriented economies can efficiently protect the environment. Furthermore, the methods chosen to put a price on commodities such as clean air, water, and use of renewable energy sources must as far as possible rely on market mechanisms. Not that these mechanisms are virtuous in and by themselves, but they are undeniably the most efficient means of allocating resources.*[11]

In any event, cash outlays are clearly only one side of the story. Many environmentally motivated actions produce solid bottom-line benefits, especially when competitors and/or other industries are less alert or able to take similar actions. Increasing revenue flows or cost reductions can transform an environmental challenge into a win–win opportunity, benefiting both the environment and the company's shareholder.

Such opportunities are discussed in a variety of eco-efficiency publications.[12] Actually, virtually without exception, technical improvements of industrial processes and/or products – often executed as part of a total quality management (TQM) initiative – result in the immediate reduction of operational costs (including compliance costs). The names given by some leading companies to their efforts leave little doubt about their expectations of bottom-line benefits from environmental measures: 3M's Pollution Prevention Pays (3P); Chevron's Save Money And Reduce Toxins (SMART); Dow Chemical's Waste Reduction Always Pays (WRAP); and Texaco's Wipe Out Waste (WOW).

Many basic environmental management practices produce savings in plant and equipment costs, such as low-energy/long-life lighting systems, energy-efficient construction (resulting in lower heating and cooling costs), and reduced maintenance expenditures. Cogeneration for the production of energy and heat can also sometimes produce spectacular cuts in both emissions and costs.

The same applies to sourcing, assembly, logistics and even office administration. A European computer manufacturer, for instance, was surprised to learn that designing a computer for easy recycling also reduced assembly costs by over 50 per cent. A herbicide producer managed to decrease its process waste, thereby cutting back its pollution by 90 per cent and lowering costs by 5 per cent. Likewise, the environmental optimization of logistics networks can lead to substantial improvements in the utilization of transport capacity, fuel, reduction of mileage costs, etc. In office administration, the replacement of paper by electronic media has led to greater efficiency of communication and decision-making. Indeed, further win–win benefits may realistically be expected from advances in information technology (IT), which promote virtual partnerships throughout the value delivery chain.[13]

The redesign of products can also lead to significant reductions in material intensity and variety, and hence to major cost savings in purchasing and storage. In fact, as argued by Friedrich Schmidt-Bleek of the Wuppertal Institute, greater material intensity is fundamental to preventing destabilization of global ecosystems. In order to create room for economic growth in developing countries, he argues, developed nations should strive for a factor-ten decrease in materials use, ie a 90 per cent cut in their use of materials.[14]

The progress made in improved product design is a source of pride in many companies. In one case, a European computer manufacturer reduced the variety of materials in its product by 50 per cent, while reducing its weight by 20 per cent. Further, current efforts to design the next generation of ultra-high efficiency cars promise similar improvements in material efficiency. Minimizing packaging also almost always creates significant savings. A German medical products manufacturer, for example, replaced individual equipment packaging with a new distribution system using trucks with padded and adjustable shelves. The result: annual savings of over $150,000 per hospital.

Another benefit of environmental measures is found in the extension of resource use: the longer a material is used, the less of it is needed. The move towards cradle-to-grave responsibility in many industries in essence optimizes the cascade of a resource, from its virgin use to its ultimate 'disappearance', by maximizing the number of vertical steps and lengthening the duration of each step. The range of such resource extension possibilities is extremely broad. It runs from the actual abolition of the need for the product (eg teleconferencing's elimination of the need for air travel), to product reuse (eg returnable packaging crates), to product repair, to material recycling (reusing a material in another product), to thermal recycling (capturing the material's energy contents through incineration), to waste incineration (burning a material to limit the volume to be disposed of).

Individual companies may also gain a sustainable competitive advantage by promoting regulation or market demand favouring a technological or business solution of their own that is difficult or costly for others to implement. In 1991, for instance, DuPont executives actively lobbied in order to 'harvest' their commercial and technological advantage with regard to CFC substitutes, by encouraging the US's Environmental Protection Agency (EPA) administrator to speed up the regulatory timetable for the fight against ozone depletion. President George Bush subsequently announced that the US would unilaterally phase out production of CFCs by the end of 1995 instead of 2000.[15] In another example, Svenska Statoil of Sweden decided to invest in petrol vapour recycling at all of its petrol stations. The company urged the regulator to support this approach, which later became obligatory. Since the company's sales-per-station were higher than the industry average, its investment costs per litre of petrol sold were lower than those of its competitors.

The promotion of specific measures or market demand does not necessarily have to be done in a proactive and aggressive manner. A soft-sell approach can also be highly effective. A number of large European supermarket chains, for instance, provided constructive leadership in shaping joint collection systems for packaging waste after the introduction of the take-back obligation. Almost certainly, this cooperative approach was partially induced by the fact that their greater economies of scale – in terms of floor space and hardware –

and especially their greater delivery frequency gave them a competitive advantage over their smaller rivals.

Similarly, major chemical multinationals actively search their technology portfolio for proprietary processes that, through either patent protection or prohibitive costs, could effectively block imitation by competitors and hence result in a cost advantage. Some European salt producers, for instance, apply a vacuum technology that produces less waste and, moreover, contains much less mercury than the traditional rock-salt-based technology. When regulators became persuaded of the merits of the new technology, and forced major industry players to adopt it, the innovating companies' competitors were unpleasantly surprised. In another example, Scandinavian paper producers have virtually eliminated the use of chlorine in their bleaching process, thus positioning themselves as primary suppliers to a growing number of organizations with environment-driven, sound-sourcing practices. In this case, NGOs did much of the lobbying by attacking major customers for their 'irresponsible' purchasing.

Win–win solutions can also be realized by pursuing green marketing opportunities. Prompted by numerous publications and the media generally, consumers are more informed, sensitive and demanding with regard to the greenness of products.[16] And many companies are responding. Following in the footsteps of Swiss Migros and a number of German supermarkets, chains in the UK have taken up the green gauntlet. Such initiatives, in turn, stimulate green product offerings from suppliers. Companies like Apple Computer and Ben & Jerry's have received excellent publicity by boycotting suppliers that fail to adhere to their codes of environmental and social responsibility.

But food retailing is not the only sector that is reacting: manufacturers of products as different as refrigerators and cars have presented a green front and benefited accordingly. Further, as Sweden's second-largest food products chain, KF, has found, the benefits are two-fold: not only does its green own-brand Änglamark produce above-average margins, it has also boosted KF's corporate image within the industry and among customers.[17]

A cautionary note should be sounded here, however. As yet, there is little evidence that many end-users/consumers are willing to pay significantly more for greenness. Reports claiming that they are ready to pay a 5 per cent environmental premium are, in fact, rarely supported by actual sales numbers.[18] For most consumers, being 'green' is equated with being hygienic and healthy, and thus it is a basic characteristic of satisfactory products. In other words, 'ungreen' products are increasingly unacceptable, while environmental friendliness is more and more commonly expected, something that is taken for granted, rather than an added feature that encourages a purchase despite its higher price.[19]

A further point is that consumers, especially when informed and prompted by critical NGOs, also are too smart to be fooled by what could be perceived as quick-fixes – one-off environmental initiatives. Corporate leaders should beware: if the green marketing effort is not in line with the overall corporate positioning, it could easily backfire.[20] When, for instance, in the summer of 2000, BP Amoco presented its new environmentally friendly corporate image – BP now stood for 'Beyond Petroleum' – to emphasize its long-term commitment to renewable energy sources, Greenpeace was quick to point out that the company spent more (estimated at $200 million) on the global advertising campaign to promote its new image than on the development of new energy sources themselves. Greenpeace also volunteered a new slogan for the oil giant: 'Burning the Planet'.

On the other hand, companies' environmental friendliness is also increasingly publicly challenged by competitors. In the early 1990s, Europe experienced its first green counter-attack lawsuit of this sort. Henkel, a German chemical manufacturer, launched a phosphate-free detergent, Le Chat, in France and immediately gained 18 per cent of the detergent market. Its largest competitor, Rhône-Poulenc, countered with a public campaign that claimed that the new product was actually more harmful to the environment than the standard brands. In the event, Henkel sued and won: Rhône-Poulenc withdrew its claim and took down posters of fish supposedly killed by phosphate-free detergent.[21]

Finally, a much-underestimated advantage of environmental initiatives is that they can often benefit from lower capital costs. Governments and other funding sources like the EU increasingly offer green investment support through low-interest loans and capital injections. Some countries even have tax incentives for green investments. Significantly, lending institutions are also refining their credit approval by assessing environmental risks, for example where contaminated sites are involved. Some leading asset managers and insurers are developing standards that will make it easier to account for the full impact of environmental issues on financial performance: 'good performers' benefit from lower rates reflecting the expectation of low long-term cash-flow volatility compared to other companies that might be more vulnerable to environmental regulation, accidents or liabilities.[22]

As an example of this trend, the Norwegian engineering company Kvaerner secured funding for a revolving credit facility of several hundred million US dollars in 1995 at a lending rate that was a few base points lower than the standard rate. Swiss Bank Corporation, Dresdner Bank, Enskilde and Chemical Bank arranged the facility. While these financial institutions are notoriously secretive about the details of such deals, none of them denied that the credit was granted on preferential terms 'in part because of (Kvaerner's) environmental performance.'[23]

Beat-the-alternative options

These measures involve actions that reach a specific environmental target at a net cost that is lower than the actions taken by competitors to the same end. For purposes of corporate strategy development, the most common beat-the-alternative options are present when both the scope and the timing of the solution are uncertain, that is, for issues in Phase 2 of the PLC. In such instances, multiple options for attaining the environmental target are often available. In many cases, none of these hold a reasonable promise for a win–win solution – that is, the economic impact is almost certainly negative. Outsmarting the competition, however, by selecting an option that destroys less shareholder value than the competitors' alternatives can still contribute to competitive advantage (Figure 4.3).

Almost invariably, beat-the-alternative options involve a degree of probability assessment. Management compares its do-nothing scenario or the solutions proposed by other players with its own alternative. It then assesses the likelihood that the competitors will actually pursue their options and the associated expectation of the economic impact. Any perceived superiority of the chosen option over those of competitors represents value created for its shareholders.

Most often, these options are open only to those companies or industries that have 'earned' such opportunities, because they generally require the cooperation or, at least, the implicit approval of

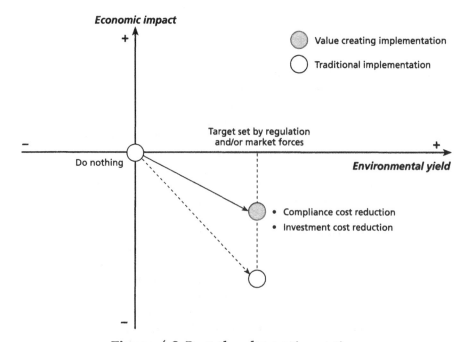

Figure 4.3 *Beat-the-alternative options*

government and/or the marketplace. Thus a key requirement is a credibility, which is built on a sustained corporate positioning vis-à-vis environmental demands. With such credibility, the opportunities to enhance shareholder value are significant indeed.

Among the beat-the-alternative options, it is useful to distinguish between those that reduce compliance costs and those that reduce investment costs.

1 Compliance cost reduction.

In the short term, a company can perhaps benefit most from a risk/liability management programme aimed at avoiding accidents and limiting the costs of liabilities and damage reparation. The experience of companies involved in major environmental incidents provides very clear evidence of how significant the costs of poor risk/liability management can be. Union Carbide, for instance, barely survived the Bhopal disaster, while Exxon lost billions as a result of the Exxon Valdez oil spill. In a more recent example, the Swedish-Canadian mining company Boliden saw its stock value plunge by $138 million after the April 1998 collapse of a tailings reservoir in Spain; the event caused toxic sludge to spill over an estimated 4200 acres of farmland and threatened to contaminate Doñana National Park, one of Europe's largest nature reserves. The initial Spanish estimates of the cleanup costs were as high as $320 million, but the company reportedly only had $70 million in insurance cover.[24]

With lower public tolerance of such incidents and increasingly tough jurisprudence, preventive measures thus pay off more than ever. This presents a simple choice for many corporations: do nothing and accept the risk of considerable costs in the case of an accident or a liability suit, or invest now in a targeted programme to reduce both the probability and the negative impact of such events.[25] From a purely economic viewpoint, risk and liability management is thus based on a probability assessment of alternatives, with the escalating penalties of a mistaken choice increasingly strengthening the case for self-initiated action.

Clearly this is an area of extreme relevance to many top management teams, especially in North America where financial and personal liabilities are much greater than elsewhere. Unfortunately, the subject requires a much more detailed discussion than is possible here, so we refer the reader to the specialized literature on the topic (see also Box 4.1).[26]

Important savings can also result from optimal participation in the policy process, which can reduce the direct costs of compliance with regulations. A certain level of direct environmental expenditure is unavoidable and, in a perfect world, is carried equally by every competitor. Regulations will continue to make target groups carry the external costs of their activities through fees, taxes and levies,

Box 4.1 Profiling current risk/liability exposure

Throughout this book we have refrained from discussing the most appropriate ways of dealing with environmental risks and liability exposure. Although the topic is of obvious importance to all business enterprises and, in our experience, generally not well covered by even large companies especially in Europe, it belongs in the realm of the functional response as defined in Chapter 1.

The 'golden lesson' on the topic was perhaps best expressed by former colleagues of the authors, Andreas Merkl and Harry Robinson in the title to their publication *Environmental Risk Management: Take it Back from the Lawyers and Engineers*.[a] Almost without exception, there is a lot of money left on the table because of poor management. Three separate elements often require specific attention:

Safety risks relate to accidents with very low probabilities and potentially very severe effects. Assessment of these risks – often mandatory as part of a permit procedure – generally includes technical risk analyses that yield the probability of plant-related (human) fatalities within a certain radius of a plant per year. Problems here include the inherent complexity of calculating a reliable overall safety risk level for a company on the bases of these analyses. The resulting risk figures also do not take into account the public perception of risks, even though perception may be a key factor in the acceptance of a company by society. Thus, the calculated figures have only limited usefulness for purposes of risk management.

Emission risks can be defined as the risks associated with known or unknown, regulated or non-regulated emissions and the ensuing damage to the environment. Probabilities are often much higher and immediate effects much less dramatic than those of safety risks. Emission risks may lead to significant costs, serious legal liability problems – for instance, in case of exceeding limits or damaging personal property – and poor corporate image. Usually, these risks can be managed systematically once they are identified; they should, however, be considered as part of an integrated risk assessment in order to form a sound basis for risk management.

A third type of risk arises from *liabilities due to past performance* – think of the costs of the US Superfund, but also the soil clean-up in The Netherlands or that in the former East Germany. Although highly relevant, for instance in case of acquisition or merger, the assessment of these liabilities most often belongs in the territory of legal and insurance experts and can be influenced only to a marginal degree by strategic management.

a Andreas Merkl and Harry Robinson, *The McKinsey Quarterly*, 1997, Number 3, p150ff and companies will continue to invest in environmental infrastructure, such as wastewater and air-treatment facilities. However, examples abound in which an entire industry or a single company has reacted sub-optimally, exposing itself to even more stringent government intervention. Specifically, the case for early and constructive involvement in the PLC is strong.

This is especially true with regard to issues that have political priority and hence may lead to regulations that are inefficient or inequitable. Naturally, regulators are first of all concerned with the effectiveness of their environmental measures: there is a problem and it must be solved. However, solutions that are also efficient and equitable require detailed business knowledge, and the regulators often have trouble reaching such solutions. Furthermore, legislation focused on effectiveness alone is at times unworkable. In the US, for example, the EPA introduced landfill standards that were prohibitively expensive to meet unless huge waste volumes were involved. Few local governments, however, were willing to accept gargantuan landfills in their jurisdictions because of the fear of uncontainable air quality problems or 'nimbyism' (not in my back yard) within the community.

The experience in more environmentally advanced countries increasingly shows that alternative approaches can yield significant economic benefits to companies that participate in the policy-making process. Industry know-how, furthermore, frequently results in meeting environmental objectives at a much lower cost. Once again, management must make a probability assessment. Delaying, softening or defeating proposed regulation often pays off in the short term. However, it also polarizes positions, possibly leading to the worse outcome of tougher and more costly policies at a later date. Even a passive approach can be sub-optimal relative to policy optimization. Usually the most sensible approach is for industry sectors or individual companies to actively participate by contributing their insights and agreeing on a proper time-frame and a practical setting of priorities; the end result thus has a good chance of reflecting both their own economic interests and those of the environment. Weyerhaeuser's behaviour in the following case is a good illustration of the benefits of such an attitude (Box 4.2).

2 Investment cost reduction.

The best alternative is often the result of management decisions about cutting compliance costs. Let's look at the main options available.

Significant shareholder value can be created by responding to regulation not with end-of-pipe solutions, but through the integrated redesign of processes. Indeed, many large companies have successfully lowered their investment costs by proposing process-integrated

---

Box 4.2 Weyerhauser Company and Georgia-Pacific

In the mid-1990s Weyerhaeuser Company faced off against forest products industry rival Georgia-Pacific in a lobbying battle. EPA investigations under the Clean Air Act threatened to lead to sizeable fines plus the obligation to retrofit their plants with millions of dollars-worth of pollution control equipment. Still, neither company was clearly guilty.

In this uncertain legal environment, the two companies responded very differently. Georgia-Pacific succeeded in inserting an amendment into pending legislation that would enable it to avoid installing expensive pollution control equipment. Weyerhaeuser was less combative; in the hope of getting the EPA to drop its investigation, it paid $1.5 million in fines to state authorities and voluntarily installed the equipment.

Next up for the company was lobbying to keep the Georgia-Pacific provision from becoming law. 'Georgia-Pacific would have gotten an unfair competitive advantage because installing and operating pollution control equipment is very expensive,' said Sara Schreiner Kendall, Director of Environmental Affairs for Weyerhaeuser. 'It would be fundamentally unfair to penalize companies for coming voluntarily into compliance.' The strategy paid off. The EPA closed its investigation of the company and the objectionable amendment, according to Kendall, 'has been very, very watered down.'[a]

a *Tomorrow*, March–April 1996, p15

---

solutions to replace a series of smaller end-of-pipe actions. The costs of control devices such as filters or scrubbers escalate sharply as the demands on their effectiveness are increased. Thus an overly narrow approach in the beginning can turn out to be quite costly in the long run. This applies in particular to industries with long investment cycles – eg the chemical and basic metals industries. Such companies pay the price of narrow initial approaches, since they can generally realize environmental objectives more cheaply through the fundamental redesign of production processes. There is a further advantage to this approach: if a company can actually exceed the regulatory targets, the authorities often are open to negotiating the implementation timeframes, thus giving the company the chance to better synchronize its environmental investments with its overall investment plans.

The reduction in investment costs and emissions can be considerable. As an example, 3M increased the level of wastewater recycling in an Alabama plant, thus lowering the required capacity for a planned wastewater treatment facility. The recycling facility cost $480,000, but the company saved $800,000 on the wastewater treatment plant.[27]

Such process-integrated solutions, however, often require solid government–business cooperation, since the regulators lack the understanding to come up with such answers. Corporations have to gain the trust of the regulators for the successful implementation of these solutions. Regulators have to be convinced that the solution will attain at least the same result – measured in overall emission targets for an entire production process – as specific technical solutions directed at each emission outlet (eg treatment plants, scrubbers and filters).

Even more substantial benefits may be garnered from the integrated redesign of products. A car manufacturer in the functional response mode, for example, can optimize compliance with emission regulations by designing a superior catalytic conversion system. A company pursuing an integrated response may go a step further and design the next generation of ultra-efficient combustion engines, or come up with a car that is easy to dismantle and recycle.

Indeed, corporations increasingly use 'design for environment' (DFE) as a basis for creating unique features that give them a competitive advantage. Xerox's Asset Recycle Management programme, for example, treats old copiers as sources of high-quality, low-cost parts and components for its 'new' machines. A sophisticated re-manufacturing process allows these parts and components to be reconditioned, tested and then reassembled into new machines. In Germany, BMW initiated a 'design for disassembly' process that it hoped would pre-empt a proposed government take-back policy. By acting as a first mover, it was able to capture the few sophisticated German dismantling firms as part of an exclusive recycling infrastructure, thereby gaining a cost advantage over competitors who were left to fight over smaller, unlicensed operators, or devote precious capital to building their own dismantling infrastructure. This move enabled BMW to build an early reputation by taking back and recycling its old products as a precursor to the introduction of its new line of DFE cars.[28]

Redesigned products can also increase customer loyalty and save costs. SC Johnson Wax has developed an insecticide that has half the volatile organic compounds (VOC) of similar products. This development has reduced VOC emissions across the US and benefits customers and wholesalers through its lower residues, improved smell and new non-inflammability. It also saves the company $2 million annually in manufacturing costs.

Sharing the burden of compliance with environmental regulations can also provide advantages to companies. Rapidly increasing costs, for instance in the collection, treatment and/or recycling of process and product waste, have inspired individual companies to pursue economies of scale and form alliances with suppliers, customers or competitors, thus sharing the burden. In a typical example, the AVR Chemie partnership brought together the eight largest Dutch chemical companies, the city of Rotterdam and the national government for the development and operation of incineration and disposal facilities for the toughest toxic waste. Based on large scale and highly qualified operational management, and underpinned by a joint policy board and equitable burden sharing, the solution was clearly both environmentally and economically attractive.

Similar initiatives are springing up all across Europe and North America: for example, in car and packaging waste recycling. As regulatory and market forces increase the pressure on manufacturers to assume responsibility for the re-use and/or recycling of their products, distribution systems are redesigned to become, essentially, two-way streets. Standard business systems – eg develop–produce–sell – are expanded to include a take-back segment. Transportation and recycling economies of scale are fostering the emergence of these new 'reverse distribution' systems. Producers, packagers, wholesalers and retailers position themselves along the two-way system, usually seeking partnerships to ensure the necessary expertise and lighten the financial burden.

One step up in the burden sharing hierarchy are the market-based approaches that allow groups of companies to come up with most economical way of meeting a specific environmental objective. Such approaches include the 'bubble' concept, whereby a number of production facilities on a single geographic location are gathered under an imaginary bubble, for which overall emission standards are established. The authorities then leave it up to private initiatives to come up with the most efficient manner of meeting them. Thus, companies requiring a vast investment to meet their fair share of the target have the option of paying the others that still have the opportunity to realize more than their share at a lower cost. The savings in such schemes can be considerable.

Kalundborg in Denmark is an example of an industrial ecology or symbiosis approach. It has a complex network of companies which use each other's waste products as inputs. A coal-fired power plant generates waste heat that is used by an aquaculture facility, which raises 200 tons of turbot and trout annually. Gypsum produced from the pollution-control equipment on the power plant's smokestack is used by a plasterboard plant instead of virgin gypsum. The waste steam from the power plant is used by a Statoil oil refinery and a Novo Nordisk pharmaceutical plant. Wastewater from the oil refinery is used by the power plant. Novo Nordisk processes sludge from its fermentation activity with chalk-lime to make fertilizer for local farming operations. A cement plant and a chemical manufacturer are also part of this interconnected system. The industrial symbiosis at Kalundborg saves $12–15 million annually, along with 19,000 tons of oil, 30,000 tons of coal and 600,000 cubic meters of water.[29]

Tradable emission rights are another version of the burden-sharing concept. In this case, however, the bubble encompasses a much larger geographical area, say a state or a country or, since the Kyoto Protocol, the entire planet. Individual companies can buy and sell emission rights, as long as overall emission targets are met. Western European utilities, for instance, have been offered less stringent measures at home in exchange for helping their Central European counterparts cut their sulphur dioxide (SO_2) and nitrous oxide (NO_x) emissions, or for planting trees in developing countries to function as a carbon dioxide (CO_2) sink. It is clear that the impact of these approaches in combating acid rain and global warming is much greater, and the investment cost much lower, than would be the case with strictly national approaches.

In all likelihood, solutions along this line will come to the public's attention as the signatories to the Kyoto Protocol prepare to meet their obligations with respect to the reduction of greenhouse gas (GHG) emissions in an efficient and equitable manner.[30] In fact, carbon trading could soon become as common as buying and selling shares on the stock market. More than a decade ago, an international clearing-house system based on these principles, with money flowing from the developed to the developing countries, was proposed by McKinsey & Company as a way of structurally combating global warming worldwide.[31] Various trading mechanisms – joint implementation (JI), the clean development mechanism (CDM) and emissions trading (ET) – are currently under discussion to deal with the political intricacies of the scheme, particularly in terms of international equity.

Here are some specific examples of emission trading activity.

- In 1998, the New York State-based utility Niagara Mohawk and Canada's Suncor Energy claimed the first international GHG emissions trade. With the help of the US NGO the EDF, Suncor bought 100,000 tons of emissions from Niagara Mohawk, with an option to purchase up to 10 million more over ten years. Niagara Mohawk will invest 70 per cent of its net profits from the sale in new projects, thus contributing to GHG reductions. Suncor has also invested in the development of wind power in Alberta and in a forest conservation project in Belize, where it is protecting 19,000 acres of forest in partnership with The Nature Conservancy.[32]
- BP Amoco will order 12 of its business units to engage in internal emissions trading. The goal is to cut CO_2 emissions by 10 per cent by 2010, twice the target agreed in Kyoto for developed countries. Despite not knowing how international trading will work, BP expects to gain a valuable first-mover advantage with the mechanism that was pushed hardest by the US in Kyoto, namely, tradable CO_2 allowances.[33]
- The UK retailer B&Q decided to become carbon neutral for all its stores and lorry fleets by the end of 1999. The goal meant offset-

ting the 110,000 tons of carbon B&Q emits yearly – 90 per cent of which comes from its lorries, 9 per cent from its stores and 1 per cent from head office.

- Mazda UK has become the first car company to sign a 'carbon offset' contract to neutralize the CO_2 emissions from its cars. For every Demio small car sold after its August 1998 launch, Mazda will give some $20 to plant five trees, which is enough to absorb the CO_2 from a typical year's driving.[34]
- Dutch utility Nuon bought 200 green electricity certificates, each worth 10,000 kilowatt hours (kWh), from UK producer National Wind Power. The electricity is sold in the UK, but without the renewables label. The Dutch company can get better value for the 'environmental benefit' back home, offering green electricity to its customers, contributing to the company's own target of sourcing 3 per cent from renewables, and getting that power exempted from the Dutch eco-tax.[35]

In an interesting twist in this move to market-based instruments, traditional smoke-stack companies, especially in the developing countries, could reap windfall benefits from developed countries, or their corporations, which are willing to pay for the modernization of the developing countries' facilities in exchange for CO_2 emission rights. As a matter of fact, such 'CO_2 emission reserves' could, when recognized, significantly change the balance sheets of the facilities' owners or even make them an attractive acquisition target.

Developing countries could benefit in other ways as well. Within the Kyoto Protocol, countries like Russia and Ukraine, which have notoriously polluting industries, agreed not to increase their emissions. But the collapse of their economies since 1990 means that they are currently emitting well below the baseline levels in any event. In other words, they will have surplus permits to sell, even without doing any cleaning up. The US is happy about this, since it sees Russia and Ukraine as the source for spare credits it could buy. Does this amount to cheating? Will it eventually result in a 'hot air' problem, when the Eastern European states begin experiencing high economic growth rates and may not be able to meet their environmental obligations as their CO_2 emissions reach ceiling levels? The experts disagree, but Russia is thought to be planning to launch its own emissions futures exchange to capitalize on the situation.[36]

Portfolio win–win options offer another version of burden-sharing. Suppose a company proposed a total environmental strategy to the authorities, whereby the negative environmental impact of one of its activities is compensated for by the positive contributions of others. In The Netherlands, for instance, power generators could use their waste heat to dry animal manure, thus tackling another of the country's major environmental problems: namely, excessive manure levels that cause serious eutrophication of ground water. The additional costs associated with the process would be more than offset if the government, as a reward for the generators' contribution to solving the manure problem, would set them lower emission targets for sulphur oxide (SO_x) and CO_2 and hence reduce their costs in meeting them. The overall economic impact of the combined measures would thus be positive. The environmental benefits of drying the manure are such that, despite losses in the battle against acidification and global warming, the net environmental yield would be clearly positive.

Although an obvious portfolio win–win opportunity, the above proposal proved too complex politically. To date, such portfolio approaches have been rare. But in early 1995, US utility Niagara Mohawk agreed to transfer 1.75 million tons of CO_2 reductions to Arizona Public Service Company in exchange for 25,000 tons of SO_2 allowances, thus effectively establishing the first interpollutant exchange rate of its kind.[37] In general, however, regulators have been too compartmentalized or risk-averse, and business has lacked the strategic overview and the trust base to engage in such experiments. Still, the mutual benefits could be very significant. In any event, looking forward it would seem that the Kyoto Protocol, with its emphasis on a range of GHGs and known exchange rates with respect to their environmental effects, invites solutions of this type. With the costs of measures escalating rapidly, a strategic clustering of options could provide major opportunities for competitive differentiation.

In our opinion, the private–public partnership approach, in which government and one or more companies cooperate in implementing 3E solutions, holds the greatest promise for the future for environmental management. The experience in The Netherlands, in particular, provides a number of excellent examples of how a playing field can be partially levelled or, even, how such partnerships can create a substantial advantage over less cooperatively-inclined competitors.

The prototype for such a partnership approach is the so-called environmental action plan (EAP). Developed to deal with the environmental issues of large production sites within an individual company, the EAP can equally well be applied to whole corporations or to a single site intended for a number of companies. In its purest form, the EAP deals with the problems that commonly arise in industrialized areas because of the expansion of industrial complexes and/or urbanization. As a result, such large industrial sites become too close to residential areas. In a few cases – Bhopal for instance – the consequences are disastrous.

The costs of correcting these creeping developments are often exorbitant. Apart from the implementation of new measures, companies have to catch up with a backlog of regulations, ranging from noise and smell abatement and the minimization of risks (leaks, explosions) to soil clean-up. Often, their reaction is to battle with the authorities on each individual regulatory element. The result is frequently sub-optimal: management scurries from one end-of-pipe solution to the next without an agreed plan that would allow the execution of process solutions aligned with normal business and investment cycles. Thus, both the medium-term environmental yield and the economic impact is excessively negative, in some cases even leading to plant closures.

The EAP, in contrast, is based on the idea that by cooperating, a solution combining a high environmental yield, lower economic impact and a greater sociopolitical acceptance can be achieved. Although many variations are conceivable, the objective is to attain the regulatory environmental targets at the very least, but to do so while creating greater implementation flexibility.

After reaching an initial agreement with the authorities with respect to the principles of an EAP, a company or site management develops its own plan. Subsequently, each relevant government agency – at municipal, regional or national levels – responds to those aspects of the EAP that fall within its mandate. Against the background of the ultimate environmental targets, the economic impact can be optimized through negotiations. In those cases where the environmental targets are not yet fixed, the environmental yield/economic impact trade-off can itself be negotiated.

The ultimate end-product is an EAP that is 'owned' by the company and signed off by the authorities. The costs of environmental measures tend to be significantly reduced, as the implementation is optimized by being streamlined with the company's regular investment plans. This often requires that the authorities agree to specific delays with respect to some actions, whereas others are brought forward. In extreme cases, when the most economically positive environmental actions are taken in the beginning and the high-cost actions towards the end of the EAP, the net present value of the total plan can conceivably be positive. Most important, however, from an environmental point of view, is the fact that management produces an overall plan with process solutions that are integrated into its business plans.

Voluntarism is evidently a key characteristic of the EAP approach. Reflecting on the advantage of this ingredient, Edgar Woolard, DuPont's CEO, said:

> *Voluntary approaches use resources more efficiently and accelerate progress more rapidly than command-and-control approaches, which have reached the point of diminishing returns. At DuPont, we have learned that 80 per cent of the environmental benefit possible in a given area can be*

obtained for the first 20 per cent of the costs. We also have found that, on average, regulation-driven work costs three times more than voluntary waste reduction for the same environmental benefit. This is probably true because regulation-driven work focuses on eliminating specific substances on a set schedule – leaving little opportunity for the synergies of an integrated approach.[38]

A further step towards true cooperative approaches is the use of covenants or contracts. A group of companies, for instance an industry sector, agrees with the authorities to realize specific environmental objectives within a given time span – for instance, a 20 per cent reduction in energy consumption in a decade, or 50 per cent cut in waste in 5 years.

The covenant process is similar to that of an EAP: the companies agree on an action plan that is approved by the government. The ultimate effect is also akin to that of an EAP: the participating companies commit to the environmental objectives but have the maximum freedom for acting in the most efficient and equitable manner. To both government and industry, the covenant approach offers the additional advantage that it is no longer necessary to go through the lengthy and resource-intensive regulatory process. This not only is economically attractive, but also may produce earlier results and hence higher environmental yields.

Jump-ahead options

Many corporate actions we've discussed so far, purposely or not, involve incremental adaptation to change. Reacting to whatever the regulator or the market demands, a company takes a series of small steps as it adjusts to changing circumstances. True, the inherent flexibility of this approach can be a source of competitive strength. However, particularly when faced with PLC Phase 1 issues, where the scope and timing of potential business discontinuities are still uncertain, such incrementalism can be costly, since companies can easily be caught off-guard: the differentiation space can expand very rapidly, seriously disrupting a particular sector. Companies capable of jumping ahead of their competitors and anticipating such disruptions can benefit immensely.

Here are a couple of examples of companies benefiting from jumping ahead: the New Jersey utility, Public Service Electric & Gas, reinforced its credibility by voluntarily reducing its CO_2 emissions in order to promote a regulatory system based on allowance trading; ARCO introduced reformulated fuel in the US, thereby increasing its market share by 2 per cent. Instances of the damage caused by disruptive changes are also widespread: the sharp drop in the price

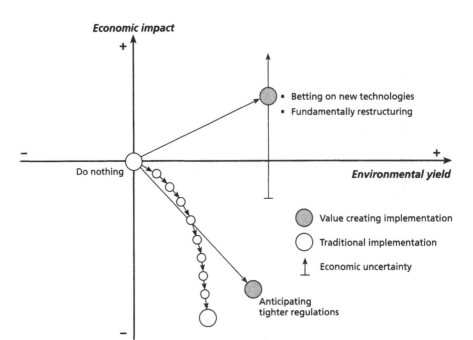

Figure 4.4 *Jump-ahead options*

of sulphur-rich oil with the introduction of legislation to combat acid rain in Europe and the US; the drop in demand for tuna caused by the consumer boycott in response to the effect of the industry's fishing practices on dolphins; and the market's punishment of German detergent manufacturers that were slow in replacing the phosphates in their products.

Anticipating such events is naturally difficult: issue areas in which jump-ahead actions can be taken are, by their very nature, uncertain, requiring cautious management assessment. The visualization of these options on the environmental option map thus reflects the inevitable trade-off involved. 'Normal' companies, which are in a functional or even an integrated response mode, would take a series of low environmental yield/low economic risk steps. Proactive companies, however, would consider an environmental quantum leap ahead with – expectedly – lower accumulated costs, but a much greater economic upside and downside. Proactive industry shapers potentially can also gain a significant advantage over their do-nothing competitors, even to the point of putting them out of business, if their beliefs in the positive economic returns of a specific high-risk option are realized. This is particularly the case when such options stem from market demands – ie if competitors are not induced to act by regulators and hence are caught off-guard (Figure 4.4).

Any jump-ahead strategy must be fed by a repeated triple-focus assessment of the positions taken by the various players in the environmental arena. But the different courses of action available can be defined. Here are three groups we have identified.

Some companies, especially in sectors in which investments can involve very long time-horizons, decide that it is better to anticipate tighter regulations rather than responding later. When considering major fixed assets plans – power plants, steel mills, refineries, etc – especially in geographic regions with currently less stringent regulation, it may be sound business strategy to implement advanced environmental measures. In such contexts management often asks itself: Will the current emission levels still be acceptable 20 years from now? Could we retrofit the plant at reasonable cost if the regulations were to be tightened, or would it be more cost-effective to build it right from the start? Here are the thoughts of Dave Buzzelli, Dow Chemical's Vice President of Environment, Health and Safety and a leading US business figure in the environmental arena:

> *A few years ago we were planning a new plant in Mexico, and decided it was going to be the best of its kind in the company. Not only would it comply with the recent Clean Air Act in the United States, it would also have a brand-new feature: all the sewers would be raised above ground, so that if they leaked we could catch the spillage. Then NAFTA came along, and we felt pretty smug. When we made the decision to build a world-class plant in Mexico, NAFTA was only a glimmer in our eye.*
>
> *Two new plants in Thailand started up in the second quarter of 1993. Again, they were designed to be the best in the whole of Dow. Thailand now has its first hazardous waste incinerator. We did not have to build it, but we wanted to avoid landfill and repeat what we had been doing in the US for many years.*[39]

As we noted in our discussion of the fourth step of the environmental hierarchy of needs, the environmental impact of corporate activity will encompass broader issues more and more. Companies considering jump-ahead options must bear this in mind. The truth is that their environmental shadows will inevitably spread. Their assessments should thus go beyond the impact of their activities on the immediate ecology, to include considerations such as spatial cohesion, social renewal and the identity of the surroundings.

But regulations don't actually have to become tighter for this sort of jump-ahead action to be worthwhile. It is frequently the case that companies face absolute environmental impact restraints. In other words, if a company wants to expand its operations, it might have to improve its environmental performance anyway. Typically, a moderate growth in a company's production of 4 per cent per year would, over a ten-year period, increase its environmental impact by about 50 per cent. Tough corporate policies would thus be needed to maintain emission volumes, waste disposal flows or traffic flows under the absolute limits.

Examples of pre-emptive corporate actions include Unilever's promotion of the sustainable fishery, Mitsubishi's funding of reforestation research and experimentation in Malaysia's Sarawak area, and Alcoa's award-winning programme of rehabilitating bauxite-mining operations in Western Australia.[40]

In May 2000, 3M announced it would voluntarily phase out production of some of its fluorocarbon-based coatings and surfactants because of concerns over environmental persistence. Derivatives of these products were detected in blood samples taken from people all over the world, even though the route of exposure as yet is not understood. The product, with annual sales of $320 million (2 per cent of the company's turnover), will be taken out of production. 'Our decision', said 3M's vice-president Charles Reich, 'anticipates increasing attention to the appropriate use of persistent materials.' External reactions have been positive. The EPA administrator, Carol Browner, gave the company 'great credit for identifying the problem and coming forward voluntarily.' NGOs, as well as interested financial parties, applauded the move, and 3M's share price rose 4.6 per cent on the day of the announcement. Industry observers also immediately pointed out that the decision put an onus on competitors such as DuPont, Elf Atochem and Clariant to offer reassurance on their fluorocarbon products.[41]

Betting on new technologies is another jump-ahead option, but it involves actions that are strategically more complex and of greater economic impact. The car industry, as is so often the case, provides colourful illustrations of widely different approaches. In the early 1990s, Japanese manufacturers led the way in focusing on low fuel-consumption technologies. Car producers in Germany and Scandinavia followed suit, while most US and Southern European producers preferred a more cautious wait-and-see approach. Some five years later, with the reality of global climate change on their minds, many major players appear to have placed their bets on new technologies ranging from fuel cells to batteries. This is a shortened version of a report on the issue published in 1999 in the Detroit Free Press:

Fuel cell technology is developing much more rapidly than many industry observers predicted just a few years ago, when battery-powered electric cars were touted as the next wave of the future.

In the mid-1990s, General Motors led the car industry in introducing a battery-powered car to consumers in California and Arizona. No large market developed because of its hefty lease price and relatively short range: the battery needed recharging after driving for a few hours.

Toyota and Honda now appear in front with hybrid-powered vehicles that run partially on gasoline and partially on a cleaner alternative fuel source such as a battery. These cars are expected to reach the US market in 2000.

Ford joined forces with DaimlerChrysler and Canadian specialist Ballard to develop the hydrogen fuel cell technology. Its first family vehicle is expected to be on the market in 2004. Feeling the heat, GM and Toyota teamed up to develop fuel cells and hybrids. Although Ford is looking good, Bill O'Neill, GM's executive director of product communication and development, insists the Toyota-GM partnership is very much in the race. 'GM took the most risk on electric-powered vehicles and we are pursuing hybrids and fuel cells with the same aggressiveness,' he added.[42]

In other industries it is no different, however. Oil giants such as BP and Shell have placed their bets on renewable energy technologies; Exxon, in contrast, is a strong advocate of the incremental approach, as shown by its pre-Kyoto lobbying activities. In the early 1990s, DuPont and ICI demonstrated the value of pre-emptive actions: they were better prepared for the fairly sudden ban on CFCs, while all their major competitors, lacking substitutes, were forced to withdraw from the industry. In some cases the moral may be simple: although the indirect environmental costs are high, the price of missing out on an environmentally benign technological break-through can be obliteration.[43]

Sometimes the new technology effectively reduces the likelihood of regulatory action. Here is DeSimone's and Popoff's description of an action taken by Cargill:

Cargill is reducing the material intensity of agriculture by applying only the required quantity of plant nutrients and agrochemicals in the sections of fields that require them. The innovation is based on a systems approach involving certified crop advisors, trained agronomists, soil testing, and application services that use the latest satellite-linked computer technology. It allows farmers to save money by buying less and benefits the environment through less runoff and contamination of groundwater by surplus products. Cargill loses sales in the short term but in the longer term has a closer relationship with more satisfied customers – and reduces the likelihood of regulatory intervention.[44]

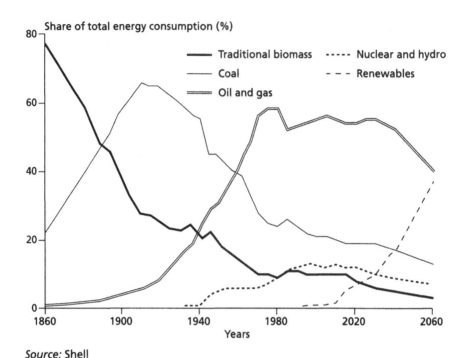

Source: Shell

Figure 4.5 *Market share of energy sources: Shell's scenario for dynamics-as-usual*

In a number of cases, the impact of changing environmental demands can lead companies to consider jumping ahead of developments by fundamentally restructuring at a business or industry level.

For instance, given the differing strategies professed within the traditionally close-knit family of the Seven Sisters, the future of the oil industry could range from the current fuel dependence to the altogether different energy sector foreseen by Shell in its scenario assessments (Figure 4.5). Similarly, and in the shorter run, it will be interesting to see how the delaying tactics of some car manufacturers with respect to a quantum leap in fuel efficiency will hold up against the response of their more advanced competitors. More relevant still, however, is the answer that even the latter will provide when it becomes evident that major increases in fuel efficiency mean little when they are offset by concomitant increases in passenger miles.

We believe that, in the long-term, structural solutions will be pressed onto industry. Given the nature of the most recent environmental issues, one must expect the necessary policies or changes in market behaviour to be far-reaching. We have already seen some examples. The phase-out of CFCs to limit ozone depletion has led to major withdrawals from the industry. Similarly, the pros and cons of chlorine will probably result in the elimination of polyvinyl chloride

(PVC) from short-life applications such as packaging materials; it is already having an impact on the paper industry, where chlorine bleaching is being replaced by oxygen bleaching. Major chlorine producers and users thus face a serious timing issue, since such changes could result in a quick and radical cut in demand for chlorine. In the chemical bulk industry this may have serious implications for the competitive positioning of players and for market stability.

Cradle-to-grave product responsibility will lead to the restructuring of many industries, ranging from packaging to cars and household appliances. And what of the effects of, for instance, much higher fees for toxic waste dumping or energy taxes, or the prohibition of food additives or pesticides? In these cases, solid preparation and pre-emptive action could limit the damage to one company or an industry sector, and actually provide others with an advantage vis-à-vis their blindsided competitors.

At an industry level, restructuring may also arise from fundamental changes in the relative bargaining power of the different players. To illustrate, the choices made by supermarket chains with respect to packaging can dictate the fortune of suppliers of base materials such as plastics or cardboard. Although sometimes disrupted by sudden developments, such as the introduction of the take-back regulation in Germany, these developments cause gradual but fundamental changes in the industry's demand and supply curves.

Referring to what he calls the 'greening up of the supply chain', Carl Frankel highlights the following corporations:

> *Among the leaders in this area are S C Johnson & Son which, starting in the early 1990s, held environmental conferences for its suppliers and publishes a regular eco-newsletter for them; McDonald's, which is purchasing over $350 million annually in recycled products under its McRecycle programme; British retailer B&Q, which requires its 450 suppliers to have an environmental policy backed by a full environmental audit and to comply with B&Q's own environmental policy; and General Motors, which, through its trademarked PICOS programme, is helping its thousands of suppliers to cut costs by becoming more eco-efficient.*[45]

A major determinant of success in formulating such a jump-ahead response is, of course, timing. Being a 'leader' in jumping ahead and avoiding environmental incrementalism is not always a prescription for value creation. Pioneers often pay a price: the environmental issue may never reach the policy formulation phase of its life cycle; the technological bet might have been placed too hastily; or the learning curve has not lowered costs. Moreover, companies cannot handle too many priorities simultaneously. It is therefore sometimes more appropriate to be an 'early adopter', as was the case of the German car industry when it followed its Japanese rivals in the area of fuel efficiency; although it lagged behind the Japanese, it was far ahead of most of its main European competitors.

Whichever jump-ahead action a company opts for, it seems to us increasingly evident that incremental approaches, particularly for large multinational companies, are more and more untenable. An excessively reactive posture, dragging one's feet and trying to block or, at the minimum, delaying environmental action, will almost certainly backfire in the form of more polarized relationships with the authorities and increased public animosity.

Frank Popoff of Dow Chemical is eloquent in his advocacy of the merits of pre-emptive actions in the chemical industry:

> *So we are saying to them: we need your help in inducing the industry to set worldwide standards employing the best available technology, and we must do this voluntarily to pre-empt the legislation that will surely come along if we do not. If we fail to act of our own accord, we will face government mandates, and they will be inefficient, punitive, and inconsistent from nation to nation – a quagmire. I am not an evangelist preaching some social cause; this is hard, cold economics. Pay now or pay a whole lot more later. Do it today or have it done unto you tomorrow. If we were not shooting for pollution prevention, I would have a hard sell. But everybody knows that that will be a part of the next generation of environmental initiatives.*[46]

ASSESSING OPTIONS FOR ACTION

So far in this chapter we have introduced the environmental option map to present a panorama of the three option groupings available to management in the light of the evolution of regulatory and market forces. Now we turn to how a specific company can identify possible actions for itself and prioritize these with a view to reaching its particular endgame.

Option assessment and selection is a bottom–up process in which business unit managers are asked to lead task forces to systematically identify and subsequently study those opportunities that combine environmental yield with shareholder value creation. Whereas the former activity generally is met with considerable enthusiasm, the latter is hard work. The end-product of this in-depth study is a short-list of preferred options, also including a best estimate of the expected benefits and costs.

Given the magnitude of the potential shareholder value impact, the assessment step must be heavily fact-based, with an emphasis on the analysis of the costs and benefits of (in-)action. At the same time, option assessment inevitably involves a significant degree of value judgement. Ultimately, there is no escaping the problem of balancing the value of, say, open space or clean air against the costs of attaining such objectives.

Many senior executives tend to be apprehensive of these 'soft' choices: they see them as too value-driven and not sufficiently fact-based. Yet the process of selecting a preferred option is no different from more traditional strategic planning, in which top management has, for instance, to trade off the 'hard' cost savings of massive personnel cuts against the 'soft' aspects of large-scale unemployment, company image or coworker morale.

Over a number of projects we have developed and tested an environmental options assessment (EOA) methodology, which addresses most of the above concerns.[47] The methodology is based on a combination of the environmental profile, introduced in Chapter 3, and the environmental option map which has been at the centre of this chapter. The environmental profile of each option is carefully assessed and determines the position of the option along the option map's horizontal axis. The cost of the action then establishes the option's position along the vertical economic axis.

The EOA constitutes a significant advance because the position of each of the different options can be directly compared on the option map on the basis of its economic and environmental impact against a base-case – or do-nothing – scenario. Managers should be primarily interested in the larger differences between the different options: they need not analyse aspects that all options share, or issues with only a minor impact. The analyses of the remaining aspects generally have to be much more detailed and complete than before, however.

To illustrate, let's look at the Dutch case in which the substitution of pinewood for PVC in window frames is assessed (Figure 4.6). The environmental profile, drawn up by a project team or in-house staff, suggests considerable benefits due to lower emissions of heavy metals and especially less problematic waste disposal. On the negative side, the substitution would cause minor contributions to, for instance, acidification and global warming.

Having acquainted themselves with the details, decision-makers are asked to combine all quantitative figures and qualitative considerations to arrive at a final conclusion concerning the total environmental yield of an option relative to the do-nothing scenario. It is here that the element of value judgement is purposely introduced. Participants must weigh the impact of, say, acidification against that of waste disposal or the depletion of resources. A crucial difference with other approaches is that within the EOA methodol-

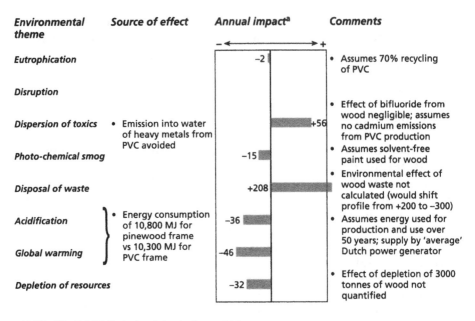

a 10,000 = 1% of total Netherlands emissions/environmental theme

Figure 4.6 *Environmental profile of an option: substitute pinewood for PVC window frames*

ogy this value judgement is made by the decision-makers themselves, rather than by a group of external experts or based on an opinion poll of a specific constituency. When the EOA is applied in a group setting with representatives of very different backgrounds, one must expect a range of environmental yield valuations instead of a single data point. Major differences in insights or opinions are thus highlighted, such that management is fully aware of issues that could require its attention.

Paralleling the environmental profile, an economic profile gives a factual overview of the net economic impact of an option. As far as possible, the option's economic effects are explicitly quantified in monetary terms, and added up to indicate a total economic impact, typically including net changes in operating and capital costs. As with the environmental profile, it suffices to focus on the major differences between options. If certain costs have to be incurred whatever the option, they can be eliminated from consideration. Long-term effects and intangibles (eg the intrinsic value of an educated workforce and the positive effects on a corporate culture or public image) which cannot be easily quantified are acknowledged in a comments column.

With all these factors in mind, decision-makers can position the selected options on an option map (Figure 4.7). Options plotted in

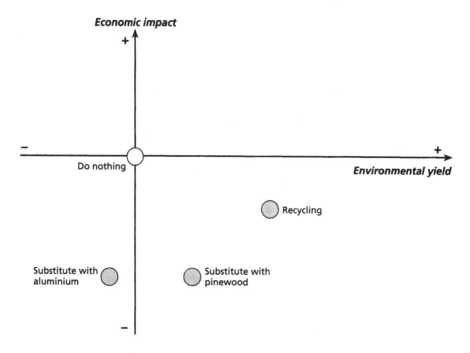

Figure 4.7 *Option mapping: PVC window frames*

the top right quadrant (ie when environmental and economic impacts are positive) would be clear candidates for immediate action, whereas options with negative environmental benefits, both left-hand quadrants, can generally be discarded. This is the case with aluminium substitution. The options plotted in the bottom right-hand quadrant require decision-makers to make trade-offs and thus constitute the main focus for the methodology.

In theory, the prioritization of options in the bottom right-hand quadrant is straightforward: scanning the map clockwise from the intersection of the two axes, those in the 'early hours' on the dial (ie just past three o'clock) are more attractive than those in the later hours. In our illustration, replacing PVC with pinewood was judged to have a positive environmental yield, but at considerable cost. A recycling option was found to be far superior, offering significant positive environmental impact – less waste disposal, and lower energy consumption and emissions due to reduced virgin material production – while incurring only moderate cost. A third option – substituting aluminium for PVC – was seen to have an overall negative environmental yield, largely due to the higher energy consumption of aluminium over the total product life cycle, even if greater use were made of hydropower.

Thus, smart decision-makers should not argue about the relative pros and cons of PVC relative to pinewood or aluminium, but should instead concentrate their efforts on optimizing the recycling valve in the PVC flow diagram.

In practice, the EOA provides a good basis for discussion and a clear way of bringing out differences in perspectives. Consistently, from one project to the next, we found it relatively easy to reach consensus among people of very different backgrounds along the environment axis of the option map. This task was much more challenging with regard to economic impact, however. Given the same fact-pack, senior representatives from industry, government, NGOs and scientific institutions generally made similar value judgements with regard to the environmental yield of a specific option (in confidential ratings, on a six-point scale, variations rarely exceeded one point). However, when presented with what most businessmen assume to be 'harder' facts about economic costs and benefits, they tended to register much greater variations, sometimes as much as four points.

The in-depth discussion of these discrepancies pointed to a rough division between industry representatives with bottom-line responsibility for the substance application (typically business unit managers) and those more distant from the bottom line, such as top managers or staff employees in industry, government officials and environmentalists. Whereas the former worried about the short-term costs and disruption, the latter placed more positive emphasis on the long-term economic impact, referring to non-defined benefits that, they suggested, usually arise as by-products of environmental measures. Thus, it must be assumed that part of the discrepancy must be accepted as a fact to be addressed in making the transition to an integrated response.[48]

We feel that the EOA methodology offers a significant advantage as a management tool. Completeness and accuracy are often of limited relevance. As with many management tasks, the comparison of options should focus on the major differences for the environment and business economics, and especially on the greatest uncertainties. If a task force can put a spotlight on these aspects, management is better able to assess the advantages and risks, and hence make better decisions. The most important advantage of the methodology is that it forces decision-makers to attach their own weights to 'soft' and 'hard' facts (including facts and opinions). Business managers thus become fully responsible for their decisions.

The EOA methodology also can take into account potential synergies between options. Suppose, on a hypothetical option map, four options are available as shown in Figure 4.8. The first three could reinforce one another and it thus would be possible to form 'packages', which can also be plotted on the map. Let us assume that the fourth option belongs in the mutually exclusive category (one cannot, for instance, simultaneously implement options to recycle a

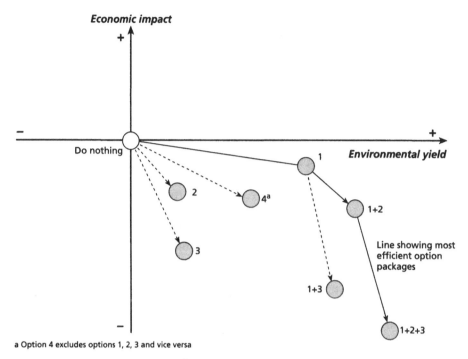

Figure 4.8 *Prioritizing options*

material and to replace the same substance). The priority sequence now would be option 1, followed by combinations with option 2 and subsequently option 3. Option 4 would not be implemented; better results could be obtained along the line showing the most efficient option packages.

Option assessment has been the subject of many recent efforts to develop appropriate management tools, in particular in connection with the life cycle analysis (LCA) or so-called ecobalances that are becoming standard ingredients of policies based on a cradle-to-grave product responsibility. In these analyses, all environmental impacts that a product has during its entire life cycle are measured. By comparing the outcome with those of other products or different material flows (eg substituting reuse by incineration), management can obtain a perspective on the environmental yield of a specific option.

Despite major progress in the technical assessments, most of these approaches appear to suffer from a lack of management perspective and high costs.[49] As Paul Allaire, Chairman and CEO of Xerox Corporation, noted: 'Our experience shows that simple LCAs can provide value in research, technology, and design decision-making. But even for a large company, the value gained does not support the prohibitive expense of conducting comprehensive LCAs.'[50]

In defence of LCA, however, it should be noted that several major corporations such as ABB have learned to work with a standardized format that greatly facilitates its use and also lowers its operational costs.[51] The investment for setting up the necessary database and other prerequisites is still considerable, however. Our greatest objection is to the technocratic nature of these methodologies. In our experience, they require a detailed understanding of environmental issues, which will generally escape the understanding of senior management. The models used are therefore essentially 'black boxes'. This would still be acceptable if the output were comprehensible. In most cases, however, the generalists' overview is missing, making it exceedingly difficult to assess the pros and cons of one option against those of another.

Many approaches based on the principles of ecobalances, moreover, have an in-built degree of automatism. As noted before, a value judgement is required for making a comparison between the impacts of, say, acidification, eutrophication and excessive noise caused by a specific strategic option. This value judgement is frequently introduced as an input factor based, for instance, on expert estimates or surveys of selected groups. Multiplying the emission levels with the predetermined weighing factors thus yields a seemingly objective quantitative assessment of the environmental impact. However, it also takes away the opportunity for a personal value judgement by the ultimate decision-makers. In our experience, this raises major barriers for a broad use, especially when a policy is developed jointly with government or NGOs.

Finally, few methods offer an integrated assessment of the environmental yield of an option together with its economic impact. Most often these decision-making parameters are treated separately, thus hampering the assessment of the relative efficiency of options.

***

Now, on the eve of change, and having assessed its options, top management has to perform some tasks to ensure that the ultimate change programme is a success. These tasks are the subject of our next chapter.

5

ON THE EVE OF CHANGE

The generation and assessment of options discussed in the previous chapter is typically task-force intensive. Only after the task forces have done most of their work does top management get involved. Once this analytical work is done and the list of appropriate actions drawn up, top managers must take centre stage in preparing for the transformation of the company's environmental future. Concretely, this means they must focus on three basic activities. First, validating the endgame – ie asking themselves whether the endgame blueprint still makes sense and, if so, whether the selected options for action will get the company there. Second – in the case of an integrated or proactive endgame – assessing the change preparedness of the organization in advance. And third – having decided to take on the challenge – preparing for the actual implementation of the change programme.

VALIDATING THE ENDGAME

All the analytic work has been done; all facts and opinions are on the table, and the best options for action have been selected. Top management must now sit back and reflect on the proper course to take. Managers have to ask themselves some basic questions: Is this what we wanted? Do we feel comfortable that the preferred options truly address the business discontinuities? Do we feel we are up to the challenge? Do we even feel thrilled by the idea of making change come about and reaching our endgame?

In effect, managers must return to their original endgame perspective and the hypotheses that set them on the road to generating and assessing options. The key to this validation process is management's ability to reflect on the endgame that may provide the company with a better competitive differentiation. Knowing what it now knows, three outcomes once again are possible. First, the opportunities for competitive differentiation are found to be relatively small after all. Particularly when other imperatives dominate the corporate agenda, a primarily functional response could still be more appropriate. A second, more likely conclusion is that the proposals for action are quite comfortable. Business managers can then be asked to integrate the selected options in their existing strategic and operational plans.

It also is conceivable, however that top management might sense that the selected options do not adequately address the (potential) business discontinuities that were identified. It could even be that new insights from the in-depth option assessment suggest the discontinuities to be greater than previously thought. Top management then has to rethink its mental model of the differentiation space and hence its view of its endgame. Could it be, for instance, that future consumer generations no longer need cleaner gasoline for their more efficient cars but hydrogen-powered cars instead? Or, because of environmental and congestion problems, no cars at all? Clearly, the differentiation space of both the oil and car industries would certainly be entirely different, and the endgame perspectives of individual corporations would have to be rethought.

It is very much this intuitive discomfort that led Bill Ford Jr of the Ford Motor Company to say that 'the last thing we should ever do is define ourselves as an automaker.... In the future, we may be selling mobility, rather than cars.'[1] His fellow CEO at DuPont, Chad Holliday Jr, echoed these concerns: 'I hope that in five years people will see DuPont not as a chemical company but [as] an environmental company. Chemicals are the route to that. But we need more products like our new herbicides and high-protein corn. If we have enough of those, people will think of us an environmental company.'[2]

In the current business environment, which is characterized by very rapid developments and major discontinuities along the technological (eg information and communications technology (ICT) and biotechnology) and sociopolitical (eg the advent of Southeast Asia as a commercial force and the global liberalization of enterprises) dimensions, the need to adjust or revamp the endgame perspective is not uncommon. In a world where entire industry sectors can suddenly disappear, and traditional powerhouses be obliterated, this is no surprise. The record shows managers who have succeeded in this task and others who have failed. But it also shows that only a small number have seriously thought through the environmental dimension of this context of rapid change. Yet, to name a few examples of potential major sources of discontinuities, the regulatory and market demands arising from the threat of climate change and the responsibility for the ecological shadow, and the opportunities of genetic modification, could fundamentally alter the playing field in many industries.

This validation is a lot to ask of most top managers, who have just gone through a series of action options, and now simply want to do a back-check on their original endgame blueprint before moving on to implementation. Still, this is the time for reflection: creative ideas do not appear on command. The circumstances that are conducive to breakthrough thinking can be stimulated, however. Referring to the specialized literature on creativity for more detail, psychologists insightfully refer to the 'bed-bath-bus' syndrome.[3] In other words, the key is to create the peace of mind that many find in a bed, in a bath or on a bus – or perhaps, currently, in an aeroplane – where the mind can creatively mull over a complex matter; we will return to this topic in the final chapter of this book. Every so often, the more fortunate among us then experience an Archimedean 'Eureka!' or 'Aha!' moment. The new endgame blueprint is crystal clear. It addresses all discontinuities. It also provides a handle for describing to others what the joint destination should be and for developing the associated action proposals. Through its clarity of purpose it can serve as the vision to drive the corporation.

Experience shows that this process of vision development often is tiresome and 'muddy': most corporate visions are more compelling with the benefit of hindsight. Not everybody will be initially happy with the possible major shifts in endgame vision resulting from the validation process. Where necessary, top management will have to ask its project teams to return to the drawing board and repeat the whole process of generating and assessing options for action, this time based on the redefined differentiation space and the associated endgame aspirations. Only after a number of iterations will the appropriately adjusted endgame vision be sufficiently crystallized to provide a good handle to make it come alive for coworkers throughout a company. Still, arriving at a well-examined and appropriate endgame vision will make the whole process worthwhile.

ASSESSING CHANGE PREPAREDNESS

Most top managers will agree that planning change is one thing but making it come about is a different matter. Plans are all very well, but like the heavyweight boxer said when informed that his opponent had a plan to beat him: 'Everybody has plans until they get hit!'[4] The attics of most major corporations are full of the remains of once-glittering change programmes that turned out to be dismal failures.

But those imaginary attics also contain treasure chests of corporate experience. As vividly illustrated by Alan Kantrow, companies too rarely draw on their abilities and experience in one area to solve problems in others.[5] The truth is that many companies will rightly have a strong sense of déjà vu when confronted by the change programme aspects in environmental management. Hopefully, their experience in other programmes will be of great help in this one.

One lesson learned from successful change programmes is that the initial effort is virtually always top–down. The introduction of IT comes vividly to mind. A small number of people are involved in implementing a big idea that affects a single, often central function – remember the huge mainframe computers of the early days of IT. Such major change programmes usually start with marginal changes in frontline management only. In time, however, the programmes lead to the full internalization of the new approaches across a whole company: in a sense they become invisible when they become part of normal business. The personal computer on everybody's desk provides a perfect example here.[6]

Will the implementation of environmental change programmes follow the same course? Pivotal jobholders – ie those whose positions in the organization are critical to a proper translation of a top–down vision into operational action – in lower organizational echelons will probably watch with apprehension. Many have been part of the preparations, for instance serving as members of task forces or participating in workshops. These are good people who want their company to be successful. Still, they have their doubts about top management's commitment; about whether they will 'walk the talk', and generally live up to expectations.

While the transition from a functional to an integrated response requires that an organization undergo an important change process, the transition to a proactive response involves changing the organization's very culture – ie 'the way we do things around here'. But organizations are living entities that over a period of years develop identities which are often hard to change. The challenge, using a sports image, for instance, would be to transform a defence-minded team into an all-out attacking group. As a first step, top management must examine the readiness of its corporation to make the change to which it aspires.

McKinsey's 7-S framework, introduced by Tom Peters and Bob Waterman in their classic *In Search of Excellence*, is a very useful means of examining the core ingredients of an organizational culture (Figure 5.1).[7] Strategy, structure, systems and skills form the classical 'hard' elements of the culture; these are often well documented and understood. The other three, 'soft' elements, however, play an equally critical role and, as a rule, are much more difficult to grasp. 'Staff' refers to the people in the organization – their background, training, motivations and aspirations. 'Style' is indissolubly connected with staff: it refers to the manner of interaction within the organization. And 'shared values' describes the uniting force in an organization, ie the banner to which it rallies.

A sports analogy may, again, help to understand each of these and particularly their inter-relatedness: one element cannot be changed

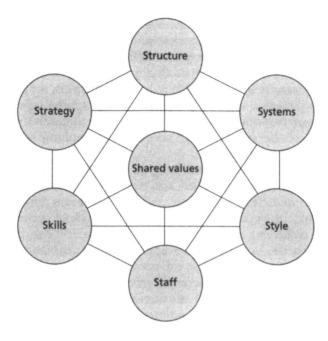

Figure 5.1 *McKinsey's 7-S framework*

without affecting the others. In a football team with a defence culture, the strategy is to wait for the opponent's attack and trying to take advantage of opportunities for counter-attacks 'on the break'. Its structure reflects this strategy; for instance, it has hardly any players for the forward positions. The manager, before the game or while in the dugout, concentrates his management systems on communicating with the goalie and the central defenders. Since the team requires defensive skills, rather than those of creative wingers or centre-forwards, the staff consists of people who expect to play mostly defensively; high-scoring matches and brilliant attacks on goal are rare (as are exuberant media reports). The style matches the culture: no frills, no fancy stuff – everything is down-to-earth and practical. The shared values most probably would reflect the pride in a job well done.

Successful organizational units also tend to have coherent cultures, in which all 7-S elements are aligned. Some, such as those in process industries, might have a culture that is geared to efficiency, whereas others, for example in sectors where innovation is crucial, aim for small-team effectiveness or even opt for highly disaggregated architectures, where very small units are stimulated to develop their own identities.

It is beyond the scope of this book to discuss the pros and cons of each culture. Still, it is obviously important that top managers examine the different features of their institution when preparing to change it. Their ability to reach a chosen endgame depends on it. For example, organizations that are inward-looking and efficiency- and/or technology-driven might have great difficulty in responding to external demands. Others might be so decentralized or disaggregated that a single corporate response is difficult to agree upon, let alone implement. Still others, with headquarters or major operations in environmental hot-spots, may, thanks to their sensitivity and front-line experience, be much better prepared for making the transition to a more advanced response.

Top management also must keep in mind that major companies are rarely homogeneous. They are made up of, and also operate within, a host of different cultures and value systems. In the words of Nigel Roome, they function in 'interdependent systems which operate at different scales in time and place.'[8] Far from being integrated entities, corporations contain what amount to multiple parallel, and often unaligned, universes, with each responding to different – and often contradictory – rules of engagement. As a result, for example, environmental management and lobbying tend to occupy entirely separate tracks within a corporation: the two tend to have nothing whatsoever to do with each other.

Carl Frankel, by way of example, refers to a Fortune 500 company with a strong environmental profile, whose chief environmental officer was genuinely shocked when he was told that his company belonged to the Alliance for Reasonable Regulation, an organization labelled by the Sierra Club as an anti-environmental corporate political action committee because of its significant campaign contributions to US senators who restrain environmental regulation.[9] He also suggests that when Bob Banks, the Chief Environmental Officer at Sun Company, points out that 'the regulatory initiatives in Washington, DC, are having no effect on our overall commitment', and when Paul Tebo, Vice-President of SHE at DuPont, says that 'you need to look at the whole spectrum of what companies are doing', they are probably not engaging in greenwashing so much as communicating their sincere assessment of a complex state of affairs. Diversified multinationals are complex organisms, often with conflicting agendas: it's unreasonable to expect consistency from them.[10]

Moreover, the – often very different – organizational units within a company are themselves made up of individuals, each with personal backgrounds and aspirations. Eventually it is the behaviour of these coworkers that top management must affect if it wants to make the transition to an integrated or proactive response. Management must therefore also go into considerable depth in assessing the readiness to change amongst its coworkers, and its pivotal jobholders in particular.

No military commander, nor sports coach for that matter, would go into battle without assessing the strengths and weaknesses of his or her cohorts. Indeed, most successful plans are designed with those characteristics in mind. Still, in our experience, managers often over-estimate their organization's environmental maturity. In fact, they almost invariably suggest that their company is in an integrated response mode – little surprise that the sense of urgency with regard to change tends to be limited.

Will, skill and thrill

What qualities do the staff members need to bring about change and reach the selected endgame? The short answer, which we paraphrase from the work of Harvard University psychologist Teresa Amabile, is will, skill and thrill.[11] If these qualities are not abundantly present among the pivotal job holders within a corporation, it is unlikely that the change process will succeed. The challenge of change therefore can be formulated in terms of top management's ability to influence the will, thrill and skill of its coworkers in terms of making the desired changes.

If coworkers have the 'will' to make the transition from a functional response to a more advanced approach, top management may be able to formulate and implement a positive value proposition that overcomes any objections from stakeholders and actually converts them into supporters. A number of current leading corporations demonstrate that it is entirely possible to quickly place the environment among their top priorities, if the will is there. This frequently happens, of course, in companies such as Shell that have been burnt by an environmental incident, but it also occurs in a more neutral setting, thanks to a change in strategy which is supported by the necessary pool of will in the organization.

Promoting a 'thrill' about the endgame is also crucial, particularly if a proactive environmental strategy is opted for. Leadership is the essential ingredient in creating thrill in an organization, especially when the going gets tough. However, this factor is no different from that required in any other corporation driven by a strong vision. Indeed, as vividly illustrated by Collins and Porras in their book *Built to Last*, it is a virtual precondition for the long-term success of major companies; we discuss this issue in Chapters 8 and 9 of this book.[12]

Although the position and the shape of the differentiation space is largely determined by externalities, the internal will and thrill that are required to act determine the degree to which a company makes the transition from a functional to an integrated or proactive response. The quality of its response is for its part heavily determined by a third factor: the adequacy of the in-house skill to execute whatever response mode it pursues.

As we conducted our surveys, discussed in Chapter 1, we were struck by the importance of these three factors in explaining the environmental management performance of the 16 companies. We

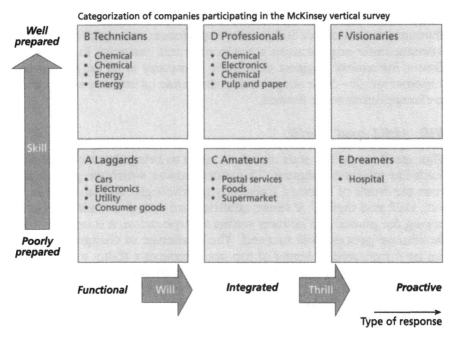

Figure 5.2 *Response categories and internal drivers for change*

found, not surprisingly, that will and skill were crucial components in the integrated and proactive approaches. Skill, in turn, determined whether or not the chosen approach would be successfully implemented: as Figure 5.2 shows, it marks the difference between the 'laggards' and the 'technicians', the 'amateurs' and the 'professionals', and the 'dreamers' and the 'visionaries'. Here, in greater detail, is how the three factors played themselves out in the surveyed companies.

1 **Laggards** Often operating in regions with lower environmental regulatory pressure – or well protected from regulatory pressures thanks, for instance, to government connections or because of more pressing concerns like employment – these companies are in a functional response mode. At the same time, they have not fully developed the expertise required to address environmental issues. This category included an electric utility with a dominant market position, but also a major car manufacturer and two consumer goods companies (electronics and food). Lacking will, thrill and skill, they cannot expect to come up with creative solutions if the need ever arises.

2 **Technicians** Typically, these organizations have considerable environmental frontline experience. However, they either remain in a functional mode – in our sample this applied to two chemi-

cal multinationals with home bases in countries with relatively lax regulations – or do not see the need to switch to a more integrated response, as in the case of an energy company with a primary focus on oil exploration and production. The companies in this group tend, however, to be excellent 'compliers'.

3 **Amateurs** These companies are often new entrants to the environmental arena, and have not been severely tested in practice, but are motivated by the opportunities offered by environmental issues. They evidently have the will to take on the challenge and to work diligently at studying options. But if they do so they take a risk, since their technical skill-base may not be up to the tasks of developing the required mental models, validating solutions and dealing with implementation problems. In our sample, examples included a large postal services organization, a major food player and a national supermarket chain, all in countries with strong environmental regulation.

4 **Professionals** Generally highly regarded by their peers within a given industry sector, these companies combine the will to act with the skill required to do so. Having integrated environmental considerations into their business strategies, they no longer think of the environment as a source of problems, but as a new challenge – a fact of life that might even offer business opportunities. In our sample, this category included major North American and Northwestern European corporations in the chemical, consumer electronics and pulp and paper industries.

5 **Dreamers** Limited in number, these companies are often motivated by highly inspired individuals who elicit the thrill required to pursue a proactive response. Their dreams can turn into nightmares, however, when they lack the required skills. If the transition is not properly managed, encompassing an in-depth skill-building programme, the cold shower of reality can cause a harsh awakening. Still, when budding initiatives are properly nurtured, they may provide the basis for the development of an entirely new mental model of the corporate direction – that is, a vision. The state-of-the-art university hospital in our surveys is typical of such belief-driven organizations.

6 **Visionaries** An increasing number of companies find themselves in a position to draw on all three qualities in shaping a proactive response. Unlike the dreamers, they have access to the skills required for hard-nosed analysis and operational execution. The ingredient that differentiates the visionaries from the professionals is the thrill factor, which is necessary to develop far-reaching solutions and to act on them. Once they make up their minds, they do not hesitate to pursue their visions. The fact that they no longer ask themselves many questions may, paradoxically, account for the fact that they did not participate in our surveys. The bench-

marking that helps other companies to understand their relative status and develop action programmes to keep up with competitors has less meaning to visionaries.

The experiences of these different company categories provide insight for managers who are considering changing their response to the environmental challenge. In particular they highlight the importance of having a balanced corporate position as a basis for change.

Balancing the corporate position

The different categories of companies produced by our surveys suggest how important it is that managers considering change pay particular attention to skill-building. A company with a weak technical skill base – ie a laggard or an amateur, to use our surveys' designations – almost certainly needs to correct this gap before moving forwards. Management must also gauge the risk of change overload that could occur when, for instance, a major environmental awareness drive coincides with a corporate priority in a different area. It also has to consider factors such as the company's environmental track record: established and credible visionaries and professionals, for instance, may expect a warmer welcome from external stakeholders when presenting creative environmental initiatives.

Balancing the corporate position is of particular importance in diversified multinational companies, where the option assessment might prompt different approaches for different business units. As an illustration, we know of a chemical company in which the management of the coatings unit – where the company is a technology and market leader – pursues a vigorous integrated response, whereas its bulk chemicals units take a functional approach.

In our opinion, this variation between organizational units is acceptable, and even desirable, as long as two conditions are met. First, the external positioning of leading units should not be damaged by less advanced units elsewhere in the same organization. And second, the mixed approach should not cause excessive uncertainty among coworkers about what the company stands for.

The importance of both points should not be under-estimated, since the risks of external criticism and consumer scepticism are high. For example, some years ago the Mitsubishi Corporation became the object of attack by the multinational NGO Friends of the Earth because of the operations of its logging company in Southeast Asia. Corporate management was caught off-guard when the media turned its critical focus to the company's much more vulnerable car group, an entity which, given the holding philosophy of the parent company, management saw as entirely autonomous.

The Mitsubishi case is not an isolated one. Time and again our surveys provide illustrations of major differences in environmental responses within large companies which, apart from increasing exposure to external criticism, also raise questions with regard to the internal conditions for change. How can top management be clear and consistent in its communication when the message differs among its businesses? How can it maintain credibility among its middle echelons if coworkers are confronted with variations in environmental aspirations when they're transferred from unit to unit?

The coordination of different environmental responses is even more relevant, and in many multinational companies acute, where they vary by geographic area. When, in our surveys, we asked coworkers about the primary driver of their environmental behaviour, they almost invariably cited the pressures from local communities, followed by state or national governments. Whereas this is perhaps understandable, it does raise doubts about the truthfulness of such common corporate statements like: 'Our subsidiaries throughout the world are obliged to apply the same standards of environmental protection and safety as in that of our home country.'

The management of this geographic dimension is a new problem to many companies. The significant environmental policy differences between the rich industrialized countries on the one hand, and the developing countries on the other, which reflect their different positions on the environmental hierarchy of needs, are particularly challenging to multinational companies. Issues that in the North are found in PLC Phase 4 – for example, the installation of sewerage systems, the control of animal plagues, or the quality control of food and drinking water – dominate the environmental agenda at the top of the PLC peak in many developing countries. Further, as we mentioned earlier, such policy-phase differences can occur even within much more homogeneous groups of countries, such as the European Union.

The international dimension is becoming even more complex, however, with consumers playing an increasingly important role in shaping the differentiation space. By way of an example: Shell International has pioneered and perfected the management philosophy of highly independent and self-standing national operating companies. This philosophy was severely challenged when, in 1995, Shell UK presented its plan to dump the Brent Spar oil platform in the North Sea. The public and political reaction triggered by Greenpeace led to a consumer boycott of its petrol stations, particularly in Germany, which reflected the greater public environmental sensitivity in that country compared to the UK. As noted by Greenpeace's campaign coordinator Jochen Vorfelder: 'Throughout the campaign in Germany, the emphasis was placed on fundamental questions of Shell's responsibilities to society as a whole. There was very little discussion of scientific issues, in marked contrast to the much narrower debate in the UK.'[13]

More recently, Monsanto, a company that aspires to environmental leadership, facilitated the import of genetically modified soybeans into the European market. Having encountered very little resistance in the US, it was surprised by the strong opposition from European NGOs and major food producers, undoubtedly prompted by unexpected consumer concerns. Again, phase differences, this time between the US and especially the UK, turned out to be greater than anticipated.

Such national differences can raise difficult internal questions for a company. What about the young manager who, after his or her first lessons in integrated environmental response at headquarters, is transferred to a developing country and finds much more 'relaxed' approaches to environmental responsibilities to be the rule? Might he or she not begin to question the sincerity of the company's commitment?

Our message is very simply that the positioning of relevant units must be based on a conscious decision and must not be the outcome, as is now most often the case, of haphazard developments. When making the transition to an integrated and possibly proactive response, the necessary change programme deeply affects many people throughout an organization and requires a serious commitment in terms of resources, share-of-mind and time. The barriers to be overcome are considerable and the prices of failure and opportunity cost are high. A consistent, thought-through top management perspective, therefore, is essential.

The internal barriers to change

Even if companies have the necessary will and thrill and the environmental skills, progress towards an endgame is often held back by a series of internal barriers. Let's look at those now.

When we studied the differences between the six categories in our survey, and particularly the lessons learned by the professionals, we discovered that organizations face remarkably similar obstacles in upgrading their environmental management approach.[14] Specifically, there appear to be five key barriers which companies must overcome on the path toward an integrated or – even more so – proactive response: lagging structure and systems; short time-horizons; over-estimation of future burdens; lack of insight into third-party imperatives; and apprehensive pivotal job holders.

Lagging structure and systems

Most companies have developed organizational structures and management systems that allow them to control their operations and implement their strategies in the – hopefully – most efficient manner.

If necessary, their structures and systems provide them with the means to effectively correct deviations as they occur.

However, organizational structures and management systems are generally only adapted long after the need for change has been recognized. Such institutional conservatism causes few problems if change is slow or if organizational requirements don't need to be radically altered. However, it is an inadequate foundation when circumstances demand rapid change and/or a transition to an integrated or proactive response.

Clearly, the amateurs – with their strategic ambitions but inadequate skills – are particularly handicapped by the virtual absence of both organizational provisions and systems support. However, even companies that are experienced in environment-related operational measures generally lack the infrastructural muscle required for an integrated response. Environmental questions have usually been added to the responsibilities of an existing health and safety department, still referred to in most companies as EHS (environment, health and safety). These departments are geared towards finding technical or administrative solutions to operational problems. They generally lack the mechanisms, skills and credibility required to assist line management with the business aspects of addressing strategic issues, such as product renewal with a view to recyclability, industry cooperation regarding product-return systems, and covenant or partnership negotiations. Many in-house environmental specialists, scarred by battles with the authorities, environmentalists or the media, can also be defensive and somewhat cynical.

Of special concern is the all-too-frequent inability of large corporations to react to emergencies and to deal with sensitive political and/or public concerns. With their EHS staff – often the best antennae in the environmental arena – wrongly positioned, and their communication or public affairs departments lacking relevant experience, managers find that their organizational processes provide them with little support. Moreover, in today's decentralized structures, national operating companies or self-standing business units effectively determine the corporate response to issues within their geographic or business territory. If these issues, from the environmental perspective, are broader in scope, the organizational structure may effectively present a barrier to the best solution.

But it is not just the organizational structure that presents problems: management systems also tend to be sub-optimal. For example, the most advanced companies in our surveys put a high priority on the environment, but most respondents felt that line managers were not sufficiently rewarded for excellent environmental performance.

Many companies are also saddled with information systems that are fully compliance-oriented. These systems supply a wealth of technical data on daily emissions of a range of substances, frequency of fire inspections, and so forth. They are largely irrelevant, however, for measuring environmental progress, let alone for such strategic management purposes as assessing the environmental performance of products from the cradle to the grave (LCA), or the economic impact of the different options for action. Frequently, a company's 'external antennae' are either insufficient or not properly wired into the management information systems. Managers therefore have no overview allowing them to set priorities and make rational, fact-based decisions. The resulting uncertainty often leads to indecision and/or 'ad-hocracy'.

Short time-horizons

People only have the capacity to handle a limited number of priorities simultaneously. Although often concerned with the long term and their ultimate objectives in life, their day-to-day concerns, which require immediate attention and action, tend to occupy them most. In terms of environmental management this trait often leads to a policy which amounts to 'staying out of trouble' by complying with regulations and preventing environmental incidents. Bhopal, Seveso, Harrisburg, Chernobyl, Love Canal and the *Exxon Valdez* are references that can still ring alarm bells at many corporate headquarters: the concern is to avoid such incidents at all costs. There is little time for more ambitious goals.

For similar reasons, senior managers tend to be largely preoccupied with operational issues such as waste disposal and water and air pollution. It was a long time before relatively new concerns such as climate change showed up in the top rankings of environmental issues in the corporate world. Even in the chemical, basic materials and processing sectors, which could be seriously affected through much higher energy prices or forced energy conservation, the pick-up was slow.

Lacking an understanding of the nature of major environmental issues, and hence of their potential impact, most business executives do not have a perspective on long-term targets. Many, in fact, fall victim to extreme 'issue overload'. As one executive told us: 'I have enough problems that find me; I don't need to go looking for more.' This makes them inclined to be very careful, and to take small steps forward, extrapolating from the recent past. While this approach certainly does not rule out progress, it leaves companies vulnerable to unforeseen developments. A producer of packaging material, for instance, which concentrates on a weight decrease of 5 per cent or a 10 per cent increase in recycling, might be blindsided by a complete material substitution that renders its product obsolete. Indeed, very few companies consider how environmental developments may

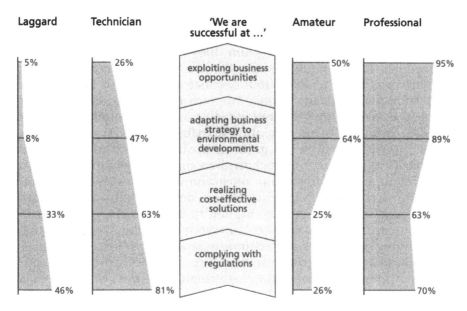

Percentage of respondents who agree

Source: McKinsey surveys

Figure 5.3 *Functionally-oriented companies less confident about strategic skills*

affect their competitive position, or are willing or able to tie such developments to long-term, over-arching business objectives.

Over-estimation of future burdens

Many senior managers of laggards and technicians pride themselves on their company's ability to comply with existing regulations. As might be expected, they are far less confident about the implementation of an integrated response, however. Business strategies do not adequately incorporate environmental developments, and new business opportunities arising from such developments are hardly exploited (Figure 5.3). Frequently, they express disappointment about what they perceive to be a lack of recognition for their environmental efforts thus far. From their perspective, governments, NGOs and other outsiders (such as the press and the public at large) have no appreciation of how much they have done, how much it has cost, and of the attractive business opportunities they had to forsake for environmental reasons.

To make matters worse, environmental issues seem to be multiplying at a frightening pace: for every problem solved two new ones seem to pop up. Under these circumstances, it is not surprising that so many leaders are much less confident about their organization's ability to meet new environmental targets and to pay the associated bills. Most notably, they tend to over-estimate required environmental expenditures or, more to the point, they under-estimate the positive effects that such expenditures may have in the longer term.

This concern is exacerbated because some of our key management tools are seriously flawed. The recent emphasis of shareholder value as a corporation's central objective has led to a reliance on net present value (NPV) or discounted cash flow (DCF) calculations. These, however, can be a significant obstacle to rational decision-making. The standard approach involves an assessment of future cash flows. True, in a world without uncertainties and, especially, without options, such methodology provides a sensible point of departure for managerial action. Still, as argued by David Pearce, professor of environmental economics at University College London, such discounting biases current decisions in favour of projects and policies that shift many of the costs into the future. In other words, it discourages management from making investment decisions whose benefits accrue in the distant future.[15]

This is particularly damaging for issues such as the environment, where the NPV or DCF estimates can be significantly altered by improvements in technology and experience gained over time. By incorporating these factors, which often amount to a more favourable NPV, managers can make better decisions. In essence, because of our ability to learn and make more educated choices with the passage of time, a fair argument can be made for basing these calculations on a lower interest rate, or setting a lower rate-of-return barrier when making go/no-go decisions.

This bias does not only affect environment-related investments. Management literature is replete with critical discussions of research and development (R&D) valuation, in which the underestimation of long-term benefits, again arising from a neglect of the management learning factor, leads to poor decision-making.[16] Improved approaches have been proposed and tested: for example, option pricing has been used to deal with stock price volatility.[17] However, the complexity of the calculations together with the apprehension that most managers feel with regard to the use of black-box models has prevented their use in environmental decision-making. As a result, most companies continue to over-estimate the 'future burden' of environmental initiatives.

The evidence that such over-estimates occur is easy to find. Time and again, even senior executives of leading corporations join together to issue warnings of the cost of taking environmental initiatives, only to retract them at a later date. A classic example occurred during the debate in the US on the 1970 Clean Air Act. Lee Iacocca, then Executive Vice-President of the Ford Motor Company, predicted that compliance with the new regulations would require huge car price increases, halving US production by 1975 and severely damaging the country's economy. The bill was nevertheless enacted and Iacocca's dire predictions turned out to be wrong.[18]

The introduction of SO_x emission-rights trading in the US offers another example. The cost over-estimate led to an over-estimate of the expected market prices, with the result that the actual development of the market was disappointing. *USA Today* thus concluded:

> *Opponents of acid rain controls said the cost of reducing sulphur dioxide would be up to $1,500 per ton. Actual market cost: $78. You can trust affected industries to cry and whine about cost, but when forced to act, you can also trust them to find cost-effective ways to comply.*[19]

Our last example of pessimistic projections of the cost of environmental measures comes from the UK Chemical Industries Association. Some years ago, the association surveyed its members annually on their estimates for environmental investments for the following three years: the outcome is consistently significantly below the estimates (Figure 5.4).[20]

In short, many managers appear to work from a worst case scenario, basing their forecasts on current technologies and full absorption of all costs. Every dollar spent on an even vaguely environmental goal seems to be held against the environment, as management ignores the potential benefits of environment-related measures, such as the learning effect within its constituencies and the possible competitive advantage. Needless to say, the perception of environmental activities as an unduly heavy burden prevents many managers from shifting from cautious functional thinking to the dynamic, strategic mindset needed for a more advanced approach.

Lack of insight into third-party imperatives

When the environmental authorities or NGOs are focused on major long-term issues such as climate change, they have difficulty in understanding the concerns of, say, a steel company faced with major excess capacity and the threat of massive lay-offs. Despite warm words to the contrary, the same is true the other way around: companies lack insight into the other participants in the environmental arena. Peter Senge wrote the following on the obstacles posed by petrified perceptions of the others and the world:

> *One thing all managers know is that many of the best ideas never get put into practice. Brilliant strategies fail to get translated into action. Systemic insights never find their way into operating policies. A pilot experiment may prove to*

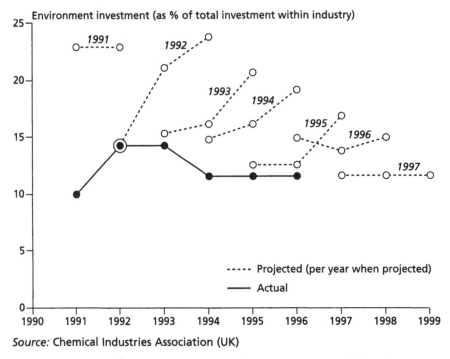

Source: Chemical Industries Association (UK)

Figure 5.4 *Over-estimating the environmental burden*

> *everyone's satisfaction that a new approach leads to better results, but widespread adoption of the approach never occurs.*
>
> *We are coming increasingly to believe that this 'slip 'twixt cup and lip' stems, not from weak intentions, wavering will, or even nonsystemic understanding, but from mental models. More specifically, new insights fail to get put into practice because they conflict with deeply held images of how the world works, images that limit us to familiar ways of thinking and acting.*[21]

The lack of understanding of third-party imperatives can be exacerbated by so-called group-think that, as experience in a large number of political and corporate decisions outside the environmental arena has shown, can lead even a highly qualified group of individuals into overly extreme decision-making, particularly in heated situations.[22] There are three reasons for this: first, a belief in the intellectual and moral superiority of one's group's viewpoint, plus excessive optimism and an illusion of invincibility, result in an over-confidence in one's position; second, the view that the opponent's stand is unintelligent and even unethical makes the group deaf to warnings and unresponsive to the possibility of negotiations and compromise as alternatives; and, third, under the pretence of cohesion, group conformity becomes an objective in its own right: self-censorship, peer pressure, a strong accent on unanimity and a selective focus on expert advice confirming the group's position. All of these promote single-mindedness and commitment to the chosen path.

The price of such attitudes can be high. As we saw in our discussion in Chapter 3 regarding the other players in the environmental arena, the increasing complexity of environmental issues and hence of environmental policies often demands that business increase its cooperation with external parties, particularly government authorities and NGOs. At the very least, companies need to keep an open mind about other stakeholders' positions and interests, and develop an explicit strategy for dealing with them. Very few management teams feel comfortable with this new challenge, however.

The polemic that arose around Shell UK's decision in June 1995 to dump its redundant Brent Spar oil production platform at sea illustrates the problems of formulating a national response to an international issue. The case provides a fascinating study of a company wrestling with the consequences of its misunderstanding of some of its stakeholders. Box 5.1 provides a selection of some of the words elicited by the Brent Spar debate.

In general, companies understand far too little about the motivations of external players, while the external players have only meagre insight into the average corporation. This mutual lack of knowledge and the history of confrontation between business and external players make it all too easy for the parties to adopt adversarial positions. This has to be avoided. Unless successful partnerships can be forged, companies are unlikely to find cost-effective solutions to environmental issues and mount a truly integrated or proactive response.[23]

Apprehensive pivotal job holders

Any change process is highly dependent on the cooperation of a few people in pivotal jobs. For companies that still respond functionally – ie laggards and technicians – the pressure is on the production managers, since they are expected to implement the primarily operational measures. When companies move towards an integrated response, however, the accent shifts to the business unit managers, who have to integrate the environmental considerations into their strategy. If these pivotal job holders lack the will and/or skill to execute major change within their own areas of responsibility, the entire change process is apt to fail. The problems are exacerbated if the pivotal job holders belong to a dominant group within the informal power structure of a company, as would be the case with production managers in many engineering-oriented organizations or business unit managers in heavily decentralized corporations.

Box 5.1 The Brent Spar

With Greenpeace leading the charge under the banner 'The sea is not a garbage can', Shell UK's project manager in charge of decommissioning Brent Spar reacted thus: 'We are trained as engineers to look at problems, analyse possible solutions, and come up with a balanced answer at the end of the day which is based on science and fact to the maximum possible extent. We can't base it on emotions.' Shell UK's Director of Public Affairs, in the same television programme, went further. 'People confronted with the campaign became emotionally disturbed,' he suggested. 'That seemed to be clearly the nature of the response, it was an emotional response.'

Indeed, Shell UK had done its national homework. Factual reports backed its position and governments supported or tacitly accepted the proposed solution. It thus was caught off-guard by the threat of a consumer boycott in continental Europe, notably Germany. Chris Fay, Chair of Shell UK, reacted by saying that 'Greenpeace are doing future generations no service in portraying industry's rational, science-based approach to environmental improvement as the enemy of sustainable development.'

His German counterpart Peter Duncan, much closer to the heat of the German boycott, had a different view, however: 'It is quite clear that all those concerned with this decision have wildly under-estimated the political implications and the inability to communicate to people what is the logic behind that.'

Eventually, with considerable damage done, the Shell Group had to step in and settle the issue. As a Group spokesperson put it: 'We said to Shell UK, it would be nice if you could reconsider. We informed them that there was no public support and no political support.'

To Shell's credit, it did subsequently develop the insight necessary to change from so-called buffering (ie preventing external stakeholders from interfering in internal operations) to a bridging (ie adapting organizational activities to incorporate the expectations of external stakeholders) behaviour. Chairman Cor Herkströter set the tone, admitting to 'a type of technical arrogance which is rather common in companies with a strong technical base. Most of us in Royal Dutch/Shell come from a scientific, technological background. That type of education, along with our corporate culture, teaches us that we must identify a problem, isolate it, and then fix it.... For most engineering problems there is a correct answer. For most social and political dilemmas there is a range of possible answers – almost all compromises. So, starting off with a strong, scientifically grounded mind-set, we tended to misjudge some of the softer issues and consequently make mistakes.'

Was Shell the only one to learn from the experience? Following fierce battles in which it made some serious mistakes, the Greenpeace leadership also reassessed its position vis-à-vis bridging. As Chris Rose, its UK Campaigns Director, put it: 'We have to move on from being hunters, hunting out and spotlighting problems, to becoming farmers, nurturing solutions.... Somehow, we have to evolve.' Thilo Bode, soon after his appointment as Executive Director of Greenpeace International, concluded: 'Industry is the main player in society.... That's why we need to talk to them.'[a]

a Alan Neale, *Business Strategy and the Environment*, May 1997, p93ff; Frans A J van den Bosch and Cees B M van Riel, *Business Strategy and the Environment*, February 1998, p24ff; and John Elkington, *Cannibals With Forks*, p146

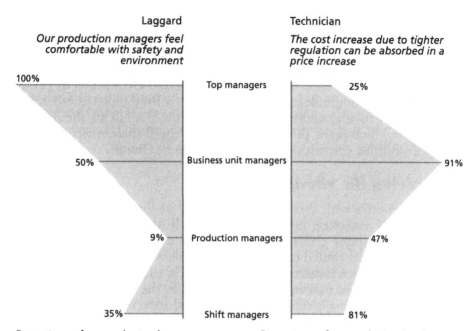

Laggard

Our production managers feel comfortable with safety and environment

Technician

The cost increase due to tighter regulation can be absorbed in a price increase

Figure 5.5 *Insecurity of pivotal job holders*

Among these pivotal job holders, there is often a marked apprehension about environmental activities, particularly in terms of their possible impact on the unit's performance. In Maslow's terms, they operate at a different echelon than their superiors and even coworkers, and often feel a sense of betrayal. Thus, our surveys show that plant managers with cost responsibility or business unit managers with a bottom-line responsibility tend to worry about the economic effect of environmental measures, far more so than their superiors or their subordinates (Figure 5.5).

Pivotal job holders are also concerned about their ability to handle this new task. In most surveys, especially among functionally-oriented companies (laggards and technicians), over 40 per cent of the respondents doubt the adequacy of the available resources. Even in some 'professional' companies, staff appear to lack the full complement of skills required to deal with environmental responsibilities: leading companies almost invariably list 'environmental training modules for managers' as their most significant need.

Adding to pivotal job holders' anxiety, there is deep-rooted scepticism about top management's commitment to a stated environmental position. Too often, especially in functionally-oriented companies, a majority of the senior line managers believe that top management's response is largely a matter of warm words but little action; only

10 per cent agree that top management has formulated an appropriate environmental perspective. There is also widespread conviction that environment-related initiatives or positions do not offer attractive career development opportunities for highly talented staff. Indeed, the experience of some environmental champions in previously leading companies that were affected by hard times or changing leadership provides some confirmation of this.[24] All in all, the uneasiness with which many pivotal job holders regard their environmental responsibilities constitutes a major obstacle to change.

Surveying the situation

Our experience with surveys has convinced us that they are often the best way of assessing how much will, skill, thrill and obstacles to change a company contains. Working with a variety of environmentally leading and skilled companies – ie professionals and technicians – we learnt that a targeted interview process of at least 100 coworkers, including top management, can provide the input to the above analysis. With the assistance of professional interviewers or use of a well-tested questionnaire, a small project team can gain a clear picture of the perceptions on the nature of the environmental challenge, the relevant attitudes and practices, and current strengths and weaknesses in the company's own response. Identifying the single most critical environmental issue to the business, coworkers also detail the threat or opportunity it offers and the best way to address this, as they see it.

The survey must tap in to all relevant coworkers, both vertically across organizational echelons and horizontally across the functions potentially affected, ranging from R&D through production to marketing, sales and service, plus the key functional areas, including environment. The subsequent analysis thus allows testing of their level of agreement with respect to the progress made and the gaps still to be filled. More importantly, it allows the identification of pockets of greater (or lesser) will and skill, and especially of apprehension. Virtually without exception, the latter provides a solid basis for the identification of pivotal job holders: these coworkers, even without a formal environmental change programme, invariably 'know' they are expected to carry a greater responsibility in this sensitive area.

Various survey methodologies can be applied, each with its pros and cons. A questionnaire, for instance, also makes it possible to benchmark the responses internally (ie among units or functions) or externally (ie against other companies). Personal one-to-one interviews, on the other hand, facilitate a deeper understanding of gaps in the organization's abilities and better identification of the barriers to change among the pivotal job holders. Experience shows that by phrasing the questions in a positive sense – for example: 'Do you feel we should tackle this challenge? What could it mean for colleagues in your position? What could be done to help them?' – most coworkers gladly volunteer their creative insights.

Often, some individual pivotal job holders, by hook or by crook, have already implemented solutions to their own challenges, which are often informal. Moreover, their names can easily be found through the organizational grapevine. The information base thus can be sensibly complemented through a limited number of focus groups, in which these informal change leaders interact in providing their insights as to the most desirable action programme.

Holding up a mirror to top management, the project team facilitates the discussion of the current stage of response as well as the gaps in the organization's abilities for reaching the next stage: How far have we progressed? How strong are our skills? What is most critical, however, is the identification of the pivotal job holders and their barriers to change. Using the five barriers discussed in this chapter as 'bulletin boards' to collect and sort the comments and suggestions made during the data gathering process, management thus gains an indispensable input for its strategy.

PREPARING FOR CHANGE

It is an unfortunate truth that a major incident is often the best stimulant for policy change, both in government and business. Too often policy is as good as the latest disaster was bad. But what does one do in a company that is not under extraordinary external pressure, and where top management is nonetheless convinced of the need for an integrated or proactive response despite the significant disruption this might mean for many of its coworkers? Although coworkers are more often than not sympathetic to an integrated or proactive environmental endgame, this is not enough to overcome the typical barriers to change we have just examined.

In our experience, we have found that a useful tool in tackling this problem has been developed by Paul Strebel of the International Institute for Management Development (IIMD) in Lausanne, Switzerland.[25] Strebel argued that the root cause of the failure to execute change programmes is in the one-sided alteration of personal contracts by top management.[26] Coworkers and organizations have reciprocal obligations and mutual commitments, both stated and implied, that define their relationship. Radical change – in our case, making the transition to an integrated or a proactive response – alters the terms of these personal contracts (Box 5.2). Before embarking on a major change programme, top management is thus well advised to re-examine the terms of the existing contracts and also assess and test the conditions it wants to propose – particularly those for its pivotal job holders.

Box 5.2 The origins of the concept of the personal contract[a]

Contracts are about exchange: each party gives and takes. In the super-market we exchange money for tomatoes. In the labour market we exchange our time, energy and expertise for a salary plus a series of rights ranging from a desk to sit at to a pension. We do not *have* to agree to such contracts: they are entered into voluntarily.

The concept of contracts can be expanded however. Jean-Jacques Rousseau wrote of the 'social contract' as an unwritten set of rights and obligations that determine the nature of the relationship between the state and its subjects or citizens.[b] He also saw this contract as having 'natural' limitations. In other words, some individual rights are inalien-able: the individual cannot give them away, nor can the state usurp them.

Management experts, such as Harvard's Chris Argyris, have recently expanded on the idea of a contract within the business arena, where it now covers the rights and obligations of a corporation and its employ-ees. According to Schein, the so-called psychological contract may be defined as an 'unwritten set of expectations operating at all times between every member of an organization and the various managers and others in that organization'.[c] The psychological contract thus not only concerns issues such as the pay to be received but also covers non-tangible, psychological issues. It thus emphasizes elements that can be subsumed under the headings of 'consideration' and 'organizational citizenship'.

Instead of pitting them against each other as 'either/or' choices, Paul Strebel builds on these three concepts by recognizing their core elements as the separate paragraphs of a single personal contract that each coworker has with her or his company.[d] Thus he also recognizes a social paragraph at the corporate rather than the state level, and clari-fies the meaning of the psychological paragraph by focusing it on the immediate working environment of each individual.

a Peter Makin et al, *Organizations and the Psychological Contract*, p4ff
b Jean-Jacques Rousseau, *The Social Contract* (Penguin Books, London; 1968)
c Edgar H Schein, *Organizational Psychology* (Prentice-Hall, Englewood Cliffs; 1980)
d Paul Strebel, *The Change Pact: Building Commitment to Ongoing Change* (*Financial Times*/Pitman Publishing, London; 1998); see also *Harvard Business Review*, May–June 1996, p86

Checking Personal Contracts

During the course of examining its approach to the environment, management inevitably comes across widely differing perceptions and opinions with regard to the wisdom of taking environmental action. Although very few coworkers will express anti-environmental sentiment, a number might doubt the need to take action immedi-ately. They might argue for a wait-and-see approach, or for following rather than leading. Others, often younger employees, might be mystified that top management is still dawdling. In their perception, the realities of the product and labour markets leave no choice: action must be taken immediately.

Not surprisingly, top management often feels caught in the middle. It probably realizes it should act on at least some of the options it has on the table, and do so soon. On the other hand it also has a range of other business issues on its plate. To avoid over-burdening the organization, priorities must be set. Before committing to a major environmental initiative it should therefore conduct one last check of how much of a management challenge it will be to bring about the endgame.

Although most senior managers have a well-developed intuition for this type of task, its relevance and complexity suggest that it pays to be systematic about it. Here, the personal contracts can be very useful. From Strebel's perspective, these should consist of three paragraphs.[27] The formal paragraph encompasses the policies and procedures that provide direction and guidelines to managers and coworkers. The psychological paragraph captures the mutual expectations and reciprocal commitments that arise from feelings like trust and loyalty, especially between managers and their direct subordinates. Lastly, the social paragraph builds on the visions and values that a company pursues and how they are translated into practice.

From the perspective of the individual coworker, a corporation is an abstract entity. To make it come alive, it is associated with specific names and faces: the contract is between people. At the operational level, the individual deals with 'the boss'. Ultimately, when talking about visions and values, a contract is also with the top of the organizational hierarchy, embodied in the corporate leaders.

Indeed, within the confines of the company, it is individuals who have reciprocal obligations and mutual commitments, both stated and implied. Any change that managers make in essence alters the terms of these personal contracts with their stakeholders. Most often the transition is handled in an implicit, unspoken manner. New managers are installed and coworkers quickly test whether existing contractual terms are still interpreted in a same manner, or whether other, often informal, terms need to be renegotiated. For example, official working hours could be from 9 a.m. to 5 p.m., but new bosses might expect work to start earlier.

Occasionally, however, the transition is too radical. Indeed, if not fully understood and underwritten, it will be perceived as a breach of contract. People know the contractual terms they have, but too often have no idea about what they'll get in changed contexts. Remember: this is the reason why pivotal job holders – the individuals who have to make the greatest changes – are apprehensive. Within the existing contract, they could face the challenge, but can they still do so under the newly proposed contract? If the breach is considered sufficiently serious and affects many, as in collective labour agreements, coworkers may resort to industrial action. In less extreme instances, they will often feel justified in 'getting even', for instance through working-to-rule, apathy and non-cooperation.[28]

Integrated and proactive management changes often involve such drastic transformations. Managers should therefore prepare for a serious renegotiation of the personal contracts, particularly with the pivotal job holders. For each of its relevant stakeholder groupings, top management should systematically analyse the height of the relevant barriers to change. Weighing these against the will, skill and thrill it expects from the members of the grouping for the proposed actions, it can get a fair understanding of the internal change challenge.

Although the differences between companies and stakeholder groupings are considerable, a number of general conclusions can tentatively be drawn. The barrier of lagging structure and systems, for instance, can be overcome by making changes in the formal paragraph of the personal contract. The earlier organizational provisions are no longer adequate. While the new ones may not yet have been developed, the gap can be filled relatively easily: it is primarily the paper organization that has to be adapted. Organizational support, for instance, should no longer be provided by an EHS function, but by a strategic staff unit that knows environmental policy-making as well as the business arena. Also, management information systems should provide relevant data in a manner that 'normal' – ie non-expert – managers can handle. Evaluation and reward systems, in turn, should recognize and incorporate the environmental priority.

Even though such progress would be significant, as Strebel notes, this is as far as many top managers get when anticipating how change will affect their coworkers. The boss–subordinate relationship – ie the psychological paragraph – is rarely examined and therefore becomes a source of uncertainty and stress, since coworkers are unsure about what is expected of them as a result of the change. Often unwritten, the old contract involves immediate obligations and unfinished business. If the boss does not 'negotiate' a new contract, resistance to change increases: coworkers have a short time-horizon and over-estimate the burden of the proposed transition to a new environmental response.

Most critical, however, are the two remaining barriers that arise from the lack of adaptation of the social paragraph of the personal contracts. Strebel emphasizes that it is often this paragraph that is most vulnerable to communication breakdown and is frequently the source of conflict. Moreover, it covers the area where top management's credibility, once lost, is most difficult to recover. Indeed, when top management presents new values to direct the company, such as a greater emphasis on the environment, but has not effectively communicated its reasons for doing so, the lack of insight into top management's imperatives can lead some coworkers to become very recalcitrant. Still more damaging, they can feel excluded and often become resentful. From their perspective, they were loyally supporting and constructively contributing to the old corporate culture, and top management suddenly 'betrays' them by changing their contract terms without even bothering to check with them. It is no wonder that the apprehensive pivotal job holders are reluctant to change.

There is a second side to the personal contracts, however, that is becoming increasingly important and which top management must take into account when considering the most appropriate course of action. As discussed earlier, an increasing number of people, particularly in the West, want their environmental needs at the fourth echelon of their individual Maslow staircases to be satisfied. Many coworkers belong to this group; they want to gain the respect of their communities and, ultimately, also the self-respect that is associated with being part of an institution that does the right things. They expect their contract partners to be increasingly responsive to these needs for a reinforced corporate vision and values that can be the source of such pride – ie that can thrill them. If top management does not meet their demands by renegotiating the social paragraph, these stakeholders may withhold their creative energy or even find fulfilment elsewhere. Especially when this group includes the pivotal job holders and/or the junior talent that most corporations are eager to attract and retain, the price for inadequate contract renegotiations can be high.

BP's CEO was made aware of these expectations as a result of an informal survey the company conducted among coworkers before it changed its position on climate change. Commenting on those surveyed, John Browne said, 'They are a pretty good representative set – they just happen to work for an oil company. We concluded they wanted to be proud of what BP is doing.'[29]

Focusing on pivotal job holders

Actually, most senior managers are quite comfortable with the renegotiation of the formal and psychological paragraphs of the contracts with coworkers. This is how they made their career: managing individuals on a personal basis, within a relatively small area of control. They tend to be much less at ease with the social paragraph, however. Like those who can comfortably communicate with a single person or a small group, they sometimes are apprehensive and awkward when addressing a large audience. They have honed their skills and built their confidence in renegotiations with other individuals. Clearly in large corporations such an approach would not be effective nor realistic: very few top managers would have the time to successfully interact with all individual coworkers.

A useful concept in dealing with this large-scale negotiation dilemma was offered a decade ago by Burger King CEO Barry Gibbons who, borrowing from bicycle racing, introduced the term 'vacuum management' as a useful approach.[30] When a cyclist leads a group, he or she creates a vacuum while the others in the pack follow in his or her slipstream. Similarly, when top managers accelerate in a specific direction in the process of implementing radical change, they create a vacuum of sorts. Those following close behind the leader create a vacuum of their own, which in turn draws in more followers – both those reporting to them and their peers, and so on. The group travels that much faster. Moreover, in an efficient pack with good momentum, a number of riders will take a turn at the head. The first leader, the initiator of change, is soon in the pleasant position of being able to 'lead from behind'.

Institutional change, in other words, need not incorporate all stakeholders simultaneously. The key, as we have seen, is to focus on the pivotal job holders. If the corporate leadership can build the will, skill and especially the thrill for them to be creative in addressing the (potential) discontinuities in their particular areas, while at the same time eliminating their specific barriers to change, the battle is half won. This group, in turn, will create the vacuum that allows others to race forwards in the direction of the desired endgame.

Once some of the pivotal job holders move forwards into the vacuum and gain initial experience and confidence working with new environmental responsibilities, they can even develop initiatives of their own. Ideally, this will allow top management's endgame perspective to be upgraded and refined, as more and more members of the organization push forwards with environmental initiatives.

The importance of the role of these pivotal job holders cannot be over-stressed. In their book *Inside Corporate Innovation*, Robert Burgelman and Leonard Sayles argue that breakthroughs generally are a product not of top–down strategic planning but of strategic recognition.[31] In other words, higher management echelons recognize the potential merit of new approaches proposed by individuals in the lower levels in the organization. The incorporation of these ideas into business strategy comes after a successful experiment has taken place through a process called 'retroactive rationalizing', which gives the innovation legitimacy. This process of strategic recognition followed by retroactive rationalization also applies to the 'leaps' in technology and business approaches needed to make the transition to an integrated or proactive response.

Given the bottom–up character of this process, management's identification of the pivotal job holders has to start at the very front-line. If, for instance, the environmental change requires new operational processes in a plant, the emphasis could very well be on coworkers directly engaged in the relevant tasks. Higher echelons must then add value by making these pivotal job holders successful by, first, lowering their barriers to change and, second, instituting the positive incentives that invite them to 'step into the vacuum'. If, while doing so, specific groups at these higher echelons in turn face major barriers to change, they also have to be considered pivotal job holders and must have the targeted support of superiors still higher up in the organization. The sales force, for instance, could be confronted with a new market approach, or the R&D staff might be requested to come up with the formula for an environmentally-friendly production process.

Although it is essential to start 'scanning' at the frontline, in many cases the pivotal job holders are located in the management echelons. For example, when companies make the transition to a functional response, it is the plant managers who need the greatest support and reassurance; indeed, our surveys highlighted their apprehensions about their ability to perform. As shown before, in the transition to an integrated response the business managers tend to be the most concerned. Top management should therefore make a targeted effort to clear their path and pull them forwards in the desired direction. Of course, the more complete transformation implied by a transition to a proactive response would typically mean that the number and diversity of pivotal job holder groupings is larger still; in fact, it can embrace almost all coworkers.

The identification of the pivotal positions within a company thus requires serious top management attention. Some individuals are better suited to this challenge than others. The first pivotal job holders to take an initiative are on dangerous ground, and need a certain degree of personal conviction to take the career risk. Moreover, as emphasized by Burgelman and Sayles, in order to retain support and stimulate cooperation from others within the organization, they have to radiate confidence and competence. If they can make the product look like a winner, others will do things to support the initiative, helping to make it a success. The personal qualities of the pivotal job holders thus play a critical role in organizational thrill-building, and when preparing for change it is up to top management to make the proper assessments before kicking off a targeted change programme.

***

We have argued here that management plays a central part in preparing a company for change. Once it has validated the endgame, assessed the organization's change preparedness and taken the first steps in preparing for change, implementation can begin. We now turn to the implementation of an integrated approach in Chapters 6 and 7, before turning our attention to the proactive approach in Chapters 8 and 9.

PART II

INTEGRATED RESPONSE

6

IMPLEMENTING AN INTEGRATED ENVIRONMENTAL MANAGEMENT STRATEGY

The transition from a functional to an integrated response is not an awesome task. The principles are straightforward, the logic appealing and the support base among coworkers usually solid. The business visions and values that drive a corporation are not affected. Indeed, the only thing that changes is the way a company incorporates the environment into its normal strategy and operations.

Despite its relative simplicity, however, remarkably few companies have been successful in making this transition. We feel that this is often because business unit managers, one of the most important groups of pivotal job holders with their bottom-line responsibility for developing and implementing business strategy, are not always convinced of top management's commitment. Our surveys show that while these individuals tend to agree that the environment should be a top priority, they often believe that their company's commitment is a matter of warm words but little action. Further, since their time horizon is often no more than three to four years – typical for strategic plans as well as career expectations in a given position – many environmental issues easily escape their attention. Lastly, this tendency is strengthened by a natural reluctance to deal with yet another business uncertainty in an area that offers limited career pay-offs.

The implementation programme we propose for an integrated approach, the environmental management programme (EMP), focuses on this task. Its premise is that the essence of the top management challenge is the careful selection of the appropriate management instruments that have to be applied, in a proper sequence and manner, to shape a programme to change from a functional to an integrated approach. Management has what might be described as a panel with four basic instrument groups that allows it to inspire, steer, reward and anchor the will to act among its coworkers (Box 6.1).

Box 6.1 The instrument panel for change management

The purpose of change management is to induce and stabilize a desired organizational behaviour, ie the will and skill to act in a specific manner.[a] To establish the organizational conditions that are conducive to this objective, management has access to four groups of instruments (see Figure 6.1), that are tailored to:

- *Inspire* by sparking a thrill among coworkers. Attitudes and values feed behavioural change. When they are flat and uninspiring, coworkers will work 9 to 5. When sparks fly, people can surmount existing barriers to change and lay a solid foundation for a shared will to act. Especially when pursuing radical change, top management must lead the way through:
    - *Information.* Stakeholders want to know: what is the problem or what are the opportunities? How bad is it or, alternatively, how promising? What type of action is required to address it? If a problem is 'bad' or an opportunity 'good' enough, existing corporate attitudes and values will generally result in action.
    - *Communication* of an overall message, such as the endgame vision. Top management must share its mental model of the future and be open to adapt it to the needs of its pivotal job holders. Stakeholders want to know what their leadership wants to do about a business discontinuity and why and how they – individually or as members of a group – fit in and can contribute.
    - *Challenge.* Unless specifically challenged to step into the vacuum and take the initiative, many pivotal job holders will not alter their behaviour. It thus is up to top management to present the individuals with a perspective that satisfies their individual needs.
- *Steer* by setting stretching but attainable operational targets. The corporate leadership must ensure its mental model is translated into clearly defined, do-able chunks of work. Three generally acknowledged elements are central to its credibility:
    - *Targets.* The ultimate goals and the milestones in-between should be expressed in quantifiable and physical terms that have meaning to the pivotal job holders and that, moreover, allow measurement and hence control.
    - *Resources.* Action plans will include requirements with regard to the means needed for implementation. Money, time, space and access to expertise all are necessary. The most critical resource, however, is generally people, notably the assignment of widely recognized 'heavyweights' to spearhead the drive.
    - *Example.* Especially when making the transition to a proactive response, the CEO and his or her senior staff must be willing to serve as role models for their coworkers to follow: actions often speak louder than words.

a The following framework was inspired by thoughts presented by Joachim Schahn in *Psychologie für den Umwelschutz* (editors: Joachim Schahn and Thomas Giesinger; Beltz Psychologie Verlags Union, Weinheim, Germany; 1993), p29ff

- *Reward* especially the first wave of pivotal job holders. The thrill that induces pivotal job holders to step forward is best provided by the feedback of actual implementation. Success breeds success: winning teams have great confidence and also a large number of followers. Three types of feedback are virtually essential:
  - *Measurement.* Progress measurement against plan forms the natural complement to the target setting and resource allocation discussed above. However, measurement also serves an important role in reinforcing values and attitudes. Stakeholders want to know whether their efforts have been productive.
  - *Counsel and backup.* Major change is inevitably associated with uncertainty. The apprehensive pivotal job holders particularly need to know that senior managers are actively interested and will back them up when a loyal best-effort turns out to be a failure.
  - *Recognition.* Positive signals can serve as strong stimuli of the first wave of pivotal job holders as well as giving powerful motivation to the rest of the organization. Strong signals also can be given through the 'punishment' of non-performers.
- *Anchor* the will to act by creating the right infrastructure. At some stage the new behaviour must become 'normal', ie it should no longer require special actions aimed at inspiring, steering or rewarding. Taking the lead from its frontline experts, top management must anchor the change by installing the following:
  - *Structure and systems.* Organizational structures and management systems (eg information, evaluation or compensation) must be upgraded to warrant continued attention to a standard already attained but easily forgotten.
  - *Training and coaching.* Formal training and coaching programmes raise the awareness and the skill level among senior managers and stakeholders. Pivotal job holders in particular must have the benefit of reflecting upon the necessity of structural change and the ways to make it come about.
  - *Facilities.* Although rarely of major importance in inducing change, a well-conceived physical infrastructure can play a highly effective and efficient role in anchoring a specific behaviour.

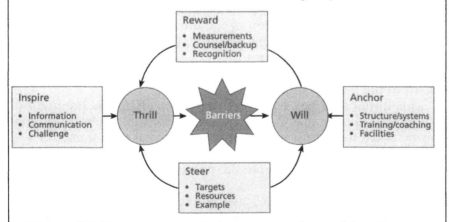

Figure 6.1 *Top management instruments for making changes*

As corporate visions and values are hardly affected and, moreover, most business unit managers have participated in strategy development and thus feel fairly comfortable with the chosen endgame and options for action, the inspiration instruments tend to have only a marginal role. Simply put, the social paragraph of the personal contracts of coworkers is not at stake in the implementation of an integrated strategy. Instead, the primary focus is on renegotiating the formal and psychological paragraphs with a limited group of business unit managers, with the purpose of inducing them to integrate the environment into their business strategy.

The key determinant for success is therefore the craftsmanship of top management in ensuring a high quality of action planning and operational execution. Its main levers in eliminating the barriers to change presented by short time-horizons and a perceived agenda overload will be the steering and rewarding instruments – familiar concepts in management. At the same time, the EMP – a factor often neglected in change programmes – should ensure that the (lagging) structures and systems are upgraded and the required training programmes instituted to anchor the will to act in daily operations.

Working directly with its business unit managers, top management needs to shape an EMP that, typically, distinguishes four roughly sequential tasks: initiate, orchestrate, activate and motivate (Figure 6.2).

INITIATE

In line with the principle of vacuum management, the corporate leadership must take steps to ensure the support of its senior management, ie the top ten or twenty people within a large company (including heads of major staff units). Not all of them will eventually be asked to take turns 'cycling' up-front; in fact, some will have little to do with the implementation of the integrated approach. Still, top management must have their support; it cannot allow too many 'dissidents' who might disrupt the flow. The initial step of vacuum management, therefore, is to initiate a joint leadership agenda with regard to the process to be followed.

This initial step has a two-fold purpose. First, it is intended to scope the challenge that each participating business unit can reasonably be asked to address within a five- or ten-year time-frame, as well as the units' readiness to fulfil the related requirements. Second, it should provide the transition to the process of outlining the relevant medium-term objectives.

` Ideally, we feel, this backcasting exercise should be the joint product of the senior management group, resulting, for instance, from one or more full-day workshops prepared by a small team of

Top management tasks

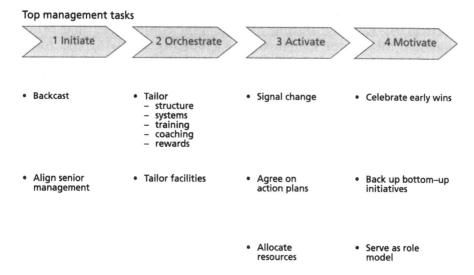

| 1 Initiate | 2 Orchestrate | 3 Activate | 4 Motivate |

- Backcast

- Tailor
  - structure
  - systems
  - training
  - coaching
  - rewards

- Signal change

- Celebrate early wins

- Align senior management

- Tailor facilities

- Agree on action plans

- Back up bottom–up initiatives

- Allocate resources

- Serve as role model

Figure 6.2 *Contours of an environmental management programme*

internal and/or external experts. The shared responsibility offers the significant benefit of the valuable strategic insight of the larger management group.

The joint workshops can promote the alignment of the relevant senior managers behind the need for change and the complications that might be expected. As discussed earlier, many forces can work against this. Sometimes senior managers have scars from previous environmental battles which make them reluctant to participate and can even blind them to the motivation of the other players in the environmental arena. They are sometimes inwards-looking, while the group-think phenomenon frequently is reflected in unnecessarily tough positions vis-à-vis 'intruders'. All too often, especially under the pressure of media attention, they have great difficulty in considering fallback positions or alternatives to their existing strategy, and develop an ability to negate new information or use it selectively.

Top management is thus well advised to adopt a number of simple rules in this closing-ranks process: it should never present its own viewpoint up-front; it should encourage others to express their doubts and criticism; and once a consensus has been reached, it should delay the final decision until the next meeting, when all the pros and cons can once again be assessed with an open, fresh mind. Also, some structural and procedural steps can enhance the effectiveness of the meetings: alternating discussion leaders; independent decision-making in two or more separate subgroups; a designated 'devil's advocate' or an external expert to challenge the group, and so on.[1]

We have developed an instrument called ECO-Match, which is particularly valuable during management conferences that bring together the senior echelons of a company. Applying the tools described in earlier chapters in an interactive one-day workshop, the participants jointly explore the main environmental issues that could have impacts on the company and the possible responses of customers, suppliers and competitors, as well as the positions that national and international government institutions and NGOs are likely to adopt. Significant time is then dedicated to the critical, but much under-rated, analysis of the internal performance. The question is: How well are we equipped to respond to the business challenges – both threats and opportunities – that have been identified? The workshop concludes with a first attempt at describing the contours of an action programme that could serve as the basis for follow-up action. ECO-Match thus facilitates the transfer of ideas from top leadership to the senior management ranks and, moreover, allows the latter to determine whether a discontinuity in a specific business segment is significant enough to warrant a truly integrated strategic response.[2]

ORCHESTRATE

For an EMP to succeed, business unit managers must be properly supported. The organizational conditions should enhance the likelihood of their success and, moreover, clearly signal top management's commitment to that success by meeting the unit managers' needs through tailored structures, systems, training, coaching and rewards. In addition, a task force should be established at the corporate level to examine the use of physical facilities as an instrument to anchor the desired behavioural change.

Tailored structure

Top management must first of all ensure that the organizational structure is geared to the needs of the business unit managers as they integrate environmental concerns into their business strategies. With its background in technical adaptations to environmental demands, a traditional EHS unit is simply not equipped to provide the business perspective required for strategic decision-making.

The organizational adaptations undergone by many large companies provide evidence of the this drawback with traditional EHS units. As we discussed in Chapter 1, during the initial reactive response stage the actual environmental responsibilities were added to the tasks of existing health and safety units. These were functional staff units, however, that were asked to find operational solutions – often of a technical nature – to problems as they occurred. The emphasis was on compliance with existing regulations. The addition of the environmental responsibility served the organization well during the reactive and functional response stages. When making the transition to an integrated response, with its focus on business strategy, the EHS unit is poorly positioned, however. It definitely is not integrated into the mainstream of events and although it prevents negative occurrences – incidents, costs of non-compliance – it is rarely of use in the pursuit of environmentally-related market opportunities.

Moreover, when the functional response requirements are adequately met, environmental staff members in principle no longer need to function as policemen or watchdogs, ensuring compliance with regulations. Instead, they can become more like internal consultants, helping operational departments achieve their goals. Organizations therefore could consider separating out the auditors, who for legal accountability reasons might be attached to health and safety departments. The consultants, in turn, should be assigned to the business units, where they should be an integral part of the strategy discipline which, in many instances, would ideally also encompass the technology function. These strategy–technology–environment (STE) staff would provide the best functional support to the frontline, as well as promote the optimal integration of operational and strategic insights with regard to the environment.

At the next organizational level, the STE staff consultant would obviously report to the business unit manager. But he or she should have a functional reporting line to a corporate STE officer (Figure 6.3). Besides strategic planning (and perhaps technology) duties, this corporate STE officer would also be responsible for proposing and auditing corporate guidelines, training and counselling, integrating the environment in corporate and business unit strategies, supporting top management so that it can be effective in partnership discussions (see Chapter 7), and warning the CEO about unwise decisions by individual business unit managers that may negatively affect other business units or the corporation as a whole.

The corporate STE officer need not necessarily have line authority for each of these tasks. Ultimately, business unit managers are responsible for their own strategies as well as any other elements, such as training, that they feel necessary. Except for proposing and auditing policy guidelines – much of which can be outsourced, if so desired – the role of the corporate STE officer is primarily one of stimulating others. It is therefore important that he or she should be seen as an organizational heavyweight, most probably at the executive vice-president level reporting directly to the CEO.

Moreover, this individual should have a special interest in the environment, ie he or she should not be a bureaucrat with another 9-to-5 task to handle. Too often we encounter highly capable functional staff leaders who have been promoted to this final-desti-

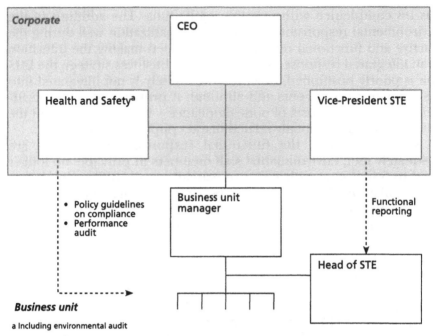

Figure 6.3 *STE support for integrated environmental management*

nation position. It is unlikely that they can serve as the respected counsellor to apprehensive business unit managers, let alone spark the thrill needed to successfully attack the new challenge.

Tailor systems

It is not only today's structures that reflect yesterday's needs. The same also often applies to other organizational elements, such as management systems and processes. For example, business unit managers lack the support they need to make the transition from a functional to an integrated response. Even worse, their operational and strategic feedback signals reinforce traditional behaviour. Major adaptations, therefore, must often be made to support an organization's will to act and/or prevent it from sliding back into earlier habits, especially when other priorities compete for attention.

Management tools must be designed to provide the level of synthesis and the timeliness of information required for decision-making. As we've seen, during the first response stages, systems and processes generally tend to be technocratic. They focus on the liability assessment of current and former production sites, public communication programmes (environmental reporting, brochures, etc), environmental performance evaluation of actual or potential business partners (eg suppliers, acquisition candidates), environmental training modules for managers, and sometimes environmental marketing programmes (eg green products, green labelling, superior recyclability). In particular, the traditional environmental audit systems existing in many industrial companies are designed to respond to legal requirements, and are far too technical and complex for strategic planning or option assessment purposes.

The key to improvement is in the overview: data have to be aggregated in a sensible manner in a management information system that will facilitate setting priorities and measuring progress against plans. Trade-offs now have to be made not only between options for environmental action (including non-action), but also between these and proposals related to other aspects of business, such as geographic expansion or new plants: each unit of currency can be spent only once. Companies also become more open about their impact on the environment and the steps they take to improve their performance. A public account, for instance an annual environmental report or periodic information to a specific community, should be based on more than public relations (PR) considerations. To this end, again, specific management information is required, but it is often unavailable.

Many companies therefore feel an urgent need for an improvement in their environmental cost accounting, to allow them to better assess environmental costs and benefits in terms of hard cash, or even experiment with the associated notion of including environmental 'capital' and 'debt' in the corporate balance sheet.[3] Although it raised some eyebrows among interested financial parties, Dutch software specialist Origin took this idea a step further in its annual environmental balance sheets. Baxter International, a healthcare products and service company, for its part, puts together an annual environmental profit and loss statement. The company's Vice-President for EHS, Bill Blackburn, says that compiling the statement has made an invaluable contribution by 'bringing together our environmental and business professionals. It enables these professionals to focus on common opportunities using a common language – the language of business – money. It has been the ultimate tool for integrating our environmental programme into our business.'[4]

Although such approaches would put environmental decision-making on a 'rational' rather than an 'emotional' footing, actual practice is fraught with major complexities that argue against dedicating excessive financial and time resources. A particular difficulty is deciding where to draw the line: Which factor costs can be specifically attributed to the environment? Should one include third-party environmental costs and benefits caused by the ecological shadow?

Although these approaches are often well-intentioned, it is our belief that, when making the transition to an integrated response, the environmental component should not be accounted for separately. Top management should bear in mind its experience with the introduction of IT over a decade ago. Initially, each company knew exactly how much its IT staff were spending: the department had constantly to justify its existence. Later, when large machines and specialized IT departments had all but vanished, few knew – or cared to know – the exact costs and benefits: IT had become integrated into the business.

This should also be the fate of environmental expenditures in a company pursuing an integrated response. Bruce Liimatainen, president of A Finkl & Sons, a Chicago-based steel forger often lauded for its clean manufacturing, notes that his company does not even bother with calculating environmental savings: 'We don't want to spend two months having employees figure out our spending payback. We just know it is right for our business.'[5] DuPont also wants to avoid the absolute quantification of environmental results in cash terms. Its chief financial officer (CFO), Gary Pfeiffer, puts it this way: 'Just as people normally think of marketing as a customary way of doing business, we want them to think of the environment as customary.'[6]

What we consider to be the ideal approach, however, goes a step further. We believe that an integrated response requires the strengthening of systems for environmental cost–benefit assessment. The cost focus used during the functional response stage should be broadened to include a first assessment of the probable benefits of a specific action. Dow Chemical's Eco-Compass tool as well as Unilever's use of an environmental profile serve exactly this purpose with respect to strategic options or business positioning.[7] Our environmental option assessment tool, presented in Chapter 4, pushes this further by combining the net environmental yield of a business option with its net economic impact. Note that in each case these are management, not financial accounting tools – relevance, not accuracy, is the objective.

The integration of the environment into business should not be limited to strategy, however. Following the earlier accent on process design during the functional response stage, the integrated response is characterized by a greater emphasis on product life cycle responsibility or, as it is more commonly known, product stewardship. A number of leading companies have made significant progress with advanced systems for product design, such as design for recycling (DFR), design for disassembly (DFD) and design for reusability (DFRE).[8]

A specific example is provided by the Scandinavian car manufacturer Volvo. The company publishes an 'environmental product declaration' which provides an overview of the environmental performance of a car. It compares performance achieved in important categories – manufacturing, operation, recycling and environmental management – of Volvo's own operations and those of its suppliers and dealerships alongside a theoretical maximum. The declaration is third-party certified according to ISO 14001. The purpose is to give buyers sufficient and meaningful information so that they can objectively compare different cars.[9]

The systems and management processes must also allow the tracking of progress against individual goals. Environmental performance should become an element in a business unit manager's overall performance evaluation.

Other management systems that require specific attention for the transition to an integrated approach include the environmental 'antennae' (eg advisory groups consisting of local community representatives or of external experts); the environmental impact assessment of major business decisions (such as investments and/or new product introductions), even if not required by law; and the strategic planning process, which must include the systematic exploration of potential business opportunities and/or environmental scenarios. Moreover, basic tools must be available for simplified LCA concentrated on material use, energy consumption and one or two company-specific, critical parameters, such as emissions of toxic substances.

Tailor training

When we ask senior managers of leading companies about their priorities for internal action, environmental training modules for managers almost invariably tops their list. As the corporate response evolves, the demands on managers require that they have a broader range of skills. Moreover, the skills build on each other: if technical skills are not properly developed, the more strategic general management skills of integrated response have an insufficient foundation to build on (see Box 6.2).

In this hierarchy of skills, those required for a reactive environmental response typically include knowing current regulations and ensuring compliance, but also managing risks and assessing liabilities (Figure 6.4). During the functional response stage, the skills required are somewhat more sophisticated and include anticipating upcoming regulation, ensuring cost-effective compliance, conducting environmental cost accounting and managing constituencies (including political lobbying).[10] Building on this foundation, under an integrated response business unit management has to hone its skills at scanning the environmental horizon, as discussed in Chapter 2, but also develop such essential qualities as assessing environmental options and external partnering (see Chapter 7).

Special attention needs to be paid to the training of what we can call 'path-finders' among the pivotal job holders. This is the small group – usually about 15 per cent of all pivotal job holders – who must come up with the breakthrough solutions. With costs and

Box 6.2 Don't run before you can walk

A special warning is due in case not all functional skills and the supporting systems are adequately developed when top management decides to pursue the transition to an integrated response. The amateurs in our vertical surveys (see Chapter 5) provide ample case illustrations. The potential losses in terms of internal and external credibility, for instance when a 'green marketing' campaign is found to be a sham or top management publicly fails when responding to a crisis, can be considerable.

Although the situation differs from one company – or even organizational unit – to another, a number of deficiencies appears to recur. Most often, a high-priority catch-up effort with respect to these functional skills is called for before making the jump to an integrated response. A general lack of overview and the resulting inability to manage risks and contingencies in cases of incidents makes companies extremely vulnerable to major public pressure and liability charges. The required skills tend to be new at an institutional level. Companies virtually always have a technically adequate manual for internal health and safety (including fire hazards) procedures, which includes sections on environment. However, most companies still do not have an integrated risk and contingency policy including priority-setting devices for management purposes.[a]

In addition, few companies appear to be truly prepared for dealing with incidents. Managing risks at a lower, technical level of the organization usually implies that top management does not have immediate access and expertise to deal with the pressure of public opinion in case of an accident. Also, its support staff are not equipped to handle such situations: communications departments are not wired-in to the technical details, EHS staff on the other hand are over-technical in their orientation. Organizational task distribution schemes put the responsibility at line management level, ie it is often the site managers who handle the first wave of public attention. The negative evidence in this regard is mounting; in numerous cases it took too much time for the CEO to personally address the issue in public.

Positive examples show a different approach is possible, however. Following the Exxon Valdez disaster, BP was faced with an oil spill in California. Although a contract carrier was to blame, BP's CEO, when asked on television if BP was responsible, replied: 'Our lawyers tell us it is not our fault. But we feel like it is our fault and we are going to act like it is our fault.' Noted risk communication expert Peter Sandman: 'Six months later they did a survey and found that BP had gained stature because of how they handled the spill.'[b] Indeed, senior executives have increasingly stepped forward to assume a corporate responsibility. However, it takes a thorough technical/procedural and especially philosophical/emotional preparation for an organization to adequately deal with such a challenge. These are 'technical' skills that must be developed as part of a functional response.[c]

Few line managers are able to effectively manipulate environmental data. First, current performance must be monitored and audited. Most companies have some kind of measuring system, even if only because it is legally required. However, the information – if adequate – is rarely used for management purposes.

a Andreas Merkl and Harry Robinson, *The McKinsey Quarterly*, 1997, Number 3, p150ff
b *Tomorrow*, March–April 1996, p20
c See, for instance, Lawrence Susskind and Patrick Field, *Dealing with an Angry Public: The Mutual Gains Approach to Resolving Disputes* (The Free Press, New York; 1996); and Kenneth E Goodpaster, *The Corporation, Ethics, and the Environment* (edited by W Michael Hoffman, Robert Federick, and Edward S Petry, Jr; Quorum Books, Westport, Connecticut; 1990) p32

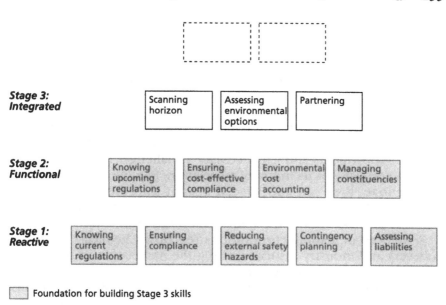

Figure 6.4 *Hierarchy of environmental management skills*

pressures growing, it becomes increasingly unlikely that 3E solutions can be found simply by tinkering. Top management must therefore support these managers in learning how to work with the new tools, such as triple-focus scanning and EOA, which can help them in their strategic decision-making and in their broader role in shaping environmental partnerships. Within their units, they will be asked to manage those solutions that can be realized through product design, and initiate the restructuring of the existing business systems, for instance through the introduction of reverse logistics concepts.

All these tasks require significant training. In-house programmes can only provide some of this. External help is not ideally geared for handling the challenge, although the World Resources Institute recently identified a number of positive initiatives at US business schools.[11] If the current gaps are not closed, however, the apprehension among these key managers might stop them from taking far-reaching initiatives.

Tailor coaching

Forward-looking environmental management requires adequate knowledge of developments identified on the environmental horizon. Many senior executives are not prepared for this task: in fact, they often share the apprehensions felt by some pivotal job holders. To support them, they need small, top-class STE staff who can help them build the knowledge, confidence and credibility they need to be able, in turn, to support their business unit managers.

They also need an understanding of the culture and the probable strategy of the main players in the environmental arena to be able to assess proposed business strategies and develop proper networks and partnerships. Senior managers must become personally involved in PLC Phase 1 and 2 discussions, and again, solid STE support is necessary here.

An external advisory board (EAB) composed of independent outsiders can reduce the risk of being blindsided. Such outside counsel supplements and – if necessary – challenges the perspectives within a company or its industry association. Serving as environmental antennae, they can add special insight into the most relevant environmental themes and the most important countries/regions, ie, the other two axes in the triple-focus methodology.

A number of leading corporations (eg Dow Chemical, Interface, Unilever) and industry associations (eg the Association of the Dutch Chemical Industry) have resorted to outside counsel. Other institutions, faced with specific environmental issues, have also chosen this course – eg the European Bank for Reconstruction and Development (investing in Central and Eastern Europe) and DuPont (biotechnology). Alternatively, a number of North American companies (eg ARCO, International Paper, Monsanto, Niagara Mohawk Power Company, Ontario Hydro) brought in one or more individuals with good environmental credentials to sit on their supervisory boards.

A number of companies have also successfully enlisted the professional help of renowned environmentalists, who increasingly work through commercial organizations, to provide sparring partners and guides for business unit management in making the transition to an integrated response. Ray Anderson of Interface, for instance, consults his 'dream team', which includes leading environmental thinkers such as Paul Hawken, Amory Lovins and Bill McDonough.[12] The combination, within a single task force, of in-depth business insight and frontline environmental experience frequently produces innovative solutions. The added advantage of this approach is that it helps bridge the culture gap between the business and environmental worlds.

In the same vein, some large corporations have formed mutually beneficial, albeit usually temporary, partnerships with NGOs in order to address a specific environmental issue of mutual concern. After a confrontational start, the cooperation of McDonald's with the EDF, for instance, has proven to be successful in reducing the waste stream of the fast-food giant. Despite the success of this type of partnership, to which we return in Chapter 7, it must be expected that they will be limited to a small number of highly visible issues. Simply put, the NGOs do not have enough qualified people to partner more than a small number of companies.

Tailor rewards

We have mentioned that our surveys suggest that a majority of business unit managers, even in leading companies, feel that excellent environmental performance is not rewarded or – even worse – doubt whether environment-related initiatives or positions benefit their careers. This does not bode well for their readiness to move to an integrated response. Top management must therefore ensure that the proper incentives are in place to stimulate initiatives and recognize performance. This is especially so during the early stages of the transition, when the business unit managers perceive the barriers to be high.

On the other hand, top management should not overdo the use of rewards. After all, business unit managers are merely asked to integrate the environment as a normal element in their strategies and operations. Thus, the emphasis should be on rewarding the exceptional; that is, the first wave of pivotal job holders and truly superior initiatives and performances, as measured by the expected value added.

Given the emerging thrill among business unit managers, their reward is partly the very existence of the initiative itself. Since they are often climbing up to the fourth echelon of their individual Maslow staircase and are surrounded by others, inside the company as well as in the neighbouring community, doing the same, many appreciate the opportunity to gain (self-) respect by being part of an environmental initiative. Top management should stimulate this interest by providing timely and public measurement of the progress being made.

One critical element, which is rarely formally stimulated, is the business unit manager's need for counsel and support higher up in the organization. The business unit managers are bound at times to be apprehensive. This might lead them to inaction or dissuade them from considering more daring options. They therefore often need somebody at a senior management level to provide them with organizational shielding. Ideally, the Executive Vice-President of STE plays an active role in this regard. However, especially in larger companies, a formal mentor system can be usefully developed, in which selected senior managers 'adopt' a number of business unit managers and serve as their sounding boards and supporters.

The mentor can provide informal – ie non-hierarchical and thus less threatening – counsel that can build confidence. He or she also can play a key role in the process of strategic recognition of bottom–up initiatives, adding the overview that often is required to tailor proposals to better fit the general corporate development. When necessary, the mentor can be instrumental in convincing top management that a specific initiative is worthwhile and will be successful if properly supported. Mentors can thus play an important part in closing the gap between top management – which has a tendency to under-estimate the degree of difficulty – and business management, which tends to do the opposite. However, the most important contribution this executive mentor can make is in championing the cases of loyal path-finders when things unexpectedly go wrong. Certainty in the support of a trusted and respected senior person is undoubtedly one of the strongest incentives for breakthrough change.

Obviously, as with all good work done by business unit managers, superior performance should be rewarded in financial and career terms. It should again be stressed that the latter provides a far stronger message across the organization: few are aware of the size of an individual bonus, but more will be aware of a promotion. As suggested earlier, environmental activities also offer significant opportunities for alternative forms of public recognition – eg awards, feature articles, internal and external presentations – that warrant serious consideration.

Tailor facilities

Most large industrial companies have extensive experience, usually dating back to their very origins, in the use of physical stimuli to induce a desired behaviour among their coworkers, and even in the communities where they are located. The availability of appropriate light-switches, paper recycling bins and separate rubbish containers in the canteen, for example, can promote the will to act.

To stimulate the transition to an integrated response and to anchor such change, top management must therefore adapt the company's facilities. Many companies have considerable experience in using physical layout and interior design to influence behaviour. Distance, for instance, has a powerful influence on who will interact with whom. In general, the more frequent the interactions, the more likely it is that informal communication will be effective. Thus, if top management wishes to integrate environmental considerations into business unit strategy, it is advisable to locate its STE staff close to the action.

Companies are also increasingly concerned about sending the right message to external as well as internal stakeholders. To this end, they often use their buildings to communicate their identity. The Dutch Ministry of the Environment, for instance, made a point of using a highly innovative construction concept to limit energy consumption to the extreme; the message was as important as the savings.

The Amsterdam-based bank/insurance company, ING, had architect Anton Alberts design its new headquarters. The bank's board of directors wanted to integrate art, natural materials, sunlight, green plants, energy efficiency and low levels of noise and water usage into the building. Following intensive and repeated consultation with its future users, ING completed the new office, arguably one of the most significant green commercial buildings in the world, in 1987. The eco-efficiency is impressive: energy consumption, for instance, is lower by a factor of two to five than in comparable buildings constructed at roughly the same cost per square metre. Art works form a part of the building fabric, and rooftops, courtyards, atria and other interior spaces are landscaped using a variety of garden styles. One of the building's unexpected side-effects is that absenteeism has dropped. Most importantly, however, the building helps to reinforce an internal and external message: ING cares about our physical environment, whether it is our working surroundings or the impact on the community of which we are guests.[13]

In the same vein, Ford Motor Company hired designers William McDonough and Michael Braungart to do a complete make-over of its Rouge industrial complex, built by Henry Ford in the 1920s. Plans include solar panels, 'living systems' that use live organisms to process waste, a grass roof that is a net producer of oxygen, and zero waste. 'We want this manufacturing facility to be what it was 80 years ago, the most copied industrial site in the world – but this time for sustainability,' says chairman Bill Ford, Jr.[14]

Care also goes a long way in stimulating the will to act in a specific manner – something the TQM experience confirms. As early as in 1934, the famous Hawthorne studies ultimately showed that it was not so much the quality of the working conditions that resulted in greater labour productivity, but the satisfaction gained by coworkers from the greater attention they received: people worked harder because top management was perceived to care. Good lighting and climate control, plants and art works, clean washrooms and neat canteens all stimulate productivity. When coworkers are made co-responsible, they invariably respond with positive environmental initiatives, ranging from overall redesign to small win–win contributions: eg more environmentally-friendly personal computers; better use of telecommunication to reduce travel or courier expenses; elimination of disposable cups; chlorine-free paper.

A higher level of management response to the needs of coworkers reaching the fourth Maslow step involves focusing on the company's impact on its surroundings. Most physical facilities within a corporation satisfy basic requirements with regard to the quality of the environment and of nature. However, few companies have developed a sensitivity to needs related to spatial cohesion, social renewal and identity.[15] For instance, companies rarely consider the larger picture of the effectiveness and efficiency of land zoning in their area, which can, for instance, lead to a wasteful fragmentation in the pattern of land use. Too often, such issues are considered to be solely the responsibility of the public authorities.

Therefore in formulating and anchoring an integrated response, top management has to address a range of unfamiliar questions. Should it be concerned about the impact on social renewal when offices, stores and plants move or close down, leaving central areas to deteriorate further? Should it worry about the fit of its buildings into their surroundings, or limit the uncontrolled sprawl of glass-mirrored offices in many new business development areas? Individually, they are perhaps attractive; collectively, however, they are a characterless mess.

And should corporate headquarters worry about the impact the company may have on the social cohesion of the community of which it is a member? Many business centres become empty, dangerous places after dark: should management care? And should it utilize the size and setting of its office buildings to reduce the feeling of alienation that architecture often creates? Could it make better use of existing facilities by making them available at night for community purposes, such as lifelong education?

When climbing the fourth echelon of the hierarchy of needs, the emphasis shifts to gaining external respect and self-respect. Providing physical facilities that signal environmental values within a company as well as how it fits into the neighbouring community, can thus provide a much under-rated, but potentially powerful, management instrument for anchoring behavioural change.

ACTIVATE

Once the first preparations for a shared framework for action and a tailored infrastructure have been made, top management can turn its attention to activating the business unit managers themselves. In doing so, it should recall the fundamental lesson of vacuum management: it should focus on a small part of the group to be managed. In this case, this is the path-finder group of pivotal job holders, since it is not strictly necessary to get all pivotal job holders to move at the same time. Top managers should also realize that, when starting, both they and their coworkers tend to be low on experience and confidence. Endgame perspectives, derived concepts and methodologies as well as organizational infrastructure are still insufficiently crystallized, and are therefore susceptible to criticism or – even worse – cynicism.

Experience shows that some 15 per cent of all pivotal job holders will typically remain sceptical, and 70 per cent will wait before placing their bets: the path-finders, as we've noted, usually constitute the final 15 per cent. It is on these path-finders that management should focus, since they will be willing and able to move forwards into the vacuum. In effect, to make sure that the essential 70 per cent join in, the path-finders must be 'managed' towards success.

In most cases, we feel, the emphasis should be on incorporating environmental dimensions in the normal budgeting and planning process. Three specific actions are called for: signal the change, agree on action plans and allocate resources.

Signalling change

Business unit managers must believe that top management is serious about the integration of the environment into business strategies and operations. They also must perceive top management's perspective as viable and understand the framework for action.

Each person must then be able to start thinking about what he or she could do to further the integration process. In our experience, it is not absolutely necessary for top management to express itself in explicit statements: the initial scoping and backcasting exercise is inevitably rough. Once good people put their mind to it and think of a problem as their own, they often prove to have an uncanny ability to come up with the right answers for their own activities.

The signal can also take a variety of forms. Many companies have, for instance, modified their corporate mission statements to include explicit environmental objectives, or have introduced a separate EHS mission statement.[16] Similarly, a public environmental report, published in parallel with a company's annual report, can be a clear statement of corporate commitment: 'We will be accountable.'[17] An increasing number of high-profile CEOs of large and highly visible corporations have resorted to public position statements as a means of communicating internally. Here, for example, are the thoughts of DuPont's Chairman and CEO, Edgar S Woolard during his first public address, which dealt with environmental issues:

> *Judging from the press coverage and other reactions that followed the London speech, we succeeded in ratcheting up DuPont's visibility on this issue several notches. A lot of this was no doubt based on surprise that a large chemical company was declaring a 'sea change' in its environmental stance. But nowhere was the surprise greater than within DuPont itself, and because the goals we set were determined with only limited assistance from the full organization, a period of definition and buy-in followed. Leadership groups within the company had an opportunity to hear from me directly and to assist in defining the specific terms of several of the goals.*[18]

More direct and, when properly executed, more effective is the internal statement. Many companies use their regular channels (eg in-house publications and management development programmes) or special ones (eg important anniversaries or unveiling new facilities) to announce new approaches and commitments.

Most powerful of all, however, are signals produced by actual business practice. For example, in 1991 the Swedish pulp manufacturer Södra Cell was in the midst of a lengthy internal debate on whether or not to introduce totally chlorine-free (TCF) pulp. When CEO Helge Eklund had sold 8000 tons of the new product, he effectively proved its commercial feasibility and definitively concluded the debate.

Agree on action plans

Once the starting signal has been properly communicated, top management should invite the path-finders among its business unit managers to share the leadership responsibility – that is, leading the pack, to use the cycling metaphor. This typically requires considerable effort, since most companies are steeped in compliance-oriented traditions. Many business unit managers are also all too aware of the career risks of moving into the vacuum. However, our experience with client organizations consistently shows that this initial scepticism can be overcome. Time and again, we found that most managers actually know the answers to environmental questions; what holds them back from taking the initiative is the fact that their superiors rarely ask the right questions or invite them to volunteer their ideas.

The annual budgeting and planning process offers an excellent vehicle to promote vacuum management practices. Basically, the process distinguishes three steps. First, top management – in interaction with its supervisory board – determines the corporate endgame to be pursued, which is subsequently backcast in medium-term objectives. As a second step, these usually ambitious but imperfect objectives provide the starting point for a business unit management, which proposes a strategy. Top management then determines the overall strategy, while taking account of other corporate programmes, for instance in the areas of technology development and human resource management. The sequence is thereafter repeated when translating the strategic plans, usually with time horizons of three to four years, into operational plans and budgets (Figure 6.5).

The third step, the development of strategy proposals by business unit management, is central to the integration of the environment into this process. The units' leaders have to inspire themselves and their coworkers to go through the loops of generating and assessing options, in order to come up with the best. The quality of this

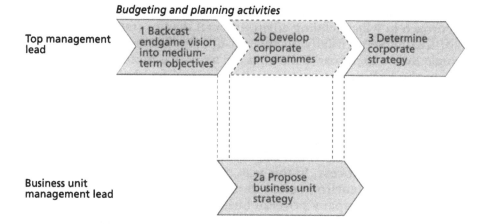

Figure 6.5 *Activation through annual planning process*

homework clearly determines that of the ultimate proposal brought to top management for validation and eventual incorporation into the overall company strategy. Equally fundamental is top management's openness to new ideas and proposed deviations from its initial medium-term objectives. In the long run, strategic recognition (by top management) and ownership (by business unit management) both argue for a strong bottom–up influence.

Using the ordinary planning process for integrating the environmental response brings with it the risk of over-burdening business unit managers. One of their routine tasks – strategic planning – now requires a very significant additional effort. The other danger is that top management and its STE support staff, due to limited experience or time constraints, might not be able to provide the critical validation needed. The result could very easily be sub-optimal and even counter-productive.

In line with the principles of vacuum management, top management therefore sometimes opts for a three-wave approach. Focusing on the personalities of its pivotal job holders and the anticipated relevance of the environmentally induced business discontinuities, a relatively small number of business units is selected to participate in a first wave of action. With top management providing close support, the emphasis is on developing methodologies and building confidence. When success has been demonstrated, the following waves are used for testing and gaining buy-in. Although the advantages of this approach are obvious, when incorporated into the normal planning process its completion requires a lengthy period, typically at least three years. Problematic in itself, this time-frame also complicates the development of corporate or cross-unit policies.

In a number of cases, we have therefore proposed an alternative approach in which leading environmental themes (rather than units) are treated sequentially. In this set-up, top management selects a single theme each year. Following the work of a triple-focus scanning team, the EAB or external experts are asked for their views on the theme's development and the accompanying policy or market response. In-house industry experts help in developing a greater sensitivity to the possible business impact of the theme. In instances where a business discontinuity is probable, the specific issue is subsequently handed over to the relevant business units as an input into their planning process. In this way, over a period of a few years, the most important environmental developments are gradually incorporated into the company's overall business strategies.

Whatever process is adopted, it must produce a number of well-defined and mutually agreed medium-term objectives, operational targets and time-frames. A common ingredient of successful change programmes is the leadership team's obsession with performance, usually manifested through frequent reviews of key numbers. Under a functional response, specific targets are often set for variables such as emissions and waste reduction – eg a 50 per cent reduction of the total process waste volume before year X. But this task is much more difficult under an integrated response, since the environmental data become an integral part of the company's operational fabric and hence cannot be singled out for quick and easy analysis. Still, a credible measurement and feedback of performance with respect to critical issues is essential. Some companies such as BMW have, for example, set themselves ambitious and publicly announced targets for the recyclability of their cars, while others, such as Coca-Cola, have done so for the contents of recycled materials in their packaging (in plastic bottles). Other companies – eg those aspiring to making a more efficient car or refrigerator – measure success in terms of energy conservation in their processes and products.

Highly creative approaches have been shown to be successful in dealing with this critical management task. To stimulate the transition to an integrated response, electronics giant Philips, for instance, asked each business unit management team to develop and market one 'flagship' product, which would clearly surpass competing products in both economic and environmental performance. Shell, in turn, found the environmental performance assessment of a business unit to be more meaningful and stimulating when conducted by a team from another unit.

Allocate resources

The planning process is completed when top management allocates money, time and talent to it. Personnel decisions are particularly important: employees have a good sense of the corporate pecking order, and recognize how top contributors are rewarded through career promotion. By appointing broadly recognized and respected path-finders among its business unit managers to lead the environmental charge, top management sends a strong signal that change is on the way. More importantly, the assignment of top talent will attract other high-calibre individuals, who want to work with winners and share in the excitement of being part of the solution to an important problem.

If, moreover, corporate leadership names a top-notch senior manager as head of the company's environmental programme, the priority it places on the environment will be taken far more seriously than if it continues to make environmental assignments a showcase for the corporate Peter Principle. An example from Dow Chemical is illustrative: after the then-CEO Frank Popoff announced the appointment of Dow Canada's top person, Dave Buzzelli, as Vice-President and Corporate Director of EHS, a manager of a large Dow site remarked: 'Now all the good people only want to work in environment.'

MOTIVATE

Having set the agenda for change, top management is in the sometimes awkward position of having to sit back and wait for good things to happen. The first responsibility for the implementation of the EMP should rest with the business unit managers and, as far as corporate programmes are involved, with the STE unit. Still, top management cannot be complacent. During the early stages of EMP implementation especially, it has to actively stimulate its path-finders by celebrating early wins, building on bottom–up initiatives and serving as a role model.

Celebrating early wins

A public spotlight on real achievements provides an important source of inspiration and satisfaction to the path-finders, and responds to their need for (self-) respect in climbing to the fourth step of their Maslow staircase. While it is important from an organizational perspective, it also builds the confidence and aspiration level of other coworkers, and hence can be instrumental in lowering their barriers to change.

The many publications of case 'victories' – typically win–win solutions that have both environmental and economic benefits – serve the celebration purpose well. Many corporations enthusiastically celebrate the reception of prestigious awards such as the World

Environment Centre's Gold Medal for Corporate Environmental Achievements, the past winners of which include 3M, Exxon, DuPont, BP, Dow Chemical, IBM, Rohm and Haas, Procter & Gamble, Xerox, S C Johnson & Son, Ciba-Geigy, Alcoa, Compaq and Philips.

As long as the celebrations do not amount to empty cheerleading, their impact should not be under-estimated. Top management therefore must be fairly sophisticated in its use of this instrument. But it should be careful not to rest on its laurels: maintaining quality environmental performance is a matter of constant monitoring and effort. Reputations can be made or broken overnight in the environmental arena. Monsanto's reputation, for instance, has varied greatly. In 1993 it was among *Fortune*'s 'Ten Laggards' list; in 1997 it was voted one of the 'Three Most Respected US Corporations' (together with 3M and Dow Chemical) by Environics International's pool of environmental experts; and over the last couple of years it has been targeted by NGOs in some European countries because of its importation of genetically modified soy beans.

Celebrating win–win actions is of course unproblematic. They tend to be easy to identify and implement, and are uncontroversial. Much more difficult to generate and validate are those actions that have a negative economic impact, but still beat the alternatives in terms of both economics and environmental concerns. Often the strategic recognition of such options requires an in-depth understanding of environmental developments and of the likelihood of political and/or market reactions. Such solutions are clearly more deserving of top management praise: they are the very essence of an integrated response that out-smarts the competition and results in a sustainable competitive advantage. Ultimately, the touchstone for celebration has to be the anticipated impact on shareholder value.

Support bottom–up initiatives

Throughout this book we point to the essence of strategic recognition: strategies are shaped when, within the boundaries of a top–down mental framework, business unit managers and their coworkers propose actions that are approved by top management. In the long run, the essence of 'leading from behind' through vacuum management is to get the organization as a whole to think, learn and propose. Only when pivotal job holders come out of the slipstream of top management and develop their own initiatives will the organizational learning process truly gain momentum (see Box 6.3). Managers who are willing to listen to and build on the ideas of their coworkers are critical to success.

Box 6.3 Organizational learning

In 1991, 80 Dutch energy distribution companies, cooperating under the umbrella of their industry association EnergieNed, voluntarily launched a campaign aimed at the containment of CO_2 emissions. Assisted by a team of McKinsey consultants, over 50 representatives of these companies developed an environmental action plan (EAP). The EAP called for stabilization of sector emissions by the year 2000 through the implementation of energy-saving measures that would reduce total consumption by 8 to 9 per cent.

Only two years later, the sector revisited its plans, this time at the request of the Dutch government which anticipated that economic growth would interfere with the achievement of national CO_2 reduction objectives. Ambitious as the original EAP was, the CO_2 emissions now were to be reduced by 3 per cent below 1990 levels, requiring energy savings of 17 per cent.

The learning effect in EAP-II led to a surprising but gratifying outcome: the increased knowledge and confidence of the sector specialist resulted in much lower cost per avoided ton of CO_2 (most measures actually save money), plus a much greater CO_2 reduction per potential measure (see Figure 6.6). Ten years later the targets, in essence, were met.

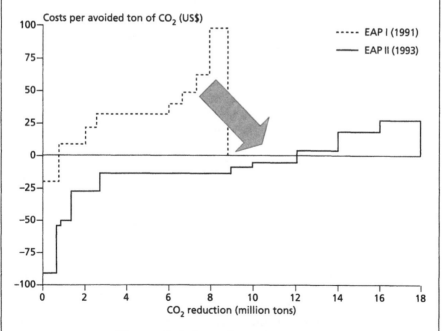

Figure 6.6 *Steep learning curves*

As they enter the relatively unknown environmental arena, many business unit managers can benefit from direct support by the corporate leadership. Whereas in their traditional business surrounding they generally develop relevant networks, they now have to create external openings to a whole range of parties outside the business. As we discuss in greater detail in Chapter 7, top management can assist them in this task by paving the way for partnerships with other business enterprises, government, NGOs and/or local communities, all of which will be of increasing relevance in developing 3E solutions.

Learning is inevitably associated with failures. Earlier we referred to the important contribution of the mentor. If top management wants its path-finders, and in subsequent waves its other business unit managers, to experiment, it must limit the associated career risks. If a loyal manager is perceived to be dropped because of his or her lack of success, the message will be registered loud and clear by all of his or her peers: 'Stay away from the EMP!' If, on the other hand, top management assumes full responsibility and stands behind the person, the organization will rally.

Serve as role model

Ultimately, corporate leaders will be judged by the degree to which they walk the talk. When the going gets tough and successes are few, or when other priorities threaten to grab the spotlight, top management must stick to its guns by reconfirming its commitment to completing the transition to an integrated environmental response. At times this is not easy, especially given the uncertainty inherent in the processes of crystallizing an endgame perspective and managing change. Many top managers are apt to have second thoughts about some of the steps that need to be taken. They must be careful not to burden the business unit managers with this additional uncertainty.

On the other hand, the transition to an integrated response does not imply that top managers suddenly have to turn into environmentalists. The integration of the environment is simply good business practice; a means of increasing shareholder value or, in the worst circumstances, minimizing its decrease. Still, CEOs and their closest colleagues often unknowingly serve as role models for many coworkers. As Frank Riddick, an experienced DuPont EHS trainer, says: 'If the first question the boss asks every day is how much did we make last night, everybody understands that production is important. If he asks did we have a safe night, did we have any environmental incidents, he makes safety and environment a routine part of the day-to-day job, just like production, quality and cost.'[19] Thus, the impact, for instance, of sceptical or cynical comments on the environment or on the efforts of the business unit managers and STE staff can be disastrous. Within an integrated response, walking the talk implies talking business.

Here is an illustration drawn from Frances Cairncross:

> *Geneva Steel, in Utah, is one of the few steel makers in the world with a good environmental reputation – and one of the most profitable ones as well. It raised eyebrows in its industry when it brought forward the timing of some large investments mainly for environmental reasons – replacing an old and inefficient open-hearth furnace with newer and much less polluting technology. 'We began more than a year before the state wanted us to,' explained Chairman Joe Canon, 'but we would have had to make the change eventually. The alternative would be to sue and fight. Litigation is expensive.'*
>
> *One consequence of their boss's known environmental inclinations has been that coworkers found some good answers to tough problems. Geneva Steel used to cool its steel in freon, an ozone-depleting substance. One of the laboratory workers waged a war with the purchasing department to persuade them to try using a much more expensive silicon-based alternative. Her trump card was to argue, 'Joe Canon wants us to think about the environment.' When the department capitulated, it emerged that a barrel of freon evaporated within a month, but the silicon-based coolant could be used over and over again. 'It turned out to be cheaper, after all, and we're no longer discharging 55 gallons of freon a month' said Mr Canon triumphantly.*[20]

***

In summary, if a top management team wants to guide its company towards an integrated response it has to focus on its business unit managers and their barriers to change. To surmount these barriers, top management must initiate its EMP through the process of backcasting and the alignment of its senior management. It must also orchestrate organizational support for its business unit managers by tailoring organizational infrastructure to their needs. Having established this foundation, it has to activate these pivotal job holders, preferably using the vehicle of the annual budgeting and planning cycle. For this purpose, it should signal change, and subsequently agree on specific action plans and the allocation of the necessary resources. Finally, during implementation, top management must motivate its coworkers by celebrating early wins, building on bottom–up initiatives and, last but not least, serving as a role model.

During this implementation phase special attention must often be paid to forming new networks with other parties in the environmental arena, some of which might evolve into mutually beneficial partnerships. We discuss the intricacies of this relevant but sensitive partnering process in Chapter 7.

7

DEVELOPING PARTNERSHIPS

We have seen that more and more people in the West have climbed to the fourth step of their environmental hierarchy of needs, a stage in which the quality of the ecosystems becomes the priority. We also noted that working towards this goal implies that all parties in the environmental arena – government, environmental scientists, NGOs and, of course, industry – have increasingly to cooperate to come up with environmental solutions that meet the criteria of effectiveness, efficiency and equity.[1] Moreover, in the discussion of the PLC, we argued that as environmental problems become more complex and their solutions more costly and cumbersome, the players begin to realize they know too little about the others to independently generate, evaluate and implement options that satisfy 3E criteria.

The case for partners is therefore strong on all sides. Indeed, companies seeking partners will frequently find interested parties; the others might even come courting themselves, believing business to be in the lead position. Paul Gilding, the former Executive Director of Greenpeace, put it this way:

> *The real leadership in the 21st century will come from the business community. This may sound strange coming from someone who has spent most of his life facing down business-people ... (but)... the environment has become a mainstream issue, from living rooms to corporate boardrooms. People's minds have been changed. The task now is to change their behaviour.*[2]

Björn Stigson, executive director of the WBCSD, welcomes such changes of heart and believes that NGOs 'must get involved in helping to find solutions that work, and cooperate with industry in implementing them. The days when NGOs could remain on the outside looking in – like theatre critics on opening night – are gone. Now, they must join the cast of the play in helping to put on an award-winning performance.'[3]

But while the formation of win–win partnership is clearly a primary management concern, two basic questions need to be answered: What partnership type? and What partnering process? Let us first sketch the three basic partnership types before examining the partnering process.

SELECTING A PARTNERSHIP TYPE

The essence of partnership is naturally that each party benefits from the cooperation.[4] From top management's perspective, there are basically three partnership types: conflict prevention, benefit exploration, and win–win.

Conflict prevention partnerships

When the ultimate objective is to prevent the escalation of mutually damaging conflicts, the partnership is based on common sense. Two or more parties – most often an environmental agency or an NGO on one side, and a company or a group of companies on the other – decide that a truce or a negotiated settlement is better than continued confrontation. Economics is quite often the underlying motivation: voluntary measures tend to be cheaper to implement than those enforced by regulation. The prevention or postponement of lengthy battles may also clear the agenda, allowing parties to focus on other pressing issues. Since resources (money, people) are often limited, particularly in relatively understaffed NGOs, partnerships of this sort often make a lot of sense.

To illustrate, in the early 1990s the forest product company Weyerhaeuser conducted a comprehensive study of the cumulative effects of timber harvesting, road construction and other forest activities on water quality, fish habitat and the public works at the Tolt watershed in the US state of Washington. In doing so, it worked with representatives of the Tulalip tribes, the Seattle Water Department, the Washington Environmental Council and the state departments of Natural Resources, Ecology, Wildlife and Fisheries. The resulting forest-management strategy was widely reported as having thrilled no one, though everyone accepted it – a sure sign of a successful negotiation. Weyerhaeuser more than doubled the forest area that was designated as logging-free, but had the comfort of knowing it wouldn't have to fight a running battle with the community parties. Indeed, the company applied the same model in some 30 other cases. Weyerhaeuser's CEO Jack Creighton acknowledges that the company 'essentially operate(s) with a franchise from the public.'[5]

Such an example suggests that a truce is not only a matter of cutting losses: it can also enhance goodwill. If a number of players are upset about seemingly unfair treatment by an 'opponent', they may unite in a much tougher resistance to other proposals. On the other hand, they may also choose to cooperate on a lesser issue in order to create favourable conditions for much more important cases. Companies such as Dow Chemical and Monsanto have, for instance, a very positive experience with the community advisory panels (CAPs), which they created for all their plants. Also, although such conflict prevention partnerships usually establish relatively unambitious, halfway-house targets, they do actually result in progress.

Given the nature of their constituencies, many politicians and environmentalists favour these solutions. They take the position that a bird in the hand is worth two in the bush: tangible, though modest, early wins are better than less certain, more fundamental long-term changes. This preference is matched by that of many managers who fear far-reaching endgame solutions, preferring to negotiate a less damaging shorter-term policy that brings them relative certainty and peace.

This cautious partnership policy – keeping one's powder dry – characterized hamburger giant McDonald's alliance on the reduction of packaging waste with the EDF. Both parties agreed on a 'walk away' provision, which stated that 'either organization had the right to terminate the project at any time if few or no substantive agreements were forthcoming ... and that if either McDonald's or EDF significantly disagreed on research findings or specific conclusions, the final report could contain separate statements reflecting these opinions.'[6]

Despite the potentially considerable short-term benefits of a truce, such partnerships do have their drawbacks, however. When they are between government and private business, outside parties such as NGOs and the media often question the effectiveness of the moderate objectives and the equity of letting business off the hook. The resulting inaction with respect to more fundamental longer-term issues may also come back to haunt the partners. Not having truly addressed the real issues, both sides frequently fail to achieve their strategic and financial goals. Many cease-fires therefore end in nasty shoot-outs or, at best, dissolution.

The 1993 Partnership for a New Generation of Vehicles, involving the 'big three' US car manufacturers and Washington, illustrates some of the problems with such agreements. The partnership was formally established for the development and production of a highly energy efficient car; one of its main results, however, was to effectively stymie the Japanese car companies' lobby in favour of more stringent regulatory standards. Thus, sceptics wondered whether the partnership reflected a solid commitment or was merely a means of deflecting political heat.[7]

Partner selection is naturally critical. If both parties are small or weak, an alliance hardly ever makes sense: together they haven't the mass to have any impact on a given environmental issue. The situation becomes more complex when one party is dominant and tries to neutralize a nuisance factor represented by the other, or a less powerful party attempts to restrain a major player. The result in either case is likely to be unsatisfactory because one party is simply too weak: for example, when a fledgling, inexperienced and under-staffed NGO enters a partnership with powerful businesses and government institution.

These initiatives are also extremely vulnerable. Take the example of a 'good neighbour' community partnership initiative by a large production plant. Such an agreement is often dependent on the efforts of a very few individuals in the company. If they are relocated to another production site or take a new job elsewhere, the partnership is threatened. Further, small businesses or local activists are frequently unable to channel their efforts, having to spread their attention over a range of issues. Large companies and major NGOs/government agencies, on the other hand, frequently are too marginally committed, entering into a relationship with many reservations or only as observers. Such factors can mean that these partnerships don't often pass the test of the 3E criteria. Although they may be well intentioned and run very efficiently and even equitably, they frequently tend to be short-lived and insufficiently effective.

However, if the partners' expectations are properly managed and their collective mass is sufficient, the conflict prevention may have merits. As long as reasonable targets are met, the greater efficiency associated with saving resources, the greater effectiveness gained by refocusing attention on more critical issues, and the long-term effectiveness and perceived equity that arises from an enhanced goodwill all can be very positive. What is perhaps even more important is that any progress, even involving modest targets, can ultimately clear the path for more ambitious partnering steps.

Benefit exploration partnerships

These partnerships frequently involve parties that have not previously worked together, but feel that they might both gain by jointly exploring solutions for environmental issues of mutual concern. Generally, the issues involved are in Phase 2 of the PLC; that is, their importance is recognized and the implementation details are being worked out: the question is not whether but how a policy is to be executed.

The parties' purpose is to minimize their resource expenditure until more is known about the problem, possible solutions and costs of alternatives. By pooling resources, they hope to attain the critical mass required to enhance understanding of the relevant issue. Such partnerships are also commonly motivated by equity considerations, the objective being to ensure that other parties, especially competitors, contribute their fair share to finding the solution.

The challenge of climatic change lends itself well to benefit exploration partnerships; indeed, these have became the strategy of choice for forward-thinking businesses in this issue area. BP Amoco entered a partnership with the EDF and, together with General Motors and Monsanto, also established links with the World Resources Institute to this end. For their part, a large number of leading Fortune 500 companies – including International Paper, Baxter International and United Technologies Corporation – teamed up with the non-profit Pew Centre on Global Climate Change to increase the scientific, economic and technological expertise to support the debate on the issue.[8]

Exploratory partnerships are therefore suitable when the objectives are limited to the study, rather than the actual solution, of a specific environmental issue. Both effectiveness and efficiency are served by pooling resources, while equity is furthered by sharing of the burden among competitors. Another example of such a partnership is the US EPA's perfluorocarbon (PFC) Emission Reduction Partnership for the Semiconductor Industry, which was launched in 1996. The PFC acronym covers six long-lived greenhouse gases with extremely high global-warming potential, including three PFCs and HFC-23. Eastman Kodak Company joined the partnership in 1998, stating the high costs of doing the necessary evaluations and lessons to be learnt from others as its major reasons for joining.[9]

However, these partnerships can also be highly effective in meeting medium-term objectives, especially when the partners are strong and compatible, and when achieving the goals requires that they work together. After two years of research and study in control technology in the above PFC partnership, for instance, the next step was to negotiate reduction goals with more than 25 participating companies, representing more than 70 per cent of PFC emissions in the semiconductor industry. In another example, Dutch electric utilities negotiated and subsequently implemented a highly successful covenant on SO_2 emission reductions with NGOs and national and regional governments. The covenant was shaped as a jointly binding agreement that fixed an aggressive schedule for SO_2 reductions in exchange for great flexibility in how the reductions were to be achieved.

As might be expected, exploratory partnerships are weakened by a lack of long-term commitments, particularly when cultural gaps separate the players and no common vision unites them. If the external conditions change or the internal enthusiasm wanes, the project might fail or one or more partners may be left in the cold. Here is a description of such a case in Northern Mexico:

> *US companies with assembly plants in Ciudad Juarez discharged treated wastewater into a sewer system full of raw sewage from municipal waste. All their efforts and expense in this Mexican twin city of El Paso, Texas, therefore had an environmental yield of zero. Led by General Motors, a 35-member Juarez Wastewater Task Force was established to combine the financial resources of the 15 US companies with the authority of the Mexican government institutions in order to develop and implement a plan for wastewater treatment.*
>
> *Four years after its 1991 inception the Task Force had met partial success. It had provided the technical expertise and planning overview to get two treatment plants on stream. However, it failed to iron out disagreements over the sharing of costs and the recovery thereof by industry. Moreover, the negotiations stagnated due to the rapid turnover of key people at both sides, also resulting from a change of government in Mexico.*
>
> *When in 1993 French contractor Degrémont provided 75 per cent of the financing for building the plants, the financial input of the US companies was no longer needed and they were left out of the deal.[10] Eventually this public–private partnership also did not work out, partly as a result of a rapid fall in the country's economy. Ground was never broken for construction and to this day Juarez' sewage goes untreated.[11]*

Particular care is required for the proper execution of partnership formation. If one of the parties uses its powerful position to force a solution on its partners, the cooperation can easily collapse when (competitive) tension develops and/or bargaining power shifts; in short, the weaker parties frequently have not truly agreed to the objectives. Also, the negotiation process itself does not always help much in promoting commitment. It is too often overly inflexible and bureaucratic – governments, for instance, frequently do not call on the input of industry experts, which could increase the likelihood of smarter responses – and industries sometimes have little understanding of the needs of the authorities or NGOs.

Many corporations join this type of partnership to ensure a level playing field. This is often made explicit: in the highly successful Responsible Care programme initiated by the North American chemical industry, the desire to minimize competitive distortion is clearly expressed. Also, European industry collaborations on, for instance, packaging waste and energy saving go to great length to prevent free riders from gaining an unfair advantage.

Unsurprisingly, it is perceived inequities, more than any other factor, that cause the breakdown of exploration partnerships. As an indication of the strong feelings against free riders, a 1995 poll of the leading negotiators of over 30 voluntary sector agreements on energy conservation in The Netherlands – whether they were from large industrial consumers, government, or the energy sector – showed that 73 per cent of those polled agreed with the statement that 'free riders in a voluntary agreement have to be handed over to the authorities'.[12]

One example where a lot of these mistakes were made is the German partnership dealing with packaging waste, the Duales System Deutschland (DSD). It is highly inefficient (costly, rigid, bureaucratic), very inequitable (many free riders, less expensive systems present in neighbouring countries), and, most importantly, not sufficiently effective, since solutions with a much greater environmental yield are conceivable. Eventually, these conditions – together with the lack of a committed leadership to unblock stalemates – make the partnership highly vulnerable.

Win–win partnerships

In this third partnership type, the parties are clearly and openly compatible and interdependent, and their alliances are essentially trust-based. In their simplest form, the agreements involve two or more players with complementary capabilities, offering significant synergy potential in meeting an external challenge. The most positive and lasting results are realized when both sides contribute equally to the partnership. By leveraging its contribution, each partner hopes to convert relatively modest investments in environmental improvement into disproportionately higher social, political or financial returns.

The advantages in terms of the 3E criteria are apparent, since the partnership combines environmental progress with economic self-interest. The truce between McDonald's and the EDF, for instance, developed into this type of alliance, when the private sector partner realized the partnership's potential as an economic and public relations mechanism. Similarly, the Dutch energy covenants, when properly negotiated and guided by credible business leaders, offer considerable merits in terms of simultaneous environmental and economic benefits: the large-scale breakthrough of cogeneration in Dutch process industry, for instance, is unparalleled. The demand-side management agreement between Pacific Gas & Electricity with the state of California, negotiated in the late 1980s, also falls into this category. By postponing, or even eliminating, the need for new plant capacity – thus limiting capital expenditures – the arrangement enabled the company to actually make money by selling less electricity. This worked because it shared the savings from energy conservation with customers and rolled investments on customer premises into the base rate.

Such partnerships, however, merit a word of caution: they can increase the risk of competitive distortion. Most current win–win agreements are negotiated between companies, or groups of companies, and government. Their primary objective is to develop a better 3E alternative to existing, proposed or anticipated regulation. However, government institutions or industry partners may be tempted to work together in a manner that distorts the competitive playing field in favour of national industries or of those companies participating.

Many observers, for instance, responded apprehensively to the US support of – in themselves – highly promising experiments in so-called joint implementation projects to meet the Kyoto CO_2 reduction targets. Clearly, the idea that private companies (usually electric utilities) finance environmental measures abroad, but receive credit for the environmental yield from their national authorities, has considerable economic appeal. To give an example, as part of a Dutch covenant, the power generators paid for SO_2 scrubbing of coal-fired power stations in Poland. Given the state of this technology, the net environmental impact per dollar invested far exceeded what could have been realized in The Netherlands – in fact, an expenditure of less than $20 million resulted in annual SO_2 savings exceeding total Dutch emissions. However, if unequally applied to competing companies, such policies could seriously upset the playing field.

On the other hand, the most significant advantage of win–win alliances is the potential they offer for self-regulation, and thus for business innovation. Indeed, win–win alliances tend to be business-to-business, though NGOs at times do take part.

The Industry Cooperative for Ozone Layer Protection (ICOLP) – now renamed the International Cooperative for Environmental Leadership – is a good example of such a partnership. In 1989, a few large industrial users of ozone depleting solvents such as Nortel, AT&T and Motorola formed the partnership with the objective of accelerating the phase-out of CFCs in the form of solvents, through the exchange of research, information and technology. The idea was to share information not just within the partnership but, most importantly, worldwide with a multitude of users endowed with fewer resources and less know-how.

ICOLP has been a great success: the participating companies have met their targets; a large number of plants in developing countries have switched to environmentally benign cleaning technology; and, according to the participants, the economics of the transition to the alternative approaches have been positive.

Government is rarely involved in partnerships of this sort: it is too big to be the small player and it has too little to add to be the big one. Still, in specific cases, government agencies can act as initiators in bringing parties to the table. The EPA actively participated in setting up the ICOLP, for instance, but not in a regulatory capacity. Its critical role consisted in convening meetings, providing funding, helping in the resolution of legal issues, serving as government-to-government liaison in the drafting of memoranda of understanding, and acting as a 'marketer' for the concept and the technologies.[13]

In many cases the net benefits of win–win partnerships are considerable. To us, the key to success is a balance not necessarily in the absolute 'weight' of the partners, but in the value they add to the partnership. In order for the partnership to be sustainable over the long term, the participants must remain interdependent. Each must contribute an essential element to the partnership, and understand and respect the motivations of the other(s).

The partners can therefore be of different sizes. In fact, the symbiosis of a large corporation and a much smaller NGO can satisfy most of the 3E criteria if the partnership combines the best features of the two infrastructures – features which either party would have a lot of trouble building from scratch. Strong professionalism or local presence are two of these features, for example. Professional infrastructures, such as can be provided by major corporations (eg know-how reservoirs, distribution networks) are costly and require superior management to be run efficiently. Local grassroots or NGO networks, on the other hand, are extremely fine-meshed and highly sensitive to outsider interference. In order to function at all, they must rely on the efforts of a few individuals who can tap into the lifelines of small communities.

Here are some further examples of win–win partnerships.

- Pharmaceutical giant Merck combines forces with the Costa Rican research institute INBio to screen rainforest biological samples. Merck thus gains access to potential pharmaceutical opportunities and INBio gets a source of funding for research, as well as a share of potential future royalties from the commercialization of rainforest products. In the process, the rainforest is protected, as it has become economically efficient to do so.
- The Tagua Initiative brings leading garment companies such as The Gap, Banana Republic and Liz Claiborne together with NGOs and Ecuadorian businesses and local workers to develop the market for tagua nuts, which are used to make shirt buttons.
- US ice-cream manufacturer Ben & Jerry's joins the Brazilian government and a number of US and Brazilian NGOs to invest in the protection of the rainforest, in exchange for economic rights to the harvested products.
- Conservation International and Croda, a worldwide leader in processing raw materials for cosmetics, cooperate in developing a new line of personal care products derived from oils and botanical extracts that are harvested by community enterprises in Guatemala, Peru and the Solomon Islands.[14]

The obvious merits of win–win partnerships make them the best form of cooperation in the environmental arena. For this reason, we dedicate the following section to the role that top management can play in making them come about. The partnering process is complex and generally consumes a lot of top management time. The outcome is also uncertain and the risks, in terms of tainting the corporate image, are considerable. More fundamentally, in a trust-based relationship a partner must earn its credibility. A company cannot simply enter and exit the environmental arena at will, but must be consistent in its role as a good corporate citizen and – if it chooses – environmental leader. The magic word therefore is commitment: if companies opt for this path they must walk it well.

LEADING THE PARTNERING PROCESS

Despite their obvious promise, most potential win–win partnerships have fallen far short of expectations. The reason, typically, is that the partnering process – ie the actions taken to agree on the partnership's objectives and procedures – is flawed. Simply put, top management has too often failed to play the leadership role that is called for by the growing strategic relevance of the business discontinuities at stake, or has not done so well enough.

Let's look now at some of the key factors behind good partnering processes. We have grouped these into factors related to understanding the process, shaping the partnerships and unblocking problems, and building networks.

Understanding the process

If partnerships are going to be a better alternative to traditional command-and-control regulation, they must provide a more effective, efficient and equitable manner of moving an environmental issue through its PLC. Good partnering experiences can teach us a lot in this regard. Our analysis – or 'reverse engineering' – of the processes that led to some 20 successful North American and European environmental partnerships between industrial parties on the one hand and government authorities and/or NGOs on the other, reveals some best practices.[15] From this analysis and five hands-on pilot projects in which we were involved, we feel it is useful to distinguish three stages in this partnership formation process. Each stage requires a distinct management structure, which is directly related to the specific environmental theme's location in its PLC (Figure 7.1).

Setting the agenda

For a partnership to come together, of course, the players have to be conscious of the need for joint action. Ideally, this happens during

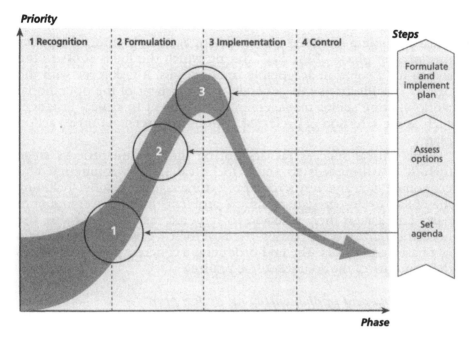

Figure 7.1 *Partnership formation process*

the transition from the PLC's recognition to its policy formulation phase, when a specific issue has reached the societal agenda but the appropriate policies have yet to be formulated. There is thus still room for negotiation to find a 3E solution; the parties have not dug their trenches, and the troops are not rallied to a fever pitch.

As a first step, the parties must agree on the purpose and scope of the partnership. Synchronizing agendas is usually complex when different interests are at stake, as in industry projects involving more than one company, and especially when working with the government and/or NGOs. In one of our pilot projects, for example, industry participants from four companies worked with senior officials from two government departments and representatives from two environmental organizations. Each of the members of the initiating steering group brought along the agenda of his or her constituency.

Our findings indicate that essential elements for successfully managing the agenda-setting typically include: a facilitator respected by all; a forum including all significant stakeholders; an open-mindedness among all participants to consider wide-ranging solutions; and, especially, a willingness to accept the realities of the imperatives of all other players. The end of this process stage is a jointly agreed charter to proceed.

Assessing options

Once a problem has been put on a joint agenda, it enters the policy formulation phase of the PLC, during which the focus shifts to the search for a solution acceptable to all parties. A task force with the proper qualifications can generally take on most of the operational work, limiting senior management involvement to critical instances such as the selection of preferred options or agreement on an action plan.

The critical success factors during this second process stage include a willingness to share technical (ie environmental and economic) data and very strong project management skills, including the ability to desegregate technical problems into their component parts and assign their solution to targeted task forces. Using the pooled expertise of all parties, the task force's objective is to build a fact-based consensus. The end-product is a concrete plan that defines the contours of the solution to be realized.

Formulating and implementing an action plan

After all this homework has been done, the environmental issue has reached the PLC peak. The accent now shifts to finalizing the agreements and preparing for execution. Clearly, the required management structures at this stage depend on the specifics of the partnership. What is indispensable, however, is that a steering group of senior representatives of each partner organization increasingly concentrate on strategic control while the various projects are executed at an operational level.

Shaping and unblocking partnerships

Even if the road to a successful partnering process seems simple, success rates are disappointingly low. To increase the partnership's chances of success, top management must show strong leadership in two tasks: agreeing on a partnership charter and breaking deadlocks.[16]

Agreeing on a charter

Top management is uniquely positioned to create external openings to pave the way for partnerships. To this end, top managers must be seen as trustworthy and as having an understanding of the culture and imperatives of the other partners: they must create the sense that all parties are 'in it together'. Moreover, a positive personal and corporate environmental track record and a willingness to take risks – for instance, by sharing information or insights which perhaps could be used against one's person or company – are also required.

It also is important for top management to acknowledge up-front that not all parties have access to equal resources or networks. In its interaction with government or especially NGOs, business will therefore often have to do the bulk of the homework or pay the lion's share of related expenses.

Further, if the gaps between the various groups are to be bridged, opening channels of communication is a high priority. This is especially relevant when the initial discussions are preceded by heated public battles. In such cases, the parties tend to be deaf to the others' viewpoints.

In cases involving a number of companies, top management should do all it can to ensure that their positions are well aligned. Negotiations and, particularly, compliance are relatively easy to organize when a single company or a small number of players are involved. Similarly, the process flows more smoothly when the sector is dominated by a few players, or when the industry association truly speaks for its members. But a larger number of non-aligned company players obviously complicates the matter.

Top management should also be aware of the two basic win–win partnership options open to it: namely, the contract and the covenant. Contracts are best suited to address issues for which standardized solutions are needed and available. Government and the industry sector (or a company) can then agree on a detailed contractual solution, instead of more time-consuming and unpredictable regulation. Covenants, on the other hand, are more appropriate when standardized solutions are not needed. Typically, this is the case when a sector is heterogeneous and the most appropriate solutions are not uniform or – as often occurs in the environmental arena – are as yet unknown.

Whereas contracts establish company-specific solutions for each company within a sector, covenants often express agreement on broad objectives – such as a 20 per cent reduction of energy consumption over ten years, or a 50 per cent increase in recycling – and leave it to the companies to tailor action plans to achieve them. Covenants therefore offer more freedom of manoeuvre than contracts, and are also better suited to tap the expertise and creativity of the participating companies to deal with newly emerging environmental issues, the solutions to which are still unclear.[17]

In shaping a win–win partnership, top management must also take into consideration the impact the initiative might have on those interested parties that are excluded from the arrangement. Generally, approaches that cannot bear public or political scrutiny will attract criticism. The agreement should therefore never be used as a means of keeping others out and to distort the competitive playing field. Any evidence of back-room dealing of this sort will damage not only the prospects of covenants as an alternative to regulation, but also the company's or industry's credibility, which, if nothing else, will affect its chances of entering partnerships in the future.[18]

The eventual charter defines the joint aspirations. A common purpose – including a definition of the problem and an appropriate ambition level (objectives, targets) – is essential to ensuring a common work focus and commitment to the process. The charter also defines both the structure and operating approach. A transparent but highly flexible decision-making process (including a dispute resolution mechanism), explicit funding arrangements, clear rules on external communications, and especially a high-level consensus on priorities – recognizing that there may be areas of fundamental disagreement, but not allowing them to prevent progress, ie 'agreeing to disagree' – are all critical to the smooth functioning of the subsequent stages of the partnering process.

Breaking deadlocks

When the differentiation space is large or when an environmental issue is not yet fully understood, it is particularly difficult to define the best 3E solution. Often the charter turns out to be sub-optimal and, over time, can actually obstruct progress. Implementation task forces or management teams must have the possibility of calling on the original negotiators to redefine the charter. Naturally, this unblocking option is not available in cases where top management is not sufficiently involved at the original stage; in such cases, arguments can be lengthy and frustrating.

The Dutch board manufacturers provide an example of effective deadlock breaking. In 1991, the companies signed a covenant with the national government, committing them to limit production volume so as to reduce packaging waste. Subsequent analysis, however, showed that this would not only have a negative economic impact, but would also actually be detrimental to the environment, because the industry effectively served as an environmental vacuum cleaner, sucking in large volumes of waste paper. The proposed downsizing of its production volume would mean less cardboard waste going to landfills or incinerators, but it also meant that there would be a net increase of the total waste volume, thanks to the newsprint, graphic paper, etc that would no longer be recycled. In 1995, the Dutch paper and board industry, chaired by Gijs van Reenen, came up with a significantly better plan. The government was receptive to the proposal, which not only was very positive environmentally but also provided the Dutch industry with a significant advantage over its competitors in neighbouring countries, such as Germany, where more rigid regulatory approaches were in force.

The central importance of deadlock-breaking actions taken by leaders, and especially business leaders, in successful partnerships is strongly confirmed in the results of our in-depth interviews with five senior officials of the Dutch Ministry of Environment. We asked them to reverse engineer what they personally considered to be the best examples of policy successes. Virtually all of the 12 cases mentioned involved partnerships, with major roles played by lower levels of government (regional or municipal) and industry. Whether by design or accident, most of these partnerships built on existing structures for communication or negotiation. Still, their success was usually a product of the personal initiatives of high-ranking individuals not only in getting the process started but in breaking deadlocks, if necessary.

Building on the foundation of mutual trust, peer group leaders from national government (ie the minister or the most senior official), lower echelons of government (usually a regional politician charged with the environmental portfolio, or sometimes the mayor of a large city), but especially top managers of a leading company were highly instrumental in deadlock breaking. Often putting their personal prestige on the line, top managers repeatedly proposed and explored new solutions.

In a hallmark case, Olivier van Royen, CEO of Dutch steel manufacturer Hoogovens, called on his peers to break a last-minute deadlock of a major energy conservation covenant. With the political winds shifting, senior executives of some of the leading participating companies had sensed they could refuse to sign the impending agreement with the national government. The covenant, reached after more than two years' negotiations, obliged the companies to reduce energy consumption per product unit by 20 per cent over ten years. Taking a long-term perspective van Royen, who was highly respected among his peers, persuaded his fellow chairs of the importance of the agreement to their credibility and the continuity of cooperation, and the hesitating companies then fell into line.

Building networks

The Dutch experience also points to the importance of building networks in the environmental arena. Even in the most advanced companies – 'visionaries' and 'professionals' in our surveys' categorization – top management tends to be poorly connected with the relevant networks. Contacts are left up to a corporate EHS staff, who are usually technically oriented, or to a safety, environment and regulatory affairs (SERA) or public affairs unit, both of which are primarily focused on legislation and lobbying. This does not provide an ideal foundation for a significant partnership. Furthermore, when top managers are involved, they tend to be insufficiently knowledgeable or too inadequately supported to be effective.

As we've already seen, the crucial role that senior managers have had in successful policy formulation shows the potential impact that individuals can exert. With the differentiation space rapidly expanding, investment in scanning the environmental horizon and cultivating a network is almost certain to pay off. This consists, in essence, of two tasks: bridging the culture gaps between the company and other relevant players in the environmental arena, and selecting the most appropriate partners by proactively looking for win–win situations.

Bridging culture gaps

Partnerships of course imply a process of give-and-take, in which all parties are truly committed to solving a problem. They require that the parties involved have a good understanding of the imperatives that drive their partners. As an example, industry representatives must learn more about the background of environmental issues and the intricacies of policy development (see Chapter 3). Unfortunately, senior executives still sometimes exhibit little respect for politicians or senior government officials. Politicians, for their part, frequently can't resist the temptation to score quick points if the occasion arises – for instance, when an incident prompts public opinion to demand drastic government action. All partners-to-be thus must bridge enormous culture gaps.[19]

Clearly, the greatest challenge for top managers is to strengthen their involvement and influence at the early phases of the PLC, when policies are being recognized and formulated. Given that their experience tends to be limited to the third, implementation phase, the task is not easy. In essence, it is reminiscent of the challenge presented by industrial marketing: getting to know the people on the other side of the table, and learning to understand their individual motivations, and those of their organizations, as the basis for a sustainable relationship that best satisfies 3E criteria.

With regard to the NGOs, this is generally not very complex. They are few in number and their leadership groups tend to be small. Also, their formal strategies are transparent and their unpredictability predictable. Moreover, there are a number of studies of environmental NGOs, which should facilitate management's understanding of them.[20]

Government environmental officials are also quite approachable. However, although much has been written about environmental policies, relatively little is known about the people who develop them. Environmental officials are less visible than environmentalists. Moreover, they are often seen to be relatively unimportant, with business lobbying efforts focused at other departments – eg ministries of industry or energy – or at politicians.

Good networking requires a bridging of the cultural gaps with officials – ie understanding their imperatives. Such an understanding can be gained, among other ways, through a study of political programmes and policy plans, complemented by a clear view of the policy-making process and its anticipated development.[21] The challenge is one of establishing contact and developing it sensibly. In our experience, senior managers who have seriously tried to understand the other parties at an agenda-setting negotiation table are frequently impressed by the high quality of government representatives. Building on early successes and often guided by a mutually respected facilitator, business leaders can bridge the culture gaps and develop fruitful cooperation.

Selecting the most appropriate partners

Given the different possible partnership types described above, it is clearly important for business to select partner(s) with a specific objective in mind. The company's endgame and the mid-term objectives can help it determine the players it wants to work with in the environmental arena.

The partnership should be composed of players of such weight and skill that they can jointly exert significant influence on the overall value chain. In order to increase their commitment to a long-term cooperation, their contributions should also be balanced – ie they must be truly interdependent for the group to be a success. The partners must be regarded by peers – competitors, customers – as 'attractive': the success and prestige of the partner is important to that of the group. Most of all, however, each partner must benefit from the partnership. It is up to the initiating management team to think through the probable motivations of potential partners, and to subsequently present the case to each of them as to when, why and how a partnership makes good sense.

An understanding of the imperatives of potential business partners is pretty straightforward. Their interest is in avoiding litigation and adverse public sentiment and, if possible, capturing real business benefits through reducing environmental costs, spreading costs equally among businesses, opening new market opportunities and improving their public profile.

Still, management has to be selective in choosing its partners. A win–win alliance, for example, requires partner(s) with an appropriate environmental track record. A company with a history of battling environmental legislation, or with a reactive response culture, will not be looked on as a good partner by the public.

Potential NGO partners, on the other hand, are difficult to select, and the process itself is complex since their cultures and partnering abilities vary tremendously.[22] Management should recognize, for example, that environmental activists, and to a somewhat lesser degree also lobbyists, are understandably concerned about compromising their chosen role by partnering a business organization. Their credibility with their membership, the media and the public at large is at stake. Concern about their standing with their business partners might also limit their freedom in dealing with another issue that, in their view, might require a less cooperative approach. Moreover, their staffs are limited and they often find it difficult to dedicate the time required for an intensive partnership relationship. These NGOs might be best suited for one-off conflict prevention partnerships, or even exploratory ones. It is doubtful whether they are adequately equipped for a committed, long-term cooperation, however.

The EDF–McDonald's partnership, as noted, grew from a highly uncomfortable truce that 'united' the two parties in a win–win alliance that analysed waste streams jointly. McDonald's invested the quality human resources who, with EDF, developed solutions that were good for the economics of their company and for the environment. As a result, the hamburger giant made a quantum leap, becoming an environmental leader in the industry. The partnership was at least as important for the precedent it set within the North American environmental community, however. The EDF move legitimized in-depth collaborations between NGOs and industry – although at some cost to the EDF, which was strongly attacked for 'selling out'. Nevertheless, virtually overnight, corporations lost their status as arch enemies and began to be seen as potential allies.[23]

Committed cooperation is something business can expect more of from the 'exploiters' NGO group. These are often quite stable organizations with a large membership, which can add considerable partnering mass thanks to the public visibility and acceptance of their attitudes. Given their focus on PLC Phases 3 and 4, and their relative lack of experience in the earlier phases, they are generally not of much assistance during policy formulation. If a company pursues a range of market initiatives, however, these NGOs can contribute significantly. In addition, a serious partnership with a leading exploiter NGO will probably limit the exposure of the company to attacks by activists and lobbyists.

An example of such an alliance is that between Unilever and the WWF, the purpose of which was to set up the Marine Stewardship Council to deal with the over-exploitation of the world's marine fish stock. The council is an independent, non-profit body which establishes general principles for sustainable fishing and sets standards for individual fisheries. Fisheries meeting the standards are eligible for certification, which can be carried on the product's package. Consumers can then select fish products that they know come from sustainably managed sources. Unilever, which has a 20 per cent share of the US and European frozen fish market, has committed itself to buying only certified fish by 2005.

Sensible exploratory alliances to deal with a specific issue that is just entering its PLC Phase 2 can often be formed through partnering with reputable environmental policy analysts. The better institutions have strong professional and often also personal ties with other NGOs. Their reputation for independence, combined with a considerable depth of understanding, can be very significant in triple-focus scanning.

Such a partnership was formed in 1998 between General Motors, BP Amoco, Monsanto and the World Resources Institute, a leading but comparatively small environmental think-tank. This 'Safe Climate, Sound Business' partnership's objective was to identify measures to reduce GHG emissions while protecting the economy.[24]

Lastly, public–private partnerships with government can lead to more cost-effective solutions. If the problem is addressed early enough, collaborative efforts may actually eliminate the need for legislative intervention altogether.

Corporate positioning is of course critical when selecting government partners, especially given the compartmentalization typically found in public administration. The lack of interdepartmental cooperation, not to speak of the obstructionism of some departments and sections, make the selection confusing at best. In addition, government departments and their political leadership often consider themselves to be single-issue promoters or the entry point for lobbyists. In the environmental arena, most new initiatives therefore stem from the environmental agencies or the department that is charged with nature conservation or occasionally physical planning. As a result, these organizations have developed units with strong PLC Phase 2 skills that closely match those of the environmental lobbyists, with which they tend to have tight ties.

Other departments – eg industry, energy, agriculture and transport – have similar lead positions in their policy fields; however, when responding to environmental policy questions, they tend to be too reactive. Their activities in the environmental arena therefore concentrate on the PLC peak, ie the last part of the second and the first part of the third phase. As a result, their senior officials and political masters usually get involved too late to influence the shaping of the policy contours. In fact, they usually engage in semi-public battles with their colleagues in environment, generally in direct cooperation with the relevant industry associations or the leading private companies.

When politicians and officials at the lower levels of government – states or provinces and municipalities – participate in national environmental debates, it tends to be to defend the interests of their constituencies. This, however, is not always the case. Local employment considerations, for instance, might take precedence over longer-term environmental needs. On the other hand, in cases of perceived serious threats to public health, the issue tends to take precedence over all others, whatever the cost: all levels of government are quickly aligned.[25]

An interesting example of authorities' placing local interests over broader environmental concerns took place in the Canadian province of Nova Scotia in 1993. The Swedish multinational Stora Kopparberg announced that its pulp and paper complex in the province was under review. With the imminent threat of closure, local politicians sought to put together a sufficiently attractive rescue package to persuade Stora management to remain. High on their list was an extension on the 1995 deadline for enhanced effluent treatment. The Liberal Member of Parliament for the area eventually proposed a five-year postponement of the regulation. The case for the extension was based on the contention that since Stora's seaboard emissions are flushed away by tidal action, they are far less threatening than equivalent emissions into fresh water river systems.[26]

Despite departmental compartmentalization, in the more advanced countries environmental responsibilities are increasingly well integrated into the tasks of non-environmental policy-makers. Their direct involvement, starting in PLC Phase 1, facilitates a healthy expansion and shift of the differentiation space. Still, management must choose with whom to form bonds. Is it with the traditional allies in industry, energy, transportation, etc? True, their Phase 3 culture with respect to environmental issues most often closely matches that of the company's own staff, so that cooperation benefits from a ready understanding of each other's imperatives. However, it might not provide the right entry for seriously influencing the contours of a new policy during the theme's transition from Phase 1 to 2 of its PLC.

Furthermore, such a partnership may not be very useful in cases where government departments are highly compartmentalized. Shell, for instance, fell victim to this trap when, in 1995, it presented the energy departments of all the nations bordering on the North Sea with its Brent Spar dumping plans, and subsequently was surprised by the extremely negative public reactions. Improved communication with the environmental departments, with their better-trained Phase 1 and 2 ears, might have alerted the company to potential problems.

On the other hand, excessive ties with environmental departments are also risky. They may upset old allies in other departments who might feel by-passed, with consequences for a company's activities in other fields. Many environmental agencies are, moreover, still weak. It often requires much effort and wisdom to develop such departments into reliable partners.

In conclusion, the key to success is to understand the imperatives driving all potential partners and their possible contribution to the company's cause. This provides the basis for establishing the partnership to be pursued and, subsequently, approaching and developing the most ideal candidates in a suitable partnering process. Only then can many large companies implement an environmental strategy that is truly integrated into its business environment.

***

Having examined the implementation of an integrated approach to environmental management, we now turn in Chapters 8 and 9 to that of a proactive strategy.

Part III

Proactive Response

8

PROACTIVE ENVIRONMENTAL MANAGEMENT: BUILDING INSPIRED CORPORATE COMMUNITIES

'Meeting the needs of the present without compromising the ability of future generations to meet their own needs'. The Brundtland Commission's broad definition of sustainability, the fifth and top step in the environmental hierarchy of needs, also represents the pinnacle of environmental management. Compared to the integrated approach which, as we've seen, involves the incorporation of environmental considerations into a company's normal strategy and operations, the proactive response demands far more: namely, a quantum leap in all aspects of corporate life and behaviour. As might be expected, the leadership tasks involved in meeting this challenge are formidable and complex, but they can be summed up in two simple words: inspiration and trust. Together, as we'll see, they provide the ingredients necessary to create the thrill required for a successful and continuous change programme. This chapter deals with the first, the development of inspired communities, and Chapter 9 with the second, with the creation of a partnership culture.

Corporations pursuing a proactive response need to become inspired communities because they need to be very sensitive and responsive to the needs of their stakeholders, particularly their coworkers and, within this group, to those coworkers who are ascending to the fourth level of Maslow's pyramid of needs: the 'fourth-echelon climbers'. What this means practically is that the proactive approach requires top management to come up with a corporate value proposition that is multifaceted. It must meet the needs of fourth-echelon climbers as well as of those internal stakeholders located on the other, lower levels of Maslow's pyramid. At the same time, however, it must inspire all of its external stakeholders to move up towards sustainability. The complexity of the task is reflected upon by Unilever's co-Chairman, Morris Tabaksblat:

Companies are made up of people. Within Unilever there are some 300,000 employees of more than 100 nationalities. All those employees communicate with one another, influence one another and help shape the company culture. A company like Unilever with such a richly varied workforce needs fundamental common values if it is to be, and continue to be successful. ... When there are so many employees, it is a given fact that many of them are members of or give donations to Greenpeace, Amnesty International, Médécins sans Frontières or animal welfare organizations. But our employees also include deeply religious Muslims who might be intensely upset by things that we, for instance, here in The Netherlands, consider acceptable. For example, the way in which references can be made to sexuality in Dutch advertising is not acceptable in predominantly Islamic countries.[1]

Tabaksblat's words suggest, moreover, that there is an added complication of the managerial task. Namely, the fact that although proactivity is essentially a response to the higher environmental needs of the increasing number of people climbing to the top level of Maslow's pyramid, these are only one set of individual needs. People live by more than greenness alone: they have economic and social needs. That their stakeholders have economic needs is, of course, nothing new to corporations. But corporate involvement in meeting their social needs, unless these are very extreme, is not so common.

This chapter attempts to help management deal with this challenge. Our discussion is divided into three parts: telling a 'story', understanding the corporate pyramid of needs, and tailoring the story to stakeholder needs.

TELLING A STORY

When we speak of a quantum transformation in the corporation, we partly mean that top management must transform both the attitudes and values of its coworkers. This requires what Harvard psychologist Howard Gardner calls excellent 'storytelling'.[2] Most managers, he suggests, simply retell their company's traditional story as effectively as possible. At best, they bring new attention or a fresh twist to the story. Such storytelling is appropriate for a functional or integrated response, where the message is essentially: 'Keep doing what you've been doing, but do it better.'

The transition to a proactive response, however, demands much more from leaders. Their objective is to inspire value change to carry the company to another level – to reinvent the corporation, as it were, both for its own and its stakeholders' sake. Burger King's CEO Barry Gibbons says that 'this means telling people what's happening to the organization, where it's been, who you are, what you're going to do, and what you stand for.'[3] In other words, it requires a solid, convincing and inspiring endgame story that can thrill all stakeholders and which drives, and in turn is fed by, their individual and collective will to act (see Box 6.1). Only then can the story have the desired impact on corporate culture.

Since sustainability is a long-term objective, the story must also have staying power and be resistant to changing conditions. This is particularly relevant when the initial launch excitement wanes and the stakeholders have not yet fully internalized the responsibility for implementation.

As Gardner stresses, the leadership's stories must compete with the many preceding stories. If the new story is to succeed in impacting on attitudes and values, it must suppress, complement or in some measure outperform these earlier stories.[4] It must also meet the challenge of the 'counter-stories', which almost inevitably will be concocted by those opposing the suggested change.

Samuel C Johnson, Chairman of S C Johnson & Son and according to *Fortune* 'America's corporate environmentalist', tells this enchanting story:

> *My grandfather once used a white-flannel test to sell the company's wax. After polishing and shining a customer's floor dressed in a smart white suit, he sat down and got them to pull him over the newly waxed floor. When he got up, his backside was clean, not a speck of dirt. My dream is to be able to conduct an environmental white-flannel test around our offices and factories to show that they operate behind a 'clean' ethic while producing goods.*
>
> *We aggressively seek out eco-efficiencies – ways of doing more with less – because it makes us more competitive when we reduce and eliminate waste and risk from our products and processes. And it saves us money. By developing products that are as safe as possible for people and the environment, we improve our market share. Of course, we're making tough decisions all the time that weight the human positives of our products against their potential environmental impact. We're always looking for cleaner, greener solutions. This is going to become increasingly important as customers become more sophisticated and demanding in this regard.*
>
> *But our actions aren't just about business. When my grandchildren first saw the big snapping turtle in the pond where I used to play and fish as a boy, they glowed with the same wonder and awe as I did. Without sustainable develop-*

*ment, it's going to be a less satisfactory planet for my grand-
children to live in. For me, those are the stakes.*[5]

In another example, Ray Anderson, founder and CEO of multinational carpet maker Interface, recounts how he was asked to kick off
an internal task force by presenting the team with an environmental
vision:

> *I offered the task force a vision: to make Interface the first
> name in industrial ecology worldwide through actions, not
> words. I gave them a mission: to convert Interface to a
> restorative enterprise; first by reaching sustainability in our
> practices, and then becoming truly restorative – a company
> returning more than we take – by helping others reach
> sustainability. I suggested a familiar strategy including:
> reduce, reuse, reclaim, recycle (later we added a very impor-
> tant one, redesign); adopt best practices and then advance
> and share them; develop sustainable technologies and invest
> in them when it makes economic sense; and challenge our
> suppliers to follow our lead.*
>
> *I then asked the original task force who would lead the
> effort to sustainability, not just here in the United States, but
> worldwide? They didn't have an answer, so I asked, 'Why not
> us?' Their response marked a tidal wave of change in our
> company.*
>
> *We look forward to the day when our factories have no
> smokestacks and no effluents. If successful, we'll spend the
> rest of our days harvesting yesteryear's carpets, recycling old
> petrochemicals into new materials, and converting sunlight
> into energy. There will be zero scrap going into landfills and
> zero emissions into the biosphere. Literally, our company will
> grow by cleaning up the world, not by polluting or degrading
> it. We'll be doing well by doing good. That's the vision.*
>
> *Is it a dream? Certainly, but it is a dream we share with
> our 6300 associates, our vendors, and our customers.
> Everyone will have to dream this dream to make it a reality,
> but until then, we are committed to leading the way.*[6]

These stories point to three personal qualities that all good storytellers have. First, they must be credible. Whatever the story's
contents, the tellers must believe in their story and, moreover, 'live'
its vision. Sam Johnson, for instance, 'walked the talk' when, upon
receiving the first alarming reports on ozone depletion in the mid-
1970s, he banned CFCs from all his company's products worldwide.
'Nobody that I knew believed it,' he recalled, 'but we did a survey
and found that housewives, our customers, were concerned. So I

asked our chemists to look into the report, and they told me it might be true.'[7]

Leaders do not have to be saintly, nor do they need to have all the answers.[8] Coworkers readily pardon the minor slip-ups of their superiors, as long as top management does not compromise on issues that touch their message's core. For this reason, Mark Moody-Stuart of Shell stresses that 'in a large organization it's important that people should know that this [commitment to sustainability] is really serious and is not something done for window dressing. The role of senior management is to look into the eyes of our people so they see we really believe it.'[9]

Second, they must be willing to retell a single story a thousand times, or, as one of the grandmasters of the art, General Electric's Jack Welch, said: 'You've got to be out in front of crowds, repeating yourself over and over again, never changing your message no matter how much it bores you. You need an overarching message, something big but simple and understandable.'[10] On each occasion that message must be tuned to the needs of a specific group of pivotal job holders; this aspect of 'management-by-speech' is frequently underestimated. The large number of coworkers in many companies means that they will be diverse and have different needs. Remarkably, however, our experience suggests that when top management zeroes in on a specific group like this, the rest of an audience tends to be intrigued, not bored.

Third, managers must learn, especially at the start when the story has not fully crystallized, to live with a sense of inadequacy and personal uncertainty with regard to the story. Most successful corporate visions look much better many years after their creation. Initially, they are frequently incomplete and clumsily worded, or, as Hanover's Bill O'Brien remembered, 'sound like apple pie and motherhood'. He concluded that 'people need visions to make the purpose more concrete and tangible. We had to learn to "paint pictures" of the type of organization we wanted to be.'[11] Contrary to most textbook wisdom, such pictures may well be impressionistic, ie the corporate vision and values do not necessarily have to be succinctly phrased. If a constituency wants to understand a message, it will fill out the gaps with further positive thoughts, often even without using words.

Actually, in reference to the story's presentation, single ideas, or even single words, can open up immense imaginative spaces to be filled-in by the receivers: 'Love', with its myriad of definitions, summarizes the New Testament; Martin Luther King's 'I have a dream' inspired millions to follow; other millions also grasped the intentions behind Michael Gorbachev's *perestroika* without having read his book. Actually, in a corporate context a somewhat open-ended story – leaving questions to be answered and details to be refined –

invites coworkers to participate in filling the spaces that the leader-ship has purposefully created.

But the story must of course address needs that coworkers perceive as real. Thus it must be preceded by, or include, the infor-mation required for people to grasp the extent of the challenge at hand. Or, as Jack Welch said: 'Start with reality. Get all the facts out. Give people the rationale for change, laying it out in the clearest, most dramatic terms. When everybody gets the same facts, they'll generally come to the same conclusion. Only after everyone agrees on the reality and resistance is lowered can you begin to get buy-in to the needed change.'[12]

The story should also provide coworkers with a direction for a future endgame that is worthy of commitment. Ultimately, people want to feel good about what they are doing. Central to the story, therefore, are the emotional building blocks which help coworkers think about who they are as individuals and as part of a group, where they come from, and where they can be heading on a higher level of their Maslow hierarchy of needs.

Lastly, our experience tells us that the best results are obtained when elements of the endgame story are framed in the form of a question. For example, after presenting a blueprint of the endgame that management proposes to pursue, it would pose the following question to the coworkers: What does this mean for you and for the way you do your job? By translating, as it were, a number of top–down elements of the blueprint into questions that are relevant to the pivotal job holders, these are invited to complement the story and thereby become co-responsible for finding the best solutions and/or upgrading the blueprint. The vision should be based on contents – ie knowledge and thorough understanding of the environ-mental challenge – and on emotion – ie the set of shared values pursued. While it should not be academic, it should certainly not be simplistic either: people do not mind missing a part of a story as long as they are taken seriously. The simple criterion must be: Can my neighbour – a person who is at ease with me and is willing to listen for five minutes – understand my story?

Focusing on fourth-echelon climbers

While the needs of coworkers situated on various levels of Maslow's hierarchy of needs have to be addressed, it is undoubtedly the satisfac-tion of the needs of the fourth-echelon climbers that will make or break the change programme. This group has to be inspired not only because its members are most likely to share the values of sustainability and self-fulfilment, but also because they have the skills and attitude needed to be successful proactive environmental managers.

Management's task in this regard is facilitated by the fact that this group – as well as others in the organization – typically feel frustrated in their environmental behaviour: they think there is little that they, as individuals, can do to protect the environment in a permanent, continuous manner. This audience is therefore receptive to management initiatives, since the corporation does have the wherewithal to satisfy this need for impact and continuity.[13] This reality was echoed by Hewlett Packard's co-founder, David Packard, shortly before his death:

> *Why are we here? I think many people assume, wrongly, that a company exists solely to make money. Money is an important part of a company's existence, if the company is any good. But a result is not a cause. We have to go deeper and find the real reason for our being. As we investigate this, we inevitably come to the conclusion that a group of people get together and exist as an institution that we call a company, so that they are able to accomplish something collectively that they could not accomplish separately – they make a contribution to society, a phrase which sounds trite but is fundamental.*[14]

Nonetheless, despite their receptivity, the fourth-echelon climbers expect management to deliver the goods: to inspire them. If top management fails them, they will turn away and look for better opportunities elsewhere. If they consider their company to be unchallenging, boring or to embody unattractive values, they will leave or not come in the first place, as the case may be. If, on the other hand, the corporate leadership can provide the quality of direction that they are looking for, these fourth-echelon climbers are the ideal partners for a thrill-building process that produces lasting loyalty and results. Thus, the essence of attracting, motivating and retaining young people is reflected in the words of business people as different as The Body Shop's founder Anita Roddick ('Especially with young people, you have to find ways to grab their imagination. You want them to feel they are doing something important'),[15] and DuPont's CEO Chad Holliday Jr ('People in their twenties like to feel good about [working for a company]. You can get people to work night and day if the cause is right').[16]

More specifically, and in line with the lessons of vacuum management, success depends on the business leaders' ability to inspire the path-finders among the fourth-echelon climbers – ie the more environmentally-driven, competent and respected among their peers. Many of these coworkers will be truly inspired when the corporate leadership presents a convincing vision based on sustainability. Anita Roddick speaks of 'creating electricity and passion that bonds people to the company'. To benefit from their constructive energy, leaders must focus on the path-finders' need for self, self-respect and self-actualization to motivate them. They want to be recognized for their individual contributions; they want the opportunity to develop and renew themselves, and to shine in public too. It's tough, as Ms Roddick notes, to get that from 'just selling shampoo and body lotion.'[17]

As the need to inspire one's coworkers and meet the demands of external stakeholders becomes the central concern in the competitive arena, shareholder value will increasingly be based on appealing shared values. Eventually, the X-factor – ie the added value that comes about when good people team up to form idea-driven communities – will usually make the difference in the competitive arena. The next challenge then clearly is: How should the endgame story be developed in order to inspire the path-finders to follow in the vacuum created by top management? To answer this, top management must have a clear understanding of the needs of its stakeholders.

UNDERSTANDING THE CORPORATE PYRAMID OF NEEDS

We turn again to Maslow's work to understand the various needs of stakeholders and thereupon to develop the all-critical endgame story. Earlier, we used his framework as a basis for the development of the environmental hierarchy of needs. But as we've said, this needs is only one set of needs: individuals must satisfy a range of other, non-environmental needs as well.

Given the large number and variety of needs, we have chosen to simplify the picture by dividing all individual needs into the three groups implicit in the 'triple bottom line' measure of corporate performance: namely, economic, social and environmental.[18] Since a corporation is made up of its individual stakeholders, one can develop a useful framework, a corporate pyramid of needs, which reflects the situation of the internal stakeholders of any given corporation. One can envisage a pyramid with three edges, representing the key measures of performance in satisfying stakeholders' economic, social and environmental needs (Figure 8.1).

As individuals ascend the pyramid, they can choose to do so on different edges, but, in accordance with Maslow's principles, they cannot get too far ahead on one without raising their levels on the other two. They might, for instance, decide to climb the third step along the economic edge, by earning more income. But having secured the desired economic foothold, they now must satisfy the environmental and social needs of the third level before proceeding further up the economic edge. The slopes between the different edges represent the areas, or battlefields, where the tensions between the two edges are revealed and resolved: the three slopes are the socioenvironmental, the socioeconomic and the environmental-economic.

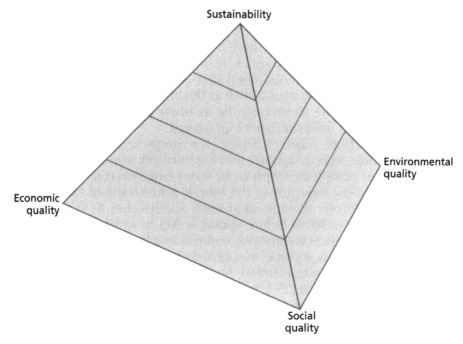

Figure 8.1 *The corporate pyramid of needs*

On the socioenvironmental slope, practical solutions have to be found – for instance, for the equitable access to natural resources, land tenure and the siting of high-environmental-impact industrial facilities. The socioeconomic slope would deal with issues such as employment creation, equitable distribution of wealth, business markers serving social needs, investment in coworker education, minority-supplier access and corporate donations. Finally, the environmental-economic slope would be dominated by eco-efficiency concerns, which we discussed in Chapter 4 – eg materials and energy efficiency.[19]

What this means is that corporations on course for a proactive response have to be sensitive and monitor all the needs of their stakeholders. Practically, it implies that all needs along the other edges of the pyramid must be fulfilled more or less concurrently. While climbing the corporate pyramid the different stakeholders are, as it were, attached to each other by an invisible rope. If some want to climb the economic edge quickly, the others, with different personal imperatives, will hold them back until their social and environmental needs at the lower echelon are satisfied as well. If, on the other hand, something goes 'wrong' along a specific edge of the pyramid that forces the corporation to descend to a lower echelon, the slide is manifested along the other edges, including the economic one.

If, for instance, the very existence of the corporation is under imminent threat, many coworkers will be very concerned about job security – typically an issue of immediate concern at Maslow's second level. Under such circumstances, it is virtually impossible to rally people for an environmental need such as noise abatement, not to speak of fourth echelon issues, such as the loss of identity of a specific neighbourhood. The factory can be as noisy and unattractive as it likes, as long as it offers secure employment.

This works both ways, of course. If management, obsessed with the bottom line, were to ignore meeting third-echelon environmental needs, such as compliance with air or water emission regulations, this would, at the very least, lower the morale and loyalty of coworkers. The point is simple: management must ensure that its coworkers' lower needs are satisfied before taking action to satisfy higher ones. However, the situation is obviously complicated by the fact that almost any larger institution is composed of stakeholders with very different needs. Even on a single echelon, leaders must continuously decide which of the stakeholder needs to satisfy first. Some will choose the economic edge, whereas others prefer the social ascent. It therefore becomes very hard to maintain an overview and understand what is or should be happening. The difficulty management has in deciphering these needs while keeping an eye on the ultimate objective is expressed by Ray Anderson of Interface in a simile:

> *I have this mental picture of a mountain that is higher than Everest. It rises steeply out of a jungle that surrounds it. Most of us, people and companies, are lost and wandering around in that jungle, and don't know the mountain exists at all. Rather, we are preoccupied with the threatening, competitive 'animals' all around us. A few have sensed the upward slope of the mountain's foothills under their feet. Still fewer have decided to follow the upward slope to see where it leads. And a very few are far enough along to have had a glimpse of the mountain through the leaves of the trees, to realize what looms ahead and above. Very few indeed have set their eyes and will on the summit.*[20]

At the top of the corporate pyramid, all needs come together in a desire for sustainability: all stakeholders – internal and external, current and future – derive from 'their' community what they personally want to derive from it, while the company as a whole is 'at peace' with its surroundings. Many business people tend to resist the notion that their corporate responsibility should encompass social as well as environmental issues. Other executives see this development as a positive challenge. Reebok International's CEO Paul Fireman put it this way:

I believe we're on the verge of what might be a genuine shift in our nation's priorities – an official end to the 'me' and 'greed' decade. We now know that the conditions of our businesses cannot be separated from the conditions of the society in which we operate, and that we must advocate, promote, and even fight for responsible business.[21]

And these are the thoughts of Bill Ford Jr, Chairman of the Ford Motor Company:

Our social obligation is much bigger than just supporting worthy causes. The responsibility to consumers – and to society – of a company our size is defined in very broad terms. It includes anything that impacts [on] people and the quality of their lives.[22]

It is beyond the scope of this text to detail options that companies have on the social and economic edges as we did in Chapter 2 for the environmental one; it would require a far-reaching assessment which, moreover, each leadership team would have to tailor to its specific situation. However, an initial glance at the kind of elements to be considered on each echelon of the pyramid may prove helpful in furthering corporate thinking in the social and economic areas.

1 Food, clothing and shelter

On the lowest echelon, the driving need is for survival. Small-scale institutions such as tribes or municipalities strive for economic security through craft activities, organized in small shops or farms, and local barter. Slave labour, prostitution, and – at best – child labour often provide the only alternatives.

Socially, a (large) family is essential as a fallback in case of poor health or old age. Isolated communities are also highly vulnerable when confronted with more developed institutions. For example, the financial, technical and managerial power of the companies is such that they can overwhelm and even destroy the culture of small tribes or local groups.

2 Safety and security

The climb to the second echelon commences with the industrial revolution in the West and its emphasis on productivity. Mass production, both in industry and agriculture, creates new economic opportunities. Physical infrastructure – roads, railroads, canals, harbours, airports – opens access to national and international markets. Functional skills are exploited in functional organizations: research, manufacturing, sales, service.

On the social side, the needs of individuals are met by better access to jobs, especially through migration and training. Active labour unions confront capitalist entrepreneurs in a struggle for job security and labour conditions, with governments providing support through regulation. The expanded social infrastructure is also critical: health care, family planning, nutrition and primary education, especially for women, combine with social legislation to create stronger safety nets.

3 Social belonging

The emphasis shifts to a sense of community: individuals want to be part of a group that they value. In the West, the information revolution provided the stepping stone to this third echelon, which is characterized by greatly increased access. New and widely available technologies, ranging from aircraft and telephones to computers and networks, accelerate the pace of innovation and differentiation of product/service offerings. Many more professional coworkers cooperate in focused business units to realize as yet unparalleled economic growth.

Socially, the most fundamental need at this echelon is job stability; labour unions are now supported by protectionist government policies. The so-called civil society comes into full bloom. The quest for belonging is translated into an active participation in institutions such as churches, schools and sports clubs. Political parties and NGOs reach out to expand membership and build cadre. Legislative initiatives are taken to eliminate discrimination based on race, gender or sexual preference.

4 Self-respect

The contours of what our colleague Mickey Huibregtsen termed the 'emotional revolution', within which people strive for this self-respect, are already apparent in the West.[23] A rapidly increasing number of fourth-echelon climbers, motivated by the magic word 'self', are demanding change. On the economic side, the market takes over from a retreating government in a process that underlies increased liberalization, privatization and competition. In the competitive economic arena, companies respond by creating networks of small, entrepreneurial units, providing the focus and freedom to satisfy both customers and coworkers. Governments and corporations globalize, freeing themselves to an extent from their national roots.

On the social side, the emphasis now is on flexibility – it is not what you learnt yesterday that counts but what you will do tomorrow. Loyalty comes at a premium; job-hopping is 'in'. Self-development is also critical to the satisfaction of non-economic needs. With governments stepping back, business and NGOs assume a greater societal responsibility outside the traditional confines of their institution. Equal opportunity, one step up from non-discrimination, becomes a reality, with minorities taking on leadership roles.

Referring directly to Maslow's framework, Hanover's CEO Bill O'Brien had this to say about this echelon:

> *I think there is something beyond competitive pressures. Our traditional organizations are designed to provide for the first three levels of Maslow's hierarchy of needs: food, shelter, and belonging. Since these now are widely available to members of industrial society, our organizations do not provide significantly unique opportunities to command the loyalty and commitment of our people. The ferment in management will continue until organizations begin to address the higher order needs: self-respect and self-actualization. This is the quest we at Hanover have been on for almost 20 years now – to discover the guiding principles, design, and tools needed to build organizations more consistent with human nature.*
>
> *My personal view is that this [the reason these organizations are timely] has to do with the evolution of consciousness. Mankind's nature is to ascend to greater awareness of our place in the natural order – yet, everywhere we look we see society in a terrible mess of self-centredness, greed, and near-sightedness. In modern society, business has the greatest potential to offer a different way of operating. The potential of business to contribute toward dealing with a broad range of society's problems is enormous. But we must show the way by example, not by moralizing, we must learn how to harness the commitment of our people – then our commitment to building a better world will have some meaning.*[24]

5 Sustainability

Lastly, the fifth echelon is reached when all needs are in harmony with all actions. Perhaps utopian, this stage is nonetheless important as an objective, as something to be striven for and approximated. Organizations are characterized by a partnership that allows individuals and groups to get the best out of themselves. Knowledge is shared globally, organizations and people learn and grow as they continuously experience and accept new challenges and pursue their self-actualization.

Socially, individuals and institutions recognize and celebrate their interdependence. Webs and networks are not built to stifle social movement, but to stimulate the interaction of different parts of a same society. Equal opportunity – of gender, ethnicity, social background or personal preference – now is a fact. 'Meeting the needs of the present without compromising the ability of future generations to meet their own needs' is the order of the day.

Again, Interface's Ray Anderson sounded the high note, also referring to Maslow:

> *At the very least we will give our people and our company a higher cause and a long-range reason for being. Abraham Maslow, describing the hierarchy of human needs, says a higher cause is important, and I agree. After compensation to meet their needs, according to Maslow, people want the opportunity to develop and grow personally and professionally. When compensation is sufficient and growth opportunity is satisfied, people want to work for a company that makes a difference, that serves a higher cause. At Interface, we have learned in a very practical way that the quest for sustainability, for the welfare of our children's children, is a powerful, binding force. It is that higher purpose.*
>
> *At the very most (let's dream a little), we'll start a trickle that will influence others – maybe you – to start their trickles; when those trickles come together into rivulets, and rivulets become streams, and streams, rivers, something good can happen.*[25]

This outline of social and economic needs complements the environmental hierarchy to form a complete picture of individual needs. We're convinced that an understanding of this reality should provide corporations with the sensitivity to effectively tailor their stories to the needs of their stakeholders.

TAILORING THE STORY TO STAKEHOLDER NEEDS

On the basis of its grasp of its corporation's pyramid, top management can then select those factors that will satisfy the specific needs of its stakeholders. In doing so, it charts a path to the top, in a difficult process that concentrates on the environmental edge while keeping close contact with the social and economic ones. As we have stressed, the climb towards sustainability is held back if the corporation has not satisfied the needs of relevant stakeholder groups at lower levels.

Thus, for instance, if a multinational company is active in a poor developing country, the pursuit of extreme fourth-echelon economic needs, such as extravagant bonuses, will in the long term create tensions if the unsatisfied first- and second-echelon needs are not appropriately addressed. In the words of Chad Holliday of DuPont and his fellow chairman John Pepper of Procter & Gamble: 'Business cannot succeed if the society around us fails.'[26] Not only would the developing country stakeholders rebel, but those fourth-echelon climbers with social concerns would also find it unacceptable if not offensive; whether they be coworkers, customers or even more distant parties such as NGOs, they would be unhappy.

The objective thus is to present an endgame story that builds towards sustainability, taking due regard of today's realities. Since the pursuit of environmental and social objectives implies some economic sacrifice, it has to be compensated for by the benefits accruing from the thrill – ie the X-factor – that such pursuits create. To present its internal and external stakeholders, including the financial community, with a valid value proposition based on a vision of sustainability, management therefore has to satisfy two criteria: first, meet the lower-echelon needs of stakeholders and, second, ensure the environment-driven vision provides sufficient inspiration for coworkers and customers.

Satisfying non-environmental lower-echelon needs

Tom Gladwin of the University of Michigan recently reached a sobering conclusion. 'After devoting my entire career toward bringing industry into harmony with nature,' he told a gathering of senior business people, 'I have become increasingly convinced that the more difficult challenge lies in bringing industry into harmony with people.' Whereas most business organizations are comfortable with the economic and (increasingly) environmental areas, Gladwin notes that the same cannot be said for the third – social – edge of their pyramid of needs. 'Genuine sustainability,' he argues, 'also demands poverty alleviation, population stabilization, female empowerment, employment creation, human rights observance and opportunity redistribution on a massive scale.'[27]

Göran Lindahl, President and CEO of ABB, also expresses this concern:

> *I believe we know quite well what we mean by both economic and environmental performance – but do we know what we mean by social performance?*
>
> *The social area is huge and very complex, and industry already has a large social responsibility, which is both regulated by local laws and driven by other factors. Yet there is increasing pressure on industry to take on more social responsibility in line with its commitment to sustainable development. But we must tread carefully and be clear [about] what we are asked to undertake.*[28]

Here, for purposes of illustration, are a few proposals and examples of corporations acting to satisfy the non-environmental lower-echelon needs of their stakeholders on different levels of the pyramid.[29]

1 Food, clothing and shelter

In developing countries, where many have yet to satisfy their most basic needs, multinational corporations are challenged to contribute to the provision of the means of survival. Within limits, they can indeed help by providing jobs and elementary assistance in areas such as water and fuel supply. If large corporations put their mind to it, and – perhaps with the assistance of grassroots community-based organizations – gain the cooperation of a local population, their purchasing behaviour can create small-scale market opportunities to strengthen local farming, mining or fishing. This can result in a degree of economic stability and hope among the population, while alleviating some of the pressure on natural resources – for example, from slash-and-burn agriculture and injudicious fishery practices.

On the lowest step of the pyramid, multinational corporations also have a significant responsibility in applying due diligence in their contacts with local populations. Particularly mining companies – with their huge environmental and social impact in many developing world host countries – increasingly provide examples that may serve as models for others.[30] Although few in number, corporations are clearly increasing their activities in this regard: for example, Placer Dome's promotion of the sustainability of displaced small-scale gold mining communities in Venezuela; Shell's involvement of stakeholders during the development of the Camisea natural gas project in Peru; BP's social investment strategy for sustainable community development in Colombia; and the social policies of both Rio Tinto and Chevron in Papua New Guinea.

The possible influence of corporations is not limited, however, to their direct interactions with local communities. Companies can also address the indirect social and environmental impact of their ecological shadow, ie the effects of the activities of their upstream suppliers. Even when very carefully handled, this impact can be significant, and corporations are increasingly expected to assume full responsibility for it.

Here are a couple more detailed cases of corporate activities in helping stakeholders with survival. These, and the others cases provided below in this chapter, are presented simply as thought-provokers rather than models. The first refers to community development and the second to cultural diversity (Box 8.1).

Box 8.1 Satisfying basic needs

The Integrated Rural Development Programme (IRDP) was established by Unilever's subsidiary Hindustan Lever in 1976 to improve milk yields from its dairy factory. The company had purchased the factory in 1963 in response to the Indian government's call for rural industrialization. Local villagers supplied milk, but after ten years of operations, despite efforts to introduce better cattle and livestock management practices, the milk supply was so poor and erratic that the plant was operating at 50 per cent capacity and incurring substantial losses.

Hindustan Lever realized that the problem could only be overcome by taking a more integrated approach, and tackling not just livestock management but also the underlying poverty in the area. The IRDP was therefore launched to address the following activities: improved dairy production through better animal husbandry and milk collection practices; diversification to pigs, poultry, complimentary crops and dual use crops; development of other income generation projects; improved healthcare, particularly immunization for mothers and children; infrastructure development, particularly the provision of basic services; literacy and training, particularly improving access for women and girls; and the establishment of village development committees.

Having started with six villages, the programme now reaches about 700 villages, with very positive results. Since 1976, milk collection has increased five-fold, and the dairy at Etah is now one of Hindustan Lever's most profitable business units. Over 10 per cent of its pre-tax profit is currently invested in the IRDP, which has also attracted increased government funding. A 1991 evaluation also found improvements in other sources of village income, increased employment, literacy, health and leisure time.[a]

The Australian mining company WMC recently evaluated the feasibility of a new copper-gold mining project on an isolated part of the island of Mindanao in the Philippines. The area is home to five traditional indigenous Bla'an communities, whose way of life (including the use of natural resources) is governed by customary laws. As these groups were not officially recognized, the concession agreement between WMC and the Philippine government placed no restrictions on the company. However, once their presence became apparent, the company put its exploration activities on hold until it had identified all indigenous communities. In the absence of any existing socioeconomic baseline data, the company initiated a comprehensive data collection programme. This included ethnographic studies, archaeological studies, evaluations of social structures and customary laws, mapping of traditional territories, and an assessment of the dependency of local communities on natural resources.

These studies formed the basis for assessing the potential socioeconomic impacts of mining, initiating a community development programme to manage and mitigate these impacts and for assisting the indigenous communities to collaboratively develop and register an ancestral domain claim. The government has recently granted a Certificate of Ancestral Domain to one of the Bla'an groups, and WMC's expectation is that the submissions by the other four indigenous groups will be successful. The company is committed to early and continuing consultation, to transparency at every stage, and to a policy of 'no surprises' in conjunction with awareness training for community leaders about potential project development. Whether the mine goes ahead or not, the various programmes are helping to raise living standards and provide greater opportunities for those many people who live in this largely rural society.[b]

a Nelson, *Business as Partners in Development*, p205
b McPhail and Davy, *Integrating Social Concerns*, p15; also see Phil Watts, Lord Holme and the World Business Council for Sustainable Development, *Corporate Social Responsibility – Meeting Changing Expectations* (WBCSD, Conches-Geneva, Switzerland; 1999), p15

2 Safety and security

When economies pick up and foreign investment tends to play a greater role, multinationals can 'adopt' local communities and assist in meeting their basic infrastructural needs. Corporations can also make an important contribution to greater socioeconomic safety and security by assisting their stakeholders through in-house training and the formation of symbiotic partnerships with local suppliers.

Most large multinationals have taken initiatives in this area. Unilever, for instance, is the largest employer in Africa, with over 50,000 coworkers active on its plantations, producing things such as palm oil. Most of the large oil corporations, through their worldwide exploration and production activities, are among the largest employers in many poor countries, and hence also have considerable economic and social impacts.

This sort of presence opens up an almost limitless range of opportunities, many of them win–win in nature, for multinationals. But the precondition is that the companies must be willing to approach the challenge from two perspectives: traditional corporate self-interest on the one hand and local needs on the other. A number of corporations, Dow Chemical for example, have promoted community initiatives aimed at improving physical infrastructure (eg roads, harbours) and social provisions (eg housing, schools, hospitals, recreation facilities). They have also put their resources to work in strengthening the access of the local population to know-how, financing and markets.

But could they go even further? For example, building on their experience in their home countries, corporations could provide the seed money and know-how for farmers' cooperatives. They could create market access for the resulting products – purchasing the products themselves, or pushing for access to often well-protected markets in the North.

Although this is a very sensitive issue, companies could also combine forces with other international and local companies in advising governments on the maintenance of a stable and attractive investment climate to stimulate inflows of capital and know-how. In the same vein, by adhering to a multinational corporation code of conduct, they can contribute to a business environment with the minimum of corruption and with fair labour conditions for local coworkers and suppliers. And why, in line with an extended responsibility for the environmental shadow of their products, couldn't corporations think in terms of a 'social shadow', as the UK's Diageo did when it joined other drinks companies in promoting sensible drinking and preventing alcohol abuse? CEO John McGrath noted: 'We can only achieve so much as an individual company [but] collectively businesses can really be an agent for social change.'[31]

Box 8.2 Providing social infrastructure

'Living and working in Latin America gives a different perspective on sustainable development from Europe or America,' reflected Erling Lorentzen, founder and Chairman of Aracruz Cellulose. The $2 billion Brazilian company is the world's largest producer of eucalyptus pulp. 'You realize that poverty is one of the world's leading polluters. That's why development is essential for sustainability, because you can't expect people who don't eat a proper meal to be concerned about the environment.'

He is proud of his company's accomplishments. 'Aracruz has created social development in a sustainable way, in areas of Brazil where hardly anything existed but poverty and misery. Aracruz today employs more than 5000 people directly and indirectly, supporting a local population of over 20,000. We have invested $125 million in creating in our community a social services infrastructure, such as schools, medical facilities and housing. And we provide financial and human resources for projects that lead to self-sustaining improvements in the living conditions of neighbouring communities.'

In fact, until recently Aracruz spent more on its social investments than it did on wages: about $1.20 for every $1 in wages. Nowadays, with a dramatically improved standard of living (as well as productivity), the company no longer needs to invest so heavily in social infrastructure.[a]

C&A, the largest chain of retail clothing stores in Europe, in 1997 registered 80 breaches of the code of conduct to which it demands its suppliers comply. In 30 cases the issue at stake was child labour; the remaining cases centred around, for instance, unsafe working conditions.

At an annual cost of $3 million, a crew of C&A inspectors make approximately 1000 field visits a year to often small companies in Asia. A breach of the code results in a cancellation of orders. Only when the producer comes up with a plan will C&A consider restoring the relationship. 'In case of child labour a supplier can, for instance, propose to pay for having the children attend a school and reimburse the parents for the missed income,' says C&A spokesman Jaap Bosman. 'If he does this, and it can be verified, we will probably place orders again.'[b]

a Schmidheiny et al, *Signals for Change*, p43, DeSimone et al, *Eco-Efficiency*, px; and Stuart Hart, *Harvard Business Review*, January–February 1997, p72
b NRC Handelsblad, May 14 1998

Here are a couple more detailed examples of corporate activities in helping stakeholders at this level of the pyramid; the first refers to social development and the second to labour conditions (Box 8.2).

3 Social belonging

In industrializing nations with high economic growth rates, multinationals can play a major role in helping to meet their stakeholders' need to belong to a community they value. They can use their geographic reach and institutional power to expand their local role to regional or national levels, and make available their professional know-how for the transfer of technology or managerial skills. We have seen that private enterprise is expected to play a more active role on the social edge of its pyramid, for instance in responding to labour unions demands – eg wage increases, improved labour conditions and training – and to those of government – eg fair trade and affirmative action.

A 'good' employer also values a solid relationship with the surrounding community. Proper siting and shaping of the company's facilities is important in this regard. The sponsoring of local organizations and activities, ranging from schools to sports and to the arts, is also a plus. Stimulating employees to pursue continued and higher education also plays a role in making sure coworkers look at their company as being more than a source of income: a sense of belonging eventually creates loyalty.

Many of these tasks are less foreign to multinationals than are those related to needs at the lower echelons of the pyramid. Most senior managers have personal experience with third-echelon needs, and many large companies, especially in traditionally industrialized areas, deal with such concerns daily. However, when many corporate stakeholders and external observers are moving up to the fourth echelons of their pyramids, what once was considered philanthropy or 'good corporate citizenship' becomes normal business practice. Also, companies are expected to actively participate in regional or national partnerships to solve industry problems – the chemical industry's Responsible Care programme was even expanded into a global initiative.

Actually, we think that companies' license to operate will increasingly depend on the solidity of their foundation in society and their contribution to it. We saw earlier, for instance, how companies with a proven environmental track record are given much more leeway by the authorities to develop solutions that meet not only their environmental but also their economic objectives.

Here are a couple more detailed examples of corporate activities in helping stakeholders to increase their sense of social belonging; the first refers to gang warfare and the second to inner-city education (Box 8.3).

Box 8.3 Addressing social belonging

Auchan is France's second-largest hypermarket chain with $24 billion in sales and 120,000 coworkers. It has 119 stores in France and expanded its international presence to countries such as Spain, Portugal, Italy, the US, Poland and Mexico. When violent gang warfare broke out leaving customers too scared to enter its stores, and a security guard was killed in the crossfire, the company took a radical stance. Taking a risk, it sought out the gang leaders and hired them to serve as security guards. It also provided retail space for several community-owned boutiques, thus addressing some of the root causes of the problems: poverty, racism and unemployment.

'The results were incredible,' said Director of Human Resources Jean-Marie Deberdt. 'Not only did it change the lives of the teenagers, it also changed how managers dealt with people.' Importantly, customers also returned to the stores.[a]

Honeywell's most prized educational effort is located right in its own headquarters. It is called New Vistas High School, and it offers pregnant teenagers and teenage mothers a chance to stay in school and get a high school diploma. The school, which opened in 1990, is a collaborative effort involving Honeywell, Minneapolis public schools, and several community and social service organizations. In addition to a standard high school education, students receive a wide range of health and social services including medical care and parenting classes.

The programme's success has been phenomenal, with most of its graduates going on to college. Says M Patricia Hoven, vice president of community and local government affairs, 'I think we do a lot of the things we're doing because we believe that communities have to be viable or companies can't function.'[b]

a Malcolm McIntosh, Deborah Leipziger, Keith Jones and Gill Coleman, *Corporate Citizenship: Successful Strategies for Responsible Companies* (*Financial Times*/Pitman Publishing, London; 1998), p216
b Makower, *Beyond the Bottom Line*, p232

---

4 Self-respect

In the industrialized and prosperous parts of the world, finally, multinationals will face the challenge of trying to reach the fourth, and ultimately the fifth, echelon of the pyramid. They must respond to the needs of their stakeholders by providing greater individual responsibility for the collective performance. To this end, for example, they have been busy flattening their organizational structures, reducing hierarchy and improving their management development programmes.

Corporations also increasingly accept a responsibility regarding social questions. Some actively participate in initiating social renewal, for instance, by stimulating small enterprises or participating in

---

Box 8.4 Dealing with workplace diversity

CEO Paul Fireman of Reebok International has become an outspoken advocate on the subject of workplace diversity. 'My industry, the sporting goods industry, ten years ago was an industry overwhelmingly dominated by blond men with long legs. Ten years ago, if you saw a black man at Reebok, you knew there was an athlete visiting for the day. And while we've started down the road to change, we still have a long way to go.'

It will be a tough road to travel, he realizes. 'In the final analysis, human diversity is about qualities that don't bunch up into convenient categories. It's about the fact that we come from different places and bring with us different stories. It's about our differences in taste and temperament. We may need laws and regulations to get us from here to there, from yesterday to tomorrow, but in the end it is not habits of compliance we seek to change, it's habits of the heart.'[a]

a Makower, *Beyond the Bottom Line*, pp202, 297

---

inner-city revival. Others form partnerships with NGOs to address issues that at this echelon have become of joint concern.[32]

The social and ecological shadow that a corporation casts through the activities of its suppliers, especially in developing countries, becomes a reality in strategic thinking. New mental models based on the integration of internal and external stakeholder interests drive corporations to initiate a variety of programmes. These can include community development programmes directed at a specific host community, or sustainable development programmes aimed at sustainable life cycles for specific products (eg tea or aluminium) or services. Many companies even venture into new technologies that promote employment and renewability.

Our detailed example in this instance refers to workplace diversity (Box 8.4).

Environmental inspiration: a two-pronged strategy

It should be evident by now that crystallizing a sustainability endgame that meets the variety of stakeholder needs is a difficult challenge. But it is one that must be met if the required thrill to drive the change programme is to be generated within the corporation. Although one frequently hears encouraging and rousing words uttered by many business leaders (Box 8.5), the truth is that companies cannot solve all the problems of all the communities in which they are active, nor can anyone seriously expect them single-handedly to lift all of their stakeholders to the fourth echelon, let alone the fifth, of their pyramid of needs.

Box 8.5 The role of business in sustainable development

Frank Popoff, Chairman of Dow Chemical: We all remember the old adage, 'Of those to whom much is given, much is expected.' Well, today, with the power of the state under challenge around the world, the resulting societal vacuum is more and more being filled by private enterprise. And business is proving that with the cooperation of other interested segments of society, it can achieve dual objectives of commercial and societal progress. They need not be mutually exclusive.[a]

Edgar S Woolard Jr, Chairman and CEO of DuPont: The only sector in modern society that can solve many of our largest environmental problems is industry. Environmental problems that we characterize as regional or global are fundamentally problems of economy and production. Other sectors can analyse the problems of and plan to deal with the infrastructure needs – such as transportation, waste disposal and land use. But the remediation of existing problem sites, the procurement of raw materials, the minimization of waste and emissions, and product stewardship are problems that only industry can correct.[b]

Antonia Axson Johnson, Chairperson of the Axel Johnson Group: Companies in general, I feel are the greatest force for change in modern society – greater than politicians, churches or even universities. What companies offer in products or services influences deeply the daily lives of most of us. In our group of companies in Sweden we meet 1 million customers every day, or almost 15 per cent of all Swedes!

As agents of change, firms therefore have a special moral responsibility to bring about what can be called 'good' changes. But how can we define these? To me, the good company does good for its owners through profits and growth, for its suppliers and customers by supplying high-quality products and services, for its employees by offering job security and development opportunities, and for society at large through a multitude of actions, of which an environmental resolve and a commitment to sustainable development is one of the greatest.[c]

Göran Lindahl, President and CEO of ABB (on climate change): One must understand and accept that politicians have a different role. Maybe we in industry are in a better position to bring about change. After all, we are used to managing complex change processes whilst generating results at the same time.[d]

Harry Pearce, Vice Chairman of General Motors: We are all responsible for this planet, but business must take the lead, because only business has the global reach, the innovative capability, the capital and, most importantly, the market motivation to develop the technologies that will allow the world to truly achieve sustainable development.[e]

Ray Anderson, founder and CEO of Interface: While business is part of the problem, it can also be part of the solution, and its power is more crucial than ever in organizing and efficiently meeting the world's needs. Business is the largest, wealthiest, most pervasive institution on Earth, and responsible for most of the damage. It must take the lead in directing the Earth away from collapse, and toward sustainability and restoration.

Phil Watts, Group Managing Director of Shell International: The challenge is no longer just to operate better, but to help change the way the world meets its energy needs. My interest in sustainable development is severely practical – philosophy is one thing but it is action that will make the difference.[f]

a Popoff, speech at Ann Arbor, MI; 1 April 1998
b Bruce Smart, *Beyond Compliance*, p198
c *Stanford Business School Magazine*, December 1992, p15. The Axel Johnson Group, based in Stockholm, Sweden, is a worldwide trading, distribution and retailing firm with some $7 billion in sales and 30,000 employees
d Lindahl, speech to oikos
e *Sustain*, June 1998, p5
f *People, Planet and Profits: The Shell Report 2000* (Royal Dutch/Shell Group, The Hague/London; 2001)

Admittedly, it is not the central responsibility of corporations to meet such needs – they have neither the mandate nor the authority to do so. Nevertheless, they undoubtedly have an important role to play in the society's efforts in this regard. Perhaps Unilever's co-Chairman, Morris Tabaksblat, expresses the best balance:

Unilever is not a political organization. We have not been set up, nor do we have a mandate from society, to formulate general principles and values, let alone impose them on others. But what we in Unilever must do is ensure that, within our sphere of activities and influence, our own principles, standards and values are maintained. And the company can also be held accountable for that. Companies cannot, however, allow themselves to be used as instruments for achieving the objectives of others, however laudable those objectives may seem to be.

I shall even go a step further: companies must not be entrusted with the job of protecting general social standards and values. Companies are not equipped to determine what those standards and values ought to be. Nor are the control mechanisms within businesses appropriate for that purpose. It is a fundamental mistake to think that companies can fill the vacuum of moral authority that may be left by governments and ethical and religious institutions.

> *It is primarily the political and ethical institutions that will have to provide a national, regional and global answer to the major questions of the 21st century. They will have to develop both the organizational and the moral authority. This responsibility should not be entrusted to companies, because they do not have a mandate, nor are they equipped for this.*
>
> *What companies can be expected to do is, by acting responsibly, to make a modest contribution to solving the problems in the world. But they must, first and foremost, be expected to fulfil effectively their most important task in society: to create prosperity.*[33]

In other words, corporations need to define the discrete manner in which they plan to accommodate the variety of different needs they face.[34]

Actually, the position of corporations is further complicated by the fact that their words and deeds worldwide are scrutinized not only by coworkers and customers but also by NGOs and the media which, based in rich regions, apply fourth-echelon criteria when examining the corporation's actions abroad. Again, subtle national differences can be significant, even between apparently similar societies. As we've seen, Shell's Brent Spar experience highlighted the different perceptions of its UK and German stakeholders. We've also seen how, more recently, Monsanto, which had been making great progress on the economic and environmental edges, stumbled badly when it decided to bring genetically modified soy beans into Europe. While the product had a favourable welcome in the US, European consumers, particularly in the UK, have been very distrustful.

Still, complex as they may be, such problems are relatively easy to solve at the international level, since they play themselves out within the context of relatively homogenous, developed countries. It is when multinationals are accused of applying different standards in very different – primarily developing world – environments that the complexities of responding to fourth-echelon aspirations become extreme. Coworkers will be confused by the perceived double standards. NGOs and media outlets, and most likely consumers, will actively express their disapproval of the corporate behaviour.

The corporation's predicament is even more convoluted when it is not just active in many countries, but in a variety of product groups as well. This reality, as we've seen, had to be faced by Mitsubishi, when the deforestation activities of one of its subsidiaries affected the reputation of its car group. Such situations are not uncommon. In fact, in our company surveys we repeatedly encountered strong evidence of wide differences in environmental behaviour between the business units of a single company. Actually, we found that specific product and market characteristics were stronger determinants of coworker responses than general corporate culture itself. The problem of avoiding a Jekyll-and-Hyde image and maintaining a consistent corporate behaviour and identity – essential to providing inspiration – thus becomes even more daunting.

To some, the obvious response to the problem of having to be all things to all people is to divide and rule – ie to vary the response along regional or even national product/market issues in line with the company's organizational structure. However, fourth-echelon climbers, inside and outside the company, could object very strongly to such a cynical approach. In any event, top management can be assured that NGO activists, with the media, politicians and consumers following on their heels, will carefully scrutinize such behaviour from their fourth-echelon perspectives.

Another answer to this dilemma is offered by Morris Tabaksblat: 'A company will have to formulate its own standards and values to supplement the laws and regulations in the various countries. It will have to ensure that these are accepted internally and complied with.'[35] This still leaves many options on the way to the top, with the ultimate objective of sustainability. Still, at this moment it would appear that few, if any, multinational companies have developed a comprehensive philosophy, let alone a strategy to deal with the challenge of the triple bottom line. Flustered by internal and external pressures, companies either try to be everything to everybody or, alternatively, they freeze and do nothing sensible. Neither approach is satisfactory.

In our view, top management's objective of inspiring the organization is best served by a two-pronged strategy for each host country the corporation is active in. The first part involves being somewhat better than its main competitors in meeting the social, economic and environmental needs of its relevant stakeholder groups on each echelon – eg it should not merely be 'good' in complying with regulations, but a notch better than other corporations operating in the same industry and geographic area. The second part is to make the company the world's best performer in one or two environmental areas of relevance to the host countries. In other words, the company plays a leading role on the environmental stage, while playing a significant secondary role on the social and economic ones.

This approach has three merits. First, on the basis of its study of the countries' pyramid of needs, a company can focus its contributions so as to have a real impact. It makes no sense, for instance, for a company to sponsor a symphony orchestra or museum in a developing country, as it might in North America or Western Europe. Similarly, it does not always make sense to apply the same environmental standards worldwide. By way of illustration, SO_2 emissions, which cause acid rain in the industrialized world, have a much smaller impact in developing countries where they usually do not challenge the ecological carrying capacity.

This strategy's second merit is that it limits the challenge – and the cost – of socially-responsible positioning to feasible proportions, while the attainment of global leadership in self-selected environmental area – such as Unilever has done in sustainable fisheries – provides a source of pride and motivation for coworkers. Fourth-echelon climbers in particular will be very pleased with the fact that their company is the world's best in promoting change in a particular environmental area.

And, third, the strategy allows the company to present a proactive, non-defensive attitude to its external stakeholders. Concretely, such single-issue leadership can be of major significance in responding to the inevitable challenges of single-issue organizations and the media. Many business executives get discouraged by the thought that, in the eye of the cynical observer, they can never win: they're never good enough. Of course, if one applies fourth-echelon standards across the board, corporations inevitably fail on many counts – their coworkers in the developing countries are paid less, have fewer benefits and more limited opportunities, and so on. However, if top management can draw the attention of the media and the interest of the NGOs to its global leadership activities, even the more critical outsiders will respond cautiously, even positively. Unaccustomed to corporate proactive leadership initiatives of this sort, they will tend to support – however awkwardly – any serious corporate action programmes.

In our discussion in Chapter 2 on forecasting the differentiation space, we pointed to a group of environmental issues whose scope and timing were uncertain, and to another group in which these elements were unknown. We feel these two categories provide good sources for corporations seeking areas in which they might acquire world leadership and which could be central components in their endgame scenarios. Emissions, climate change, biotechnology, fertility issues, indoor air: any one of these offers companies a chance to gain a global profile and inspire their coworkers.

There are a number of works that can have proved to be useful to executives in making this choice. Interface's Ray Anderson, for instance, drew from Paul Hawken's *The Ecology of Commerce*,[36] with its clear and appealing recipe for sustainability, and on the thoughts of Swedish scientist Karl-Henrik Robèrt and his compelling Natural Step movement.[37] Others were inspired by the perspectives of thought leaders like Lovins, Galbraith, Handy and Piel.[38]

When placing the environment on its corporate banner, top management must develop its own story to excite its stakeholders. The overarching purpose of such visions is to contribute to a better world, where there is no separation of the environment, the organization and the self. Still, mere intuition – ie knowledge that cannot be expressed in words – is not sufficient; words quickly become airy and may easily be perceived to be politically correct cocktail talk. Deep thought and introspection are required before asking stakeholders to commit to the new vision.

Once again, the rapidly expanding literature on the 'ecocentric' school of strategic management can help executives in this regard.[39] Two main lines of thinking are apparent: an emphasis on corporate ethics and societal responsibility, and insights derived from a spiritual understanding of the connection of humans with the environment.[40] Whatever the approach chosen, it pays to think before you leap. Whereas the first road has the appeal of a rational business perspective, top management's beliefs will be quickly tested with specific cases. On the other hand, cynics are apt to challenge the more spiritual approach as being quasi-religious or dreamy. In any event, as that most enthralling of storytellers, Kermit the Frog of The Muppets, put it: 'It ain't easy being green.'

***

Sparking a proactive response starts with storytelling. Somehow, to draw coworkers throughout the corporation forwards and to inspire other stakeholders, top management must perfect its skills by practising this art. Most importantly, it must build a compelling story – a vision of the company as it could be and why it wants to get from where it is to its endgame. The framework of the corporate pyramid of needs underpins the major components of this story.

Such inspiration is not sufficient, however. Trust is the other ingredient that is needed. In Chapter 9, we concentrate on how corporations can develop this trust by redefining personal contracts with their coworkers, and then kick-start the change process through an aspirations-based change (ABC) programme.

9

Developing a Corporate Partnership Culture

The transition to a proactive response is unusual in that it is one in which process is as important as the story itself. While a superb story can lift individuals over an inspiration threshold, it takes superior interaction processes to cross the trust barrier, which is essential for the renegotiation of personal contracts. Together, inspiration and trust produce the thrill which propels a fragmented group of individuals towards an inspired partnership (Figure 9.1).[1]

Good stories evolve over time. An ideal interaction process prompts inspired coworkers to retell the story to other members of the organization. In doing so, they invariably tailor the story to the needs of these subgroups, thereby enhancing the relevance and persuasiveness of the leader's original story. The subgroups, in their turn, do the same; and so on, down the line, in a process that ultimately encompasses all coworkers. At each iteration the story is adapted and embellished, so that top management, when later credited with its depth, can happily – and modestly – acknowledge that the constantly evolving story has become the property of the group as a whole: it has become 'our story', comprising the essence of all coworkers' personal contracts.

But the notion of reopening the personal contracts is not always an easy one for business leaders. After all, not so long ago, their predecessors believed 'employees' should be happy simply to have a job. In the same vein, they often find the salary, holiday and career demands of today's university graduates unreasonable. They are disappointed by how much it takes to 'buy' their loyalty, and by the 'crazy' things these young men and women believe the company should be doing to improve society and the environment. Still, as we've repeatedly argued, if such demands are not adequately met, many fourth-echelon climbers will be difficult to attract and retain.

That is today's reality. Moreover, it is a reality characterized by an increasingly competitive, seller's labour market: the employer is no longer king. Most importantly, it is a world where the X-factor – ie

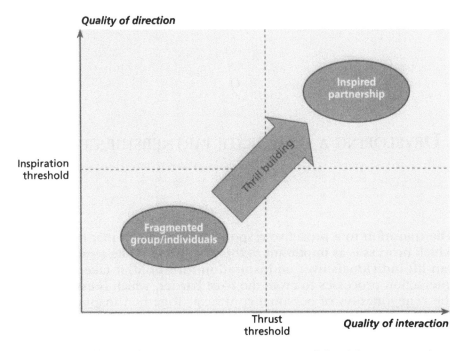

Figure 9.1 *Two dimensions of thrill building*

the added value that comes about when good people team up to form inspired communities – often makes the difference between success and failure in the marketplace. In short, corporations are more dependent than ever on their talented coworkers.

The process of renegotiating personal contracts is demanding and requires careful preparation. We have divided our discussion of it into three sections. In the first, we discuss how change can be facilitated. Then, we delve deeper into the often neglected anchoring of personal contract terms once renegotiation has been completed. Having established what it wants to be done, top management can subsequently accelerate the change process by initiating an ABC programme; this is the subject of the final section of this chapter.

FACILITATING CONTRACT RENEGOTIATION

How can leaders facilitate this personal contract renegotiation?[2] It is important to realize up-front that coworkers do not have to come to the negotiating table. Especially in apparently good times, when the need for drastic change is not fully recognized at all levels of the organization, many will question the need to make the transition to a proactive response. Top management in these cases has to be able to build on a foundation of goodwill.

In the old corporate world, people's personal interests were just that: personal. All the corporation wanted from its employees was 'an honest day's work for an honest day's pay'. The transition to a proactive response, in contrast, involves a blurring of the personal–institutional boundary. Coworkers will only be thrilled by new institutional values if these align with what they feel personally, with their needs and their values. The renegotiated personal contracts must incorporate these. They must also establish top management's commitment to supporting the full development of each coworker, and the latter's reciprocal willingness to actively cooperate in realizing the endgame.

Robert Haas, Chairman of Levi Strauss, echoes this theme:

> *In the past we always talked about the 'hard stuff' and the 'soft stuff'. The soft stuff was the company's commitment to our work force. And the hard stuff was what really mattered: getting the parts out the door. What we've learned is that the soft stuff and the hard stuff are becoming increasingly intertwined. Values are where the hard stuff and the soft stuff come together. A company's values – what it stands for, what its people believe in – are crucial to its competitive success. Indeed, values drive the business.*
>
> *It's the ideas of a business that are controlling, not some manager with authority. Values provide a common language for aligning a company's leadership and its people.... The most visible differences between the corporation of the future and its present-day counterpart will be the make-up of its work force, relationships of its people, not the types of products they make or the equipment they use in factories – although these certainly will be different. But who is working, how they will be working, why they will be working, and what work will mean to them.*[3]

In our discussion of the implementation of an integrated response in Chapter 6, we noted that environmental considerations were introduced in the business strategy within a strict framework of 'factual' outputs, requiring a proper use of the steering and rewarding instruments. Now these instruments have to be applied on a far wider scale to reach the much larger group of pivotal job holders involved in a proactive response: indeed, in this case practically all workers are part of the pivotal job holder group.

Proactivity also requires the expert use of inspiring and anchoring instruments. In this regard, the process goes far beyond the environmental management programme. It encourages the open exploration by coworkers of different endgame visions and alternative options, and allows for a greater emphasis on 'soft' issues such

---

Box 9.1 From personal visions to shared visions[a]

How do individual visions merge to create shared visions? A useful metaphor as presented by Peter Senge is the hologram, the three-dimensional image created by interacting light sources.

If you cut a photograph in half, each part shows only part of the whole image. But if you divide a hologram, each part shows the whole image intact. Similarly, as you continue to divide up the hologram, no matter how small the divisions, each piece still shows the whole image. Likewise, when a group of people come to share a vision for an organization, each person sees his own picture of the organization at its best. Each shares responsibility for the whole, not just for his piece. But the component 'pieces' of the hologram are not identical. Each represents the whole image from a different point of view. It's as if you look through holes poked in a window shade; each hole would offer a unique angle for viewing the whole image. So, too, is each individual's vision of the whole unique. We each have our own way of seeing the larger vision.

When you add up the pieces of a hologram, the image of the whole does not change fundamentally. After all, it was there in each piece. Rather, the image becomes more intense, more lifelike. When more people come to share a common vision, the vision may not change fundamentally. But it becomes more alive, more real in the sense of a mental reality that people can truly imagine achieving. They now have partners, 'cocreators'; the vision no longer rests on their shoulders alone. Early on, when they are nurturing an individual vision, people may say it is 'my vision'. But as the shared vision develops, it becomes both 'my vision' and 'our vision'.

a Senge, *The Fifth Discipline*, p212

---

as environmental yield. Crucially for the self-development of cowork-ers, the approach should also explicitly promote harmony between their personal development and satisfaction on the one hand, and the operational and strategic needs of the business on the other (Box 9.1).

GE's Jack Welch sees it this way: 'My job is to listen to, search for, think of and spread ideas; to expose people to good ideas and role models. I'm almost a maître d', getting the crowd to come sit at this table: "Enjoy the food here. Try it. See if it tastes good." And they do. When self-confident people see a good idea, they love it.'[4]

To create the conditions for this sort of active coworker involve-ment in the process, coworkers have to be stimulated to be part of two corporate structures, one active and the other reflective. These are the parallel structures identified by our McKinsey colleague Michael Jung.[5] Apart from the active structure of normal everyday behaviour, coworkers also have to be involved in a new structure, within which they can reflect on corporate attitudes and values as well as their most rewarding contributions (both personally and for the company).

The company's organizational architecture must recognize that active and reflective modes of interaction involve such different success factors that they are best kept apart. One structure should be geared for operations; the other should be geared towards validating and subsequently renegotiating the terms of the personal contracts, particularly the social paragraphs – that is, aligning each individual's aspirations with those of the company.

During the early stages of the transition to a proactive response, this second, reflective structure is key to establishing the conditions for involving coworkers in the creative process. Within this structure, they are to be invited to share top management's proposed endgame vision, and generate and assess options for improving on it and realizing it. To this end, the reflective structure makes extensive use of the inspiring instruments discussed in Chapter 6.

In effect, the reflective structure provides pivotal job holders with the vehicle for in-depth communication and for the alignment of their personal challenges with those of the corporation. After all, individuals who want to break away from mental models of the past need time and space for reflection, and for the validation of the endgame. The central question is: Is the proposed endgame truly an improvement over the current approach, as top management suggests? The situation also must allow for a direct interaction with top management: prior to making a serious commitment, pivotal job holders will want to renegotiate the social paragraph of their personal contracts. It is crucial to the quality of the result that top management should not pull rank and dictate the outcome: having told its story, it should allow its endgame vision and the associated medium-term objectives to grow, based on the bottom–up input of the pivotal job holders.

For these purposes, the reflective structure should be tuned to the needs of the pivotal job holders and particularly of the path-finders among them. As a rule they share one concern: fully aware as they are that not all efforts succeed, the transition represents a considerable career risk. On the other hand, especially in large corporations, path-finders tend to form diverse groups with varying insights, knowledge and experience. Their individual needs and aspirations will also differ. In general, it does not make sense therefore to group them together: this at best produces discomfort and, at worst, anxiety. Instead, the path-finders should be grouped on the basis of relevant expertise and shared concerns, in the same way that focus groups are formed in consumer marketing.

The formation of such groups serves two purposes. First, path-finders are, in any event, few in number and hence lonely. Like members of breakthrough schools in science and art, they are keen on finding meaningful communities to share their aspirations and apprehensions. Such groups – which are in the beginning usually loosely-knit networks – provide them with this company. The second purpose is to foster new thinking: being around like-minded, imaginative people is one of the strongest ways of promoting creativity. As in a jazz band, the quality of the players and of their interaction determines the creative quality of the musical outcome. The same applies to the interactive storytelling process: creativity and thrill require groups that are intelligently selected and brought together. Indeed, such contagious creativity is really what the process is all about.

A further advantage of well selected groups of path-finders is that top managers who work with them in this process are spared the awkwardness they might experience in dealing with large, anonymous crowds. Communication can be very personalized if the target group share backgrounds and concerns, and the story can easily be tailored to the needs of different groups. Interaction is also of greater value to leaders if they are able to interpret what they are hearing better because they know their interlocutors well.

The risk of such a managed approach, of course, is that the group pre-selection produces predictable responses. As shown by our colleague Jon Katzenbach and his Real Change Leaders (RCL) team,[6] unexpected volunteers – the jokers in the pack – sometimes turn out to be the RCLs, making the best contributions to the original story. When organizing the reflective structure, therefore, top management should take care not to be too directive. An open invitation to all pivotal job holders to participate, ample room for modifying the agenda, and the possibility of switching membership or participation in different groups must all be part of the house rules.

The resulting organizational ambiguity can be difficult to handle for many business leaders. This is hardly surprising given that they commonly build their careers by eliminating, or at least limiting, uncertainty and the associated confusion. Reflective structures challenge them to relax and let go. Indeed, many coworkers will also experience difficulties when moving from the active to the reflective structures. Accustomed to receiving orders or knowing fairly accurately what is expected of them, they are now asked what they think and what they want. Although most will appreciate the experience, they will sometimes be apprehensive.

Indeed, it could well be that trust, rather than inspiration, is the magic word in the management of proactive change. If top management does not accept the vulnerability implicit in reaching out, its likelihood of success is nil. Trust starts with giving; or, as risk management expert Peter Sandman said: 'The paradox of trust is that it builds faster when it isn't demanded.'[7]

Although some good texts have been published on the topic, the theory concerning this scarcest of resources appears underdeveloped.[8] Thus, leading corporations make their way into this unknown territory through experimentation, their experience providing others with a sense of the way ahead.[9] In this context, Jean-René Fourton, CEO of French chemicals and pharmaceutical company Rhône-Poulenc, expanded on the concept of vacuum management thus: '*Le vide* [the vacuum] has a huge function in the organization. If you don't leave *le vide*, you have no unexpected things, no creation. There are two types of management. You can try to design for everything, or you can leave *le vide* and say, "I don't know either; what do you think?"'[10]

Proper facilitation is at the core of dealing with these problems. The physical setting of the process can, for instance, also help create the right, relaxed environment to reduce apprehension: away from the workplace, no telephones, casual dress only, short agenda with lots of inefficient time built in, late night socializing: the list of dos and don'ts is predictable, though demanding. A number of companies have gone so far as to create separate physical surroundings for the reflective structure, eg the corporate 'university' or academy.

From a classical management perspective, such processes are, almost inevitably, very inefficient, with coworkers sharing responsibility for their own development as well as that of the institution. We feel, however, that this is a small price to pay to build the culture required for rethinking and subsequently renegotiating the terms of the personal contracts and, ultimately, assuring the organization's long-term success. The road ahead is demanding and, as Shell's Group Managing Director Jeroen van der Veer concluded, 'change cannot take place overnight'. Still, he feels there is no alternative:

> *Real and lasting change requires more than clear leadership from the top. For change to be truly effective, it has to be 'owned' by all of our staff, and to become an everyday part of our working lives. In this way we are seeking greater responsibility and accountability from all of our staff. In the future, there needs to be a greater and more deliberate overlap between our individual personal values and our business values. Our personal approach to the environment, for example, should be reflected in our business approach and vice versa. But realistically, this isn't going to happen overnight or by itself.*[11]

The theory underlying the use of reflective structures for the transition to a proactive response seems simple enough, but experience to date demonstrates how difficult the process is in practice.[12] Current state-of-the-art corporations have invested many years and considerable amounts – in the order of $100 million or more – to establish their corporate universities, for instance. Moreover, top managers must remember that they are instituting a continuous process which will demand their time on an ongoing basis. They must be willing to act as very visible integrators of the active and reflective structures, spending significant time being sparring partners. Again, however, despite the apparently high cost, through its co-creation by excited and trust-based learning communities throughout the organization, the reflective structure is the only manner of unlocking the potential of a proactive response.

ANCHORING RENEGOTIATED CONTRACT TERMS

Eventually all reflection on personal as well as corporate attitudes and values should result in behavioural change, ie a transformation in the active mode of working. Time and again, experience shows that making change come about is difficult, but making it last is even more so. When the novelty of the transition to a proactive response has worn off and immediate pressures from the active structure demand attention, the priority given to the reflective mode, with its emphasis on joint thrill building, often fades.

Therefore, neither management nor coworkers can be satisfied with the renegotiation of the social paragraphs of the personal contracts alone. In order to assure the proper anchoring of the intended values and attitudes throughout the company, they have to be incorporated in the daily interactions of coworkers – ie in the psychological and formal paragraphs of the personal contracts. In the next sections we discuss two aspects that require attention in this respect.

First, although the main instruments for anchoring are the so-called 'hard S's' – organizational structure, systems and skills – these cannot be separated from the 'soft S's', which form an integral part of the organizational culture. Indeed, if top management is truly committed to making the transition to a proactive response it should, as part of its preparations, redefine the corporate culture.

Second, we want to highlight a management tool – the tailoring of physical facilities – which is no panacea, but is of considerable significance in anchoring the intended behavioural change and is often ignored by change managers.

Redefining corporate culture

Ultimately, the behavioural change arising from the transition to a proactive response has to be reflected in the corporate culture – ie in 'the way we do things around here'. With the passage of time, top management should not have to steer and reward special action programmes, since the behaviour should be fully internalized by coworkers (Box 9.2).

Box 9.2 Learned behaviour

'I'm fascinated with the concept of distinctions that transform people,' said Monsanto's CEO Robert Shapiro. 'Once you learn certain things – once you learn to ride a bike, say – you life has changed forever. You can't unlearn it. For me, sustainability is one of those distinctions. Once you get it, it changes how you think. A lot of our people have been infected by this way of seeing the world. It's becoming automatic. It's just part of who you are.'[a]

Ninety-nine per cent of the decisions each of us takes are indeed taken without conscious thought. At some stage of our personal development we learnt some behaviour that, for instance, our parents, teachers or bosses thought was appropriate. To be a respected member of a desirable group, we refrain from some actions and overdo others. Thus we adapt our 'soft S's – style, staff (ie aspirations) and shared values – to suit the group's culture. Hardly questioning the driving forces behind our behaviour, we 'behave' ourselves: our behaviour has become learned.

As we grow up, we also come to recognize and interpret the stimuli in our everyday activities. Easily accessible rubbish bins or waste-paper baskets, for instance, stimulate us to collect and separate waste. After a while, their use becomes part of our routine, second nature to us. Through learning we have developed a mental model that, when called upon, allows us to instantaneously generate an acceptable option that with minimal study and validation provides a basis for action. In this manner, such action requires so little share-of-mind that we can handle multiple tasks simultaneously.

This is extremely useful, as it allows us to concentrate on activities that do require conscious thought, such as talking with others. Thus, we attain something remarkable: we can talk and drive a car at the same time. Still, even experienced drivers stop talking when they get lost in an unknown town, or the traffic conditions change dramatically.

a *Harvard Business Review*, January–February 1997, p79ff

Ideally, the organizational and physical stimuli should automatically, as if by reflex, produce the desired will to act, therefore requiring minimal managerial attention. For this reason the renegotiation process must address hard 7-S elements that play an important part in anchoring the desired behaviour: structure, systems and skills. But even this will almost certainly not be sufficient: the culture itself must be transformed, including its soft elements such as style, staff (ie expectations) and shared values.

Most major corporations today are inadequately prepared for this challenging task. Historically, their focus has been on action: their entire culture is tailored for either effectiveness or efficiency. Such a fundamentally active culture is generally not very receptive to unusual ideas like those needed for anchoring the change to a proactive response. As Levi Strauss's Robert Haas put it:

> *It's difficult to unlearn behaviours that made us successful in the past: speaking rather than listening; valuing people like yourself over people of different genders or from different cultures; doing things on your own rather than collaborating; making the decision yourself instead of asking different people for their perspectives. There's a whole range of behaviours that were functional in the old hierarchical organization that are dead wrong in the flatter, more responsive organization that we're seeking to become.*[13]

The problem, in essence, is that the transition to a proactive response requires all coworkers to think for themselves. The culture of the reflective structure has to stimulate this concentration on the self. To ensure a strong anchoring of the behavioural change throughout the corporation, the culture then has to emphasize self-control and mutual trust. Top management must ask its coworkers to share responsibility, to become partners in the daily process of making the joint vision come alive. Their personal interests must remain continuously aligned with those of the corporation, and vice versa.

As a virtual precondition for this, all members of the partnership must be willing to accept certain restrictions on their individual decision-making as a small price to pay for the common good. In a nutshell, this amounts to freedom within bounds. In terms of the 7-S framework, the culture thus would be characterized by the cooperation of individuals who feel proud to be the guardians of the shared values and trust others to feel this way as well. Indeed, they would be co-responsible, in a bottom–up process, for adding meaning to the endgame of sustainability. They must be alert to opportunities for renewing the shared values and making them come alive in their own positions within the company. The structure of the reflective mode of working is that of a franchise: each member is a direct beneficiary of the joint efforts but also must contribute to the collective wellbeing. Pride and dedication are key words for ultimate success.

The development of such a partnership culture presents a significant challenge. Behaviours typical to active structures are not always useful in reflective ones, and top management and coworkers alike thus have to learn. The idea of managers 'bossing' coworkers about is of course obsolete, to give an example. There is a second issue, however, that makes top management's predicament tougher in this respect. Earlier, in Chapter 7, we suggested that people naturally find it difficult to live and work in two cultures simultaneously. The need to switch from one set of S's to another is extremely demanding.[14] As Robert Haas says, learned behaviours, for instance, do not automatically apply: many traditionally non-conscious actions have to be thought through again.

We feel strongly, however, that there is no alternative to the reflective partnership culture for leaders who are serious about making the transition to a proactive response, and are thus intent on renegotiating the personal contracts of their coworkers. Since a reflective culture is indispensable, top management is obliged to adapt the culture of its active structure to become more closely parallel with that of a partnership.

For large corporations especially, this transition may be major. Ultimately, as Michael Jung suggests, such an active partnership culture is characterized by coworkers who function in a decentralized network made up of relatively small units, with a high degree of freedom of action.[15] Their motto might be said to be 'self-responsibility and accountability in the pursuit of general corporate objectives'. In such a culture, where all are responsible for the whole, no one can take his or her eye off the ball; all must be continuously alert to all possible important signals and respond immediately. When success or failure in the increasingly competitive product and labour markets is a matter of inches or seconds, team pride and mutual trust are crucial to winning.

It is easy to recognize that such partnership communities would readily satisfy many of the needs of the fourth-echelon climbers among a corporation's stakeholders. The word 'self' returns in its guise of responsibility and accountability. Still, the essence of the partnership culture is in that other word: trust. If the quality of the interaction among the members of an institution does not surpass the trust threshold, the organization will not develop from fragmented (groups of) individuals into idea-driven communities.

As a possible tribute to corporate foresight, many business leaders have already taken steps towards the establishment of such a culture in their companies. Indeed, virtually without exception, large corporations have implemented major changes in their organizational architecture. The number of layers has been reduced, authority has been delegated downwards and operational freedom greatly expanded, thus creating more rewarding opportunities within newly-flattened and open networks of small and autonomous units. Indeed, their corporate architectures are increasingly based on the sort of franchised partnerships discussed above. Even share ownership has been extended to cover a much larger group of stakeholders.

These all are significant moves in the right direction, but they are not sufficient to create the inspired partnership communities that can make a proactive response come alive in a meaningful manner. For instance, many have not come close to completing the task of breaking down the thousands of small hierarchies at all levels of the company to allow for true partnerships.

All in all, it is clear that the initial change is easier to realize than its anchoring. Management is faced with a series of tough questions in this regard: Do we have to go that far, or could we limit ourselves to renegotiating the personal contracts of our fourth-echelon climbers or, even more restricted, of the path-finders among them? Should we consider much greater structural disaggregation to create still smaller units, which would provide the rewarding opportunities our coworkers want? Could it be that these units would be better suited than the more amorphous corporation, as a whole, to serve as the basis for the inspired communities we are pursuing? If so, what's the point of having the corporation in the first place?

The answers to such questions can obviously have radical implications. More so than in the past, companies have to be based on values and visions that coworkers can warm to and identify with, all the more so when pursuing a proactive approach. They also have to provide the partnership culture that allows a mutual trust to grow. Only then can a joint thrill building lead to the desired inspired communities.

Let's leave the closing words on this issue to Shell's Mark Moody-Stuart:

> *If you run a global organization that is decentralized and very local in many areas, you can't control and direct. The only way of making sure that an individual on the spot at any one time makes what, from a corporate point of view, would be the right decision is to share common values. It's a question of trust, really. I know what other people are doing out there, and those people know, as a matter of trust, what I am going to do. If I have a discussion with someone – a head of state, say – to me it's of critical importance that people all around the Shell world know, on the basis of our values, what sort of things I am going to say and how I will behave, and vice versa.*
>
> *One of the reasons I have stayed with Shell all these years is that I have never found a conflict between my personal values and those of Shell. People here can always challenge things on the basis of values.*
>
> *That will be very important for us in this process of change. If we talk about sustainable development, our policies on investment and everything else will have to be congruent with that; otherwise it will fall apart.* [16]

Tailoring physical facilities

We have seen that a transition to a small-scale active culture will require expert application of anchoring instruments like structure and systems, and skill building. In this regard, we again refer the reader to the change management literature. Most of these analyses, however, neglect or under-rate the role of the third instrument:

namely, the use of physical stimuli, notably physical facilities, to anchor change. As Sir Winston Churchill put it: 'We shape our buildings and then our buildings shape our lives.'

Physical facilities are of course part of any personal contract. For instance, the formal paragraphs describe, often in great detail, the square-footage of office space and the size of desks. More importantly, the psychological paragraphs incorporate the coworker's 'rights', ranging from a window with a view to an individual space in the cafeteria or art works on the wall. Any manager who has attempted to take away these rights without proper renegotiation recognizes the problems involved.

Nevertheless, this aspect is often under-rated. Actually, physical facilities, more than any other instrument, offer an inherent possibility of influencing the behaviour of large groups of people on a permanent, low-maintenance basis. Decorated spaces make people feel more comfortable than undecorated spaces; pleasant environments increase their willingness to help each other.[17] Having a view over a natural setting helps people cope with stress. The physical facilities also have an impact on external stakeholders: as houses reflect their residents, so too do office buildings, warehouses and factory sites.

Still, business people who excel at consumer marketing and make extensive use of product design to provide a specific stimulus in a group of customers rarely apply their skills to induce or maintain proactive behaviour among their coworkers. They also, of course, miss an opportunity to communicate to external stakeholders what their corporation is all about.

The simplest – but admittedly also fairly ineffective – way to stimulate the will to act among coworkers is by urging them through reminders and prompts. We are all familiar with environmental slogans such as 'only you can prevent forest fires', 'every litter bit helps' (on rubbish bins) or – in many guises – 'empty rooms love darkness'. But these can only have an impact when such cues are given as the person is considering a specific action and an alternative is readily available – eg signs on the lawn saying 'We frown on those who trample the grass', or next to the light switch reminding people to turn the lights off on their way out.[18]

The results are even better, however, when a signal provides an immediate feedback on (in-) action. A dripping tap causes most people to close the valve, not just because of the disturbance but also because the sound provides a reminder of senseless waste. Far fewer people have the same reaction when they leave the lights on or door open when leaving a room. Apparently, emissions of light and heat are not recognized as being as wasteful as a dripping tap. Perhaps this would be otherwise if a meter ticked loudly or the lights dimmed briefly every time a kilowatt-hour were consumed – the use of such 'econometers' has prompted motorists to drive with greater fuel-efficiency.

If people rather than a mechanical device are the source of the reminder, then the impact on behaviour is stronger yet. Family members or colleagues telling others to close the door or turn off the lights are more effective at cutting consumption than the best insulation or the highest efficiency heaters.

Peer pressure can in fact go a long way towards influencing people. If a specific behaviour is accepted as the norm – for instance, when well-known public figures or, in a corporate setting, the perceived leaders of a group are willing to serve as path-finders – most other members will follow. Fairly quickly, the group as a whole, unthinkingly and without personally-felt sacrifices, will behave accordingly. For many years, for instance, consumers were stimulated to take glass bottles back to shops using the incentive of a return deposit. When the policy became uneconomic and was aborted, the return-your-glass reflex was sufficiently internalized to make the glass collection bins a surprising success. In The Netherlands, over 80 per cent of all bottles are now collected in this way.

Management must therefore create the physical conditions that stimulate the anchoring of a proactive response among its coworkers. Earlier we spoke of the impact that the shaping of offices and factories can have on those working in them. If every aspect of a building is in line with eco-efficiency – if, as in green buildings,[19] the internal atmosphere radiates care; if factors such as the impact on social renewal, social cohesion and community identity are taken into account in the location and design of new buildings, then there is little doubt that coworkers will register the message and, over a period of time, adapt their behaviour.

Physical facilities for the reflective structure are often specifically designed for reflective use. They promote a horizontal interaction and a relaxed atmosphere. As we've seen, leading corporations are increasingly experimenting with corporate universities to stimulate the matching culture of the normal operational organization, ie the active structure. The challenge of the proactive response will be to minimize the gap between the two structures: coworkers should not have to live in two worlds.

A corporate environment offers the advantages of a close community and close control: the possibilities for creating the right physical conditions for anchoring the will to act in a desired manner are thus ideal. Typically, however, the responsibility for much of the organizational infrastructure – usually with the exception of top structure, corporate logos and new headquarters – is delegated far down the ranks. Top management thus deprives itself of one of the most powerful change instruments that, because of its scarce and unsophisticated use by most companies, provides ample opportunity for competitive differentiation.

GETTING STARTED WITH ABC

Designing and implementing a programme for institutionalizing a reflective structure (to facilitate contract renegotiations) while adapting the active structure to anchor the modified contract terms is undoubtedly a huge challenge. The task is further complicated by the fact that top management must allow things to happen – ie it must relinquish control over much of the developments and trust its coworkers, especially the path-finders among them, to take a lead. There is perhaps consolation in the thought, however, that top management's predicament can best be compared with the one we all face when organizing a party. The hosts cannot order people to have fun, but they can definitely help by selecting the guests and orchestrating the conditions – setting, choice of music, drinks and snacks – to suit their probable needs.

But companies don't have to do this from scratch, of course. The proactive response is the last in a sequence of responses, as we've seen. In order to make the transition to proactivity, a corporation must have successfully completed the transition to an integrated response. To the necessary degree, it must also have networked itself into the various types of partnership that are required for the 3E implementation of such a response. Managers as well as many coworkers, therefore, should at this point have broad experience with environmental change. Indeed, they likely have a solid understanding of the most probable developments in the environmental arena and are comfortable with the steering and rewarding instruments (see Box 6.1).

But as Shell's Chairman Mark Moody-Stuart said, when referring to this situation: 'We have done the relatively easy parts of the job, by developing some key management tools to change the way we make decisions. You would expect no less from a group with a commitment to thoroughness and professionalism – but the real challenge is in making this come alive in the hearts and minds of all Shell people.'[20] To shape and internalize a proactive response, top managers now have to further hone their skills in applying the inspiring and anchoring instruments. In partnering, they also have to reach out to a more diverse group which, at a minimum, includes all internal stakeholders.

The proactive response itself requires what we call an aspirations based change (ABC) programme. This builds on the elements of the EMP, but these must now be further perfected to allow for the renegotiation and anchoring of the personal contracts of pivotal job holders. As we noted above, under a proactive response this means virtually all coworkers.

The ultimate objective of the ABC programme is the acceptance of new responsibilities as a normal part of the corporate culture. The combination of the appropriate stimuli and the essential will, skill and thrill building, as discussed in Chapter 5, requires real top management dedication in terms of leadership and interaction. Inspiration and trust prompt people to climb to the fourth echelon of their pyramid of needs, while thrill building encourages coworkers, the path-finders in particular, to take initiatives of their own, and thus ultimately enable top management to lead from behind.

It is against this background that we present points to think about, or 'thought starters', in the following sections. We use the term 'thought starters' purposefully, since the full shape of an ABC programme for a specific company can only be determined through the direct interaction of the top management team with its coworkers.

ABC methodology

If making the transition to a proactive response is comparable to organizing a party, the ABC methodology is about actually getting the festivities rolling. This is especially true during the initial establishment of the reflective structure. MIT's Donald Schön uses the metaphors of a jazz combo and a good conversation – both important ingredients of a good party – to describe the delicate balance that has to be struck between up-front orchestration and improvisation (Box 9.3). As we've seen, it is up to top management to select a theme, ie to provide its coworkers with an initial endgame perspective. Each participant, on the basis of her or his own expertise and aspirations, is then invited to build on this foundation and contribute to making it come alive and gain shared significance.

Practically, this means an ABC programme must satisfy three criteria. First, it must 'stretch' pivotal job holders, encouraging them to look beyond today's clouds to the far-away horizon, and to think about what the company could be in, say, ten years' time. Second, it must ensure these job holders keep their collective feet on the ground, so that the needs at lower echelons of the corporate pyramid are not neglected, and any new thinking is based on a realistic assessment of current business positions and skills. Third, the pivotal job holders must buy in to the endgame through an active participation in the reflective structure. Clearly a 'classical' strategy process, as described in Chapter 6 for making the transition to an integrated response, would not satisfy these three criteria.

The ABC methodology involves a funnel-like mechanism. It begins with a broad-brush sketch by top management of the endgame aspirations to be pursued and the associated change programme. Subsequently, it is narrowed down to a more detailed action plan in an interactive process between top and business unit/functional management, with the latter increasingly taking over the leadership. Finally, it narrows into a very specific action plan, in which the front-line takes on the operational lead.

Box 9.3 Organizing a party[a]

When good jazz musicians improvise together, they ... display reflection in action smoothly integrated into ongoing performance. Listening to themselves, they 'feel' where the music is going and adjust their playing accordingly. A figure announced by one performer will be taken up by another, elaborated, turned into a new melody. Each player makes on-line inventions and responds to surprises triggered by the inventions of the other players. But the collective process of musical invention is organized around an underlying structure. There is a common schema of meter, melody and harmonic development that gives the piece a predictable order. In addition, each player has at the ready a repertoire of musical figures around which he can weave variations as the opportunity arises. Improvisation consists in varying, combining and recombining a set of figures within a schema that gives coherence to the whole piece. As the musicians feel the directions in which the music is developing, they make new sense of it. They reflect-in-action on the music they are collectively making – though not, or course, in the medium of words.

Their process resembles the familiar patterns of everyday conversation. In a good conversation – in some respects predictable and in others not – participants pick up and develop themes of talk, each spinning out variations on his or her repertoire of things to say. Conversation is collective and verbal improvisation. At times it falls into conventional routines – the anecdote with side comments and reactions, for example, or debate – which develop according to a pace and rhythm of interaction that the participants seem, without conscious deliberation, to work out in common within the framework of an evolving division of labour. At other times there may be surprises, unexpected turns of phrase or directions of development to which participants invent on-the-spot responses. In such examples the participants are making something. Out of musical materials or themes of talk they make a piece of music or a conversation, an artefact with its own meaning and coherence. Their reflection-in-action is a reflective conversation with the materials of a situation – 'conversation', now, in a metaphorical sense. Each person carries out his own evolving role in the collective performance, 'listens' to the surprises – or, as I shall say, 'back talk' – that result from earlier moves, and responds through on-line production of new moves that give new meanings and directions to the development of the artefact. The process is reminiscent of Edmund Carpenter's description of the Eskimo sculptor patiently carving a reindeer bone, examining the gradually emerging shape, and finally exclaiming, 'Ah, seal!'

a Donald A Schön, *Educating the Reflective Practitioner* (Jossey-Bass, San Francisco; 1998) p30

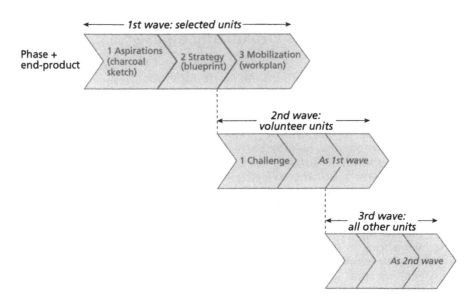

Figure 9.2 *Contours of ABC programme*

Whereas the initial vision development, ie the crystallization of the endgame, must be top–down, the change programme must take as its point of departure the frontline. Indeed, cultural change always starts from the needs and personal aspirations of the pivotal job holders nearest the frontline. As discussed in Chapter 5, higher echelons must add value by making these pivotal job holders success-ful in their efforts.

Clearly, this combination of top–down vision development and bottom–up implementation design adds significant complexity to the process. This problem is aggravated, particularly in large, diversified companies, by the risk of agenda overload among the STE staff and especially the pressing need to build momentum. As we noted earlier, one can expect that some 15 per cent of all coworkers, intent on pursuing a proactive response, will readily step forwards into the vacuum created by top management. Another 15 per cent will, for a variety of reasons, be unwilling, while about 70 per cent will prefer to wait and see. For top management, getting this last group moving may seem an impossible mission.

We have found that a three-wave approach to vacuum manage-ment (Figure 9.2) is an effective means of tackling this task. During a first wave, top management takes the lead in assessing the initial situation and the approximate implications of the conceivable long-term options, using these as the basis for drawing a sketch of the initial aspirations. This endgame model in turn provides the point of departure for three or four business unit management teams. These units are selected on the basis of the quality of their integrated response and the expectation that they comprise a relatively high percentage of potential path-finders. By managing these teams to be successful, whatever the cost, the corporate leadership hopes to bring forward the path-finders who, in turn, within their unit and during subsequent waves, can be instrumental in creating a vacuum for others to follow.

Thus, working in close interaction with top management in the reflective mode, business unit management is invited to turn the initial sketch of the endgame into an action plan. As we've seen, it is critical to the building of a thrill in their midst that their individual self-development visions should be aligned with those underlying the business, and with the organizational development perspectives held by top management. The interaction therefore must allow for, and actually invite, in-depth challenges to the initial model with such questions as: 'Suppose this is the endgame that we jointly may wish to pursue. What would it mean for you and for the way you do your job?' By making the endgame personally relevant to the coworkers, these can be drawn into generating and assessing options for action.

Coworkers will often be struck by the unprecedented nature of the process: for the first time they are not being told but asked what to do. They are also urged to consider their own position and aspirations, and how these might be interwoven with those of the model proposed by top management.

What must be realized is that solutions provided within the boundaries of an endgame can lead to incremental innovation. They offer an improvement on existing thinking, but do not result in new thinking. However, only new frameworks can lead to the generation of breakthrough responses allowing an organization to make a quantum leap. Therefore, it must be hoped that the path-finders not only find better options of their own to improve beyond top management's endgame perspective, but that they actually suggest that the corporate leaders themselves re-examine their story. Such an occurrence is often considered threatening by the corporate leadership, and receives a 'not-invented-here' cold shoulder. It might also force a repetition of earlier steps and therefore cause a delay. Still, this is how organizations learn, and ideally the input of the path-finders results in improved proposals which will be more quickly embraced at the next iteration.

The resulting action plan must eventually produce an assessment of medium-term strategic options and the tailoring of steering and rewarding instruments to the needs of pivotal job holders within the business and functional units affected. This plan is directly relevant to the active mode. However, as critical end-products of this second phase, the business unit managers, together with top management, should first produce a definition of the boundary conditions for the frontline mobilization in the reflective mode and, second, a proposal for the best way to anchor the renegotiated contracts in the everyday active structure. As a further by-product, the corporate STE staff must codify the thinking developed during the first wave, so that the other business units can build on the learning of their predecessors in the change process.

The final phase of the first wave then should represent the essence of vacuum management. With top management providing support and backing, it is now the selected business unit management teams that must lead their coworkers into behavioural change. Having fine-tuned the corporate mental model to their business environment as well as their personal aspirations, they now should use this basis for inviting their frontline coworkers to participate in the reflective mode. The rules of the game are the same as those they themselves experienced before, but the composition of the focus groups of pivotal job holders requires particular attention. In order to facilitate the renegotiation of personal contracts, such groups must be meaningful to the participants and their individual aspirations. They therefore should be neither too 'foreign' (ie too distant from the individual's perspective), nor too narrow (ie requesting input only on a person's operational expertise). The groups can stretch over multiple business units, as long as coworkers feel their input is valued and contributes to a better and more appreciated personal contract.

During the last phase of the first wave, top management can embark on the second wave. This involves inviting a larger group of volunteers from its business and functional units to step forward and repeat the three-phase process as indicated above. At this point, top management's initial model will probably have been refined and its wording improved.

Still, it is important that the aspirations of each specific unit be fine-tuned and, especially, the benefits of the bottom–up input from the management teams and their coworkers be incorporated into the process. The initially rough process and clumsy tools will have been improved both in terms of their effectiveness and efficiency. Thus, the time-span for the second wave's process probably can be shortened, and direct top management involvement reduced. The STE staff also will gain experience and confidence so that the support of external experts may be less necessary. Among the end-products of this second wave of perhaps ten business units would be a refined and tested manual.

The third wave involves rollout to remaining business units. Actually, in terms of vacuum management, it is more appropriate to talk about securing the 'buy-in' of these units. They must be drawn forward and develop their own strategies for dealing with contents as well as process. At the same time their more advanced sister units may already be well into the development of second and third generations of the model, geared to the needs of their business.

The overall ABC process may take as long as three to four years. During this period it should kick-start the transformation process, with each relevant unit having participated in at least one wave of reflective action. Undoubtedly, this will not be sufficient to realize the desired degree of alignment between the personal development visions of the individual pivotal job holders, and the corporate ones for business and organizational development. Behavioural change will, moreover, require a solid anchoring of the renegotiated contract terms. The ABC start thus has to be succeeded by a structural follow-up. Yet the improvements in the quality of a joint direction and of interaction within relevant communities will hopefully allow most pivotal job holders to cross the thresholds of inspiration and trust.

Clearly, leading such a programme sets high requirements for top management, especially regarding share of minds and energy. Sparking a thrill among coworkers drains energy that will flow back to the corporate leaders only after a period of time and proven success. Still, the final quote rightfully goes to one of the grandmasters of change, Jack Welch: 'Trust is enormously powerful in a corporation. People won't do their best unless they believe they'll be treated fairly – that there's no cronyism and everybody has a real shot. The only way I know to create that kind of trust is by laying out your values and then walking the talk. You've got to do what you say you'll do, consistently, over time.'[21]

***

Idea-driven communities evolve when the thrill factor takes over. People only get truly excited when the topic is real and relevant to them as well as to their business. Sustainable development, as discussed in this chapter, has this quality. When a flame is lit, the total becomes more than the sum of the parts and the members of the newly developing community will be willing to drop their traditional guards. Role conformity, which used to be necessary as a stabilizing factor, no longer suffocates creativity, and the path-finders are free to break away from the mental models of the past and contribute to a workable model for the future. Individual pivotal job holders may then seek self-actualization through the meshing of their personal development and business endeavours.

EPILOGUE

Management is about people and what motivates them. Whoever best satisfies the needs of customers and stakeholders – shareholders, coworkers and host communities – can gain an advantage over competitors. We have argued in this book that the environmental dimension of doing business offers just such a differentiation opportunity. A 'right' or 'wrong' management response can elicit positive or negative public reactions and may affect consumer behaviour. More importantly perhaps, a correct response can be a major factor in aligning the personal objectives of stakeholders with those of 'their' company and vice-versa. The associated thrill can turn a fragmented group of individuals into an inspired partnership. The purpose of this book has been to support top management in responding correctly.

In fact, a growing number of senior managers worldwide are ready and willing to give it a go. But their task, though exciting, is also sometimes complex. To assist them, we have offered the insights and the tools they need, particularly for those making the transition to an integrated or even a proactive environmental management response. Still, they must expect to write part of their own manual: there is a lot to learn yet – for all of us.

There is no single path to excellence in environmental management. As we've seen, the needs of stakeholders, both internal and external, vary from one company to the next and from one generation to the next. There are 'a thousand shades of green' as suggested by our title. Eventually, however, for harmony to reign, all stakeholders must be able to recognize their personal story in the one told by the leaders. The thousand shades of green then together colour the company's path towards sustainability. It is up to top management to lead the way.

NOTES

INTRODUCTION

1 Throughout this book we use the terms 'NGOs' and 'environmental organizations' interchangeably although, strictly speaking, the term 'NGOs' encompasses a broader range of organizations, including, for example, industry associations.

2 The positions we attribute to those people, primarily business executives, whom we quote are those that they held at the time they were speaking or writing.

3 Antony Burgmans, speech at WWF Conference, Lisbon, 25 September 1998.

CHAPTER 1

1 Abraham H Maslow, *Motivation and Personality* (Harper and Row, New York; 1954); see also Abraham H Maslow with Deborah C Stephens and Gary Heil, *Maslow on Management* (John Wiley & Sons, New York; 1998) and Deborah C Stevens (ed), *The Maslow Business Reader* (John Wiley & Sons, New York; 2000).

2 See, for instance, Peter J Makin, Cary L Cooper and Charles J Cox, *Organizations and the Psychological Contract: Managing People at Work* (Praeger, Westport, Connecticut; 1996), p113ff.

3 For a historic review of the global shaping of the environmental arena see Clive Ponting, *A Green History of the World* (Penguin Books, London; 1992).

4 Donald Kaniaru, 'First Anpez Lecture on the Environment and Development', Port Harcourt, Nigeria, 18 March 1998.

5 The Dutch experience, arguably the most advanced in this regard, is extensively described by Paul E de Jongh with Seán Captain in *Our Common Journey: A Pioneering Approach to Cooperative Environmental Management* (Zed Books, London; 1999).

6 World Commission on Environment and Development, *Our Common Future* (Oxford University Press, Oxford; 1987), p43.

7 We return to the concept of sustainable development and its implications for business leadership in Chapters 2, 8 and 9.

8 *The McKinsey Quarterly*, 1993, No 4, p53ff.

9 This systems-based approach is discussed in great detail in, for instance, Richard Welford (ed), *Corporate Environmental Management: Systems and Strategies* (Earthscan, London; 1996).

10 Jan-Olof Willums, *The Greening of Enterprise: Business Leaders Speak Out* (International Chamber of Commerce, Paris; 1990), p60.

11 Bruce Smart, *Beyond Compliance: A New Industry View of the Environment* (World Resources Institute, Washington, DC; 1992), p102.

12 *Harvard Business Review*, November–December 1995, p195.

13 ibid, p196.

14 Also called the 'ecological footprint' or 'Rücksack' (backpack). See, for instance, Friedrich Schmidt-Bleek, *Wieviel Umwelt braucht der Mensch?: MIPS – das Maß für ökologisches Wirtschaften* (Birkhäuser Verlag, Berlin; 1994) and Claude Fussler with Peter James, *Driving Eco-Innovation* (Pitman Publishing, London; 1996), p160ff.

15 See, for instance, Ernst von Weizsäcker, Amory B Lovins and L Hunter Lovins, *Factor Four* (Earthscan, London; 1997).

16 ibid, p224.

17 Bruce Smart, *Beyond Compliance*, p245.

18 *Harvard Business Review*, January–February 1997, p83.

19 Specifically, the surveys were designed to benchmark the relative stages of environmental management and to identify perception gaps between management layers. Typically, a brief questionnaire was distributed to over 100 members, representing the top three or four managerial layers in the organization. The results showed this approach to be a highly effective and efficient means of identifying barriers to change within companies and differences in the perceptions of managers, both horizontally (ie between units) and vertically (ie between layers).

20 Similar conclusions were reached by Arthur D Little; see, for instance, Management Consultancies Association (MCA), UK plc on the World Stage in 2010, *Book 4: Business and the Environment* (MCA, London; 2000), p69ff.

CHAPTER 2

1 Personal communication. See also Ulrich Steger, *Umweltmanagement: Erfahrungen und Instrumente einer umweltorientierten Unternehmenstrategie* (Frankfurt Allgemeine Zeitung für Deutschland, Frankfurt am Main, and Gabler, Wiesbaden; 1993), p237ff.

2 Jan-Olof Willums and Ulrich Goluke, *From Ideas to Action* (ICC Publishing and Ad Notam Gyldendal, Oslo; 1992).

3 Stephan Schmidheiny with the World Business Council for Sustainable Development, *Changing Course* (MIT Press, Cambridge, Massachusetts; 1992).

4 See, for instance, Claude Fussler with Peter James, *Driving Eco-Innovation*, and Livio D DeSimone and Frank Popoff with the World Business Council for Sustainable Development, *Eco-Efficiency: The Business Link to Sustainable Development* (MIT Press, Cambridge, Massachusetts; 1997).

5 Charles Handy, *The Hungry Spirit* (Broadway Books, New York; 1998), p158.

6 See, for instance, the constructively critical analyses presented by Frances Cairncross, *Green, Inc* (Earthscan, London; 1995); John Elkington, *Cannibals With Forks: The Triple Bottom Line of 21st Century Business* (Capstone, Oxford; 1997); and Carl Frankel, *In Earth's Company: Business, Environment and the Challenge of Sustainability* (New Society Publishers, Gabriola Island BC, Canada; 1998).

7 Also see Jan-Olof Willums with the World Business Council for Sustainable Development, *The Sustainable Business Challenge: A Briefing for Tomorrow's Business Leaders* (Greenleaf Publishing, Sheffield, UK; 1998), p37ff.

8 For relevant thoughts on this and on the associated subject of the decrease in cultural diversity, see, for instance, Norman Myers, *Ultimate Security: The Environmental Basis of Political Stability* (WW Norton, New York; 1993), and Daniel Druckman, *Global Environmental Change: Understanding the Human Dimensions* (National Academy Press, Washington, DC; 1992), p159.

9 Pieter Winsemius and Walter Hahn, *Columbia Journal of World Business*, Fall/Winter 1992, p248.

10 For a comprehensive and authoritative pilot analysis of global ecosystems by the UN Development Programme, the World Bank and the World Resources Institute, see *World Resources Report 2000–2001 – People and Ecosystems: The Fraying Web of Life* (World Resources Institute, Washington, DC; 2000). Insightful environmentalist perspectives on some of the major issues are provided by John Elkington, *Cannibals with Forks*, and Jonathon Porritt, *Playing Safe: Science and the Environment* (Thames & Hudson, New York; 2000).

11 See, for instance, Peter Schwartz, *The Art of the Long View* (Doubleday, New York; 1991), Joseph F Coates, John B Mahaffie and Andy Hines, *2025: Scenarios of US and Global Society Reshaped by Science and Technology* (Oakhill Press, Greensboro, North Carolina; 1997), and Gill Ringland, *Scenario Planning: Managing for the Future* (John Wiley & Sons, New York; 1998).

12 Allan Hammond, *Which World? Scenarios for the 21st Century* (Island Press, Washington, DC; 1998).

13 World Business Council for Sustainable Development, *Exploring Sustainable Development: WBCSD Global Scenarios 2000–2050* (WBCSD, Paris; 1997); see also Phil Watts and Ged Davis, *A Commitment to Sustainable Development* (WBCSD, London; 1998). Building on the expertise of its industrial membership the WBCSD has also initiated topical studies such as *Biotechnology Scenarios, 2000–2050: Using the Future to Explore the Present* (WBCSD, Conches-Geneva, Switzerland; 2000) as well as comprehensive sector studies in, for instance, the cement, mining and pulp and paper industries.

14 See, for instance, World Resources Institute, *Frontiers of Sustainability: Environmentally Sound Agriculture, Forestry, Transportation, and Power Production* (Island Press, Washington, DC; 1997), and the many other publications by this and other environmental think-tanks.

15 *Business Week*, May 3, 1999.

16 *Green Futures*, September–October 2000, p22.
17 Iain Anderson, speech at Rabobank International Conference, Zeist, The Netherlands; May 29, 1998.
18 Also known as endocrine blockers or pseudo-oestrogens; see Theo Colborn, Dianna Dumanoski and John Peterson Myers, *Our Stolen Future: Are We Threatening Our Fertility, Intelligence and Survival?* (EP Dutton, New York; 1996).
19 See, for instance, Philip Ball, *H₂O: A Biography of Water* (Weidenfeld & Nicolson, London; 1999), and *Industry, Fresh Water and Sustainable Development* (WBCSD, Conches-Geneva, Switzerland, and UNEP Nairobi, Kenya; 1998).
20 See, for instance, Sylvia A Earle, *Sea Change: A Message of the Oceans* (GP Putnam's Sons, New York; 1995).
21 On the use of competitors' experience see, for instance, Francisco Szekely, Thomas Vollman and Annette Ebbinghaus, *Environmental Benchmarking: Becoming Green and Competitive* (Stanley Thornes, Cheltenham, UK; 1996).
22 Noah Walley and Bradley Whitehead, *Harvard Business Review*, May–June 1994, p46.
23 Speech to Society of Automotive Engineers, The Greenbrier, October 14, 2000.

CHAPTER 3

1 Public relations expert Bruce Harrison wrote a highly readable book *Going Green: How to Communicate Your Company's Environmental Commitment* (Business One Irwin, Homewood, IL; 1993) on relating to the news media, investors, and especially the government and NGOs. The importance of understanding other players' interests and of equity concerns in conflict resolution are vividly described by Michael W Morris and Steven K Su, *American Behavioral Scientist*, Vol 42, No 8, May 1999, pp1322–1349.
2 Also see Anne Grafé-Buckens and Anna-Fay Hinton, *Business Strategy and the Environment*, July 1998, p124, and Jacqueline Cramer, *Business Strategy and the Environment*, July 1998, p162.
3 Pieter Winsemius, *Guests in Our Own Home* (McKinsey & Company, Amsterdam; 1990).
4 Ulrich Steger actually recommends quantifying the PLC curve on the basis of the number of media references to the issue; see Steger, *Umweltmanagement: Erfahrungen und Instrumente einer umweltorientierten Unternehmenstrategie* (Frankfurt Allgemeine Zeitung für Deutschland, Frankfurt am Main and Gabler, Wiesbaden; 1993), p249.
5 Rachel Carson, *Silent Spring* (Houghton Mifflin, Boston; 1962), and Donella H Meadows, Dennis L Meadows, Jørgen Randers and William W Behrens III, *The Limits to Growth* (Universe Books, New York; 1972).
6 A more detailed discussion of the interaction between business and NGOs is provided by Matthias Winter and Ulrich Steger, *Managing Outside Pressure: Strategies for Preventing Corporate Disasters* (John Wiley & Sons, Chichester, UK; 1998).

7   See, for instance, Ruud Pleune, *Strategies of Dutch Environmental Organizations* (International Books, Utrecht, The Netherlands; 1997).

8   See, for instance, Monroe Friedman, *Journal of Social Issues*, Vol 51, No 4, 1995, p197.

9   For an in-depth treatment of the development of the US environmental movement, see Philip Shabecoff, *A Fierce Green Fire* (Hill and Wang, New York; 1993).

10 Paul C Stern, Oran R Young and Daniel Druckman (eds), *Global Environmental Change: Understanding the Human Dimensions* (National Academy Press, Washington, DC; 1992), p145.

11 See Steger, *Umweltmanagement*, p95ff.

12 See, for instance, Robert Repetto, Roger C Dower, Robin Jenskins and Jacqueline Geoghegan, *Green Fees: How a Tax Shift Can Work for the Environment and the Economy* (World Resources Institute, Washington, DC; 1992); Tim O'Riordan, *Ecotaxation* (Earthscan, London; 1996); and OECD, *Environmental Taxes and Green Tax Reform* (OECD, Paris; 1997).

13 See, for instance, André de Moor and Peter Clamai, *Subsidizing Unsustainable Development: Undermining the Earth with Public Funds* (Institute for Research on Public Expenditure, The Hague, and Earth Council, San José, Costa Rica; 1997).

14 See, for instance, Huey D Johnson, *Green Plans: Greenprint for Sustainability* (University of Nebraska Press, Lincoln, Nebraska; 1995); and De Jongh and Captain, *Our Common Journey*.

15 See, for instance, Marian R Chertow and Daniel C Esty, *Thinking Ecologically* (Yale University Press, New Haven; 1997).

16 David W Pearce and Jeremy J Warford, *World Without End: Economics, Environment, and Sustainable Development* (Oxford University Press, New York; 1993), Chapters 7–10.

17 Also see Raymond Vernon, *Environment* (June 1993), p13ff.

18 Ans Kolk, *Economics of Environmental Management* (Pearson Education, Harlow, Essex, UK; 2000), p33ff. Hans Grünfeld, in his doctoral thesis *Creating Favorable Conditions for International Environmental Change through Knowledge and Negotiation* (Delft University Press, Delft, The Netherlands; 1999), skilfully applies the lessons learned from the Rhine Action Programme and the Second Sulphur Protocol to provide a vivid insight into the intricacies of inter-national policy-making.

19 For in-depth treatises on international environmental policy-making, see RE Munn, JWM la Rivière and N van Lookeren Campagne, *Policy Making in an Era of Global Environmental Change* (Kluwer Academic Publishers, Dordrecht, The Netherlands; 1996); the publications of The Royal Institute of International Affairs, for instance Caroline Thomas, *The Environment in International Relations* (The Royal Institute of International Affairs, London; 1992) and Tony Brenton, *The Greening of Machiavelli* (Earthscan, London; 1994). Insider accounts of specific issues may add to a further understanding of the intricacies of the inter-national arena, eg Richard E Benedick, *Ozone Diplomacy* (Harvard University Press, Cambridge, Massachusetts; 1991); and Jim MacNeill, Pieter Winsemius and Tazio Yakushiji, *Beyond Interdependence* (Oxford University Press, New York; 1991).

CHAPTER 4

1   *Tomorrow*, March–April 1998, p19.
2   *Sustainable Strategies for Value Creation: Reflections from a Learning Journey* (The Performance GroupOslo, Norway; 1998), p30.
3   Arthur D Little in *Prism*, Fourth Quarter, 1998, p22ff.
4   See, for instance, Karl H Dreborg, 'The essence of backcasting', *Futures* No 28, p813. A fascinating illustration of this technique is also provided in Paul Weaver, Leo Jansen, Geert van Grootveld, Egbert van Spiegel and Philip Vergragt, *Sustainable Technology Development* (Greenleaf Publishing, Sheffield, UK; 2000) where, taking a sustainable future vision as a starting point, it is used to develop the contours of a medium-term research programme.
5   Jacqueline Cramer 'Philips sound and vision', in Pier Vellinga, Frans Berkhout and Joyeeta Gupta (eds), *Managing a Material World* (Kluwer Academic Publishers, Dordrecht, The Netherlands; 1998), p243, and Op Weg naar Duurzaam, *Ondernemen* (SMO, The Hague; 1999).
6   Private communication.
7   Smart, *Beyond Compliance*, p245.
8   *USA Today*, December 9, 1992.
9   Private communication.
10 We have not included the business opportunities that may arise from selling environmental products and/or services, as these involve no management trade-offs between environmental yield and economic impact: strategic decisions are motivated by economic considerations only.
11 *The Columbia Journal of World Business*, Summer 1993, p9.
12 The eco-efficiency concept was introduced by Schmidheiny and the Business Council for Sustainable Development; see Schmidheiny et al, *Changing Course*, p10. See also Fussler and James, *Driving Eco-Innovation*; DeSimone et al, Eco-Efficiency; Von Weizsäcker et al, *Factor Four*; OECD, *Eco-Efficiency* (OECD, Paris; 1998); and Judith E M Klostermann, Arnold Tukker, Jacqueline M Cramer, Adrie van Dam and Bernhard L van der Ven, *Product Innovation and Eco-Efficiency* (Kluwer Academic Publishers, Dordrecht, The Netherlands; 1998).
13 See, for instance, Josephine Chinying Lang and Andrew Chinpeng Ho, 'Virtual teams for corporate environmental excellence', in John Moxen and Peter A Strachan (eds), *Managing Green Teams* (Greenleaf Publishing, Sheffield, UK; 1998), p237ff.
14 Friedrich Schmidt-Bleek, *Wieviel Umwelt braucht der Mensch?*, Chapter 5. Similarly, Ernst von Weizsäcker et al, in *Factor Four*, make a convincing case for the need for greater energy efficiency and the many opportunities for doing so.
15 James Maxwell and Forrest Briscoe, *Business Strategy and the Environment*, November 1997, p283.
16 See, for instance, John Elkington and Julia Hailes, *Green Consumer Guide: From Shampoo to Champagne, High-Street Shopping for a Better Environment* (Gollancz, London; 1988), and *Manual 2000: Life Choices for the Future You Want* (Hodder & Stoughton, London; 1998).

17 IVA, McKinsey and the WWF, *Environmental Management: From Regulatory Demands to Strategic Business Opportunities* (IVA: Royal Academy of Engineering Sciences, Stockholm; 1995), p85ff. A variety of textbooks provide the interested reader greater depth. See, for instance, Jacquelyn A Ottman, *Green Marketing: Challenges and Opportunities for the New Marketing Age* (NTC Publishing, Lincolnwood, Illinois; 1992), and Martin Charter, *Greener Marketing: A Responsible Approach to Business* (Greenleaf Publishing, Sheffield, UK; 1992).

18 The debate about the economic advantages and disadvantages of advanced environmental policies is also heated and inconclusive at the macroeconomic level. Among the optimists are former US Vice-President Al Gore, *Earth in Balance: Ecology and the Human Spirit* (Penguin Books, New York; 1993) and strategy guru Michael Porter, *Scientific American*, April 1991, p168. Porter writes that 'the conflict between environmental protection and economic competitiveness is a false dichotomy' (p168). On the other hand, as recently as 1998, Shell's Chairman Mark Moody-Stuart noted that his peers in other large multinationals thought Shell management had lost its head when it decided to become more deeply concerned with environmental and social issues. *Financial Times*, January 19, 1998.

19 Richard Ford, 'Green Marketing', in Dominik Koechlin and Kaspar Müller (eds), *Green Business Opportunities: The Profit Potential* (Financial Times/Pitman Publishing, London; 1992), p68.

20 See, for instance, Jed Greer and Kenny Bruno, *Greenwash: The Reality Behind Corporate Environmentalism* (The Apex Press, New York; 1997); also see the Corporate Watch website (www.corpwatch.org), featuring Greenpeace's monthly award for the 'most outrageous' corporate environmental advertisement.

21 Patrick Carson and Julia Moulden, *Green Is Gold: Business Talking to Business about the Environmental Revolution* (HarperCollins, Toronto; 1991).

22 See, for instance, Michael Silverstein, *The Environmental Factor: Its Impact on the Future of the World Economy and Your Investments* (Longman, Chicago; 1990); and Jerald Blumberg, Åge Korsvold and Georges Blum, *Environmental Performance and Shareholder Value* (WBCSD, Geneva; 1995).

23 Blumberg et al, *Environmental Performance*, p15.

24 *Business and the Environment*, June 1998, p3.

25 See, for instance, Andreas Merkl and Harry Robinson, *The McKinsey Quarterly*, 1997, Number 3, p150ff.

26 See, for instance, *The Presidential/Congressional Commission on Risk Assessment and Risk Management, Framework for Environmental Health Risk Management* (Washington, DC; 1997); Martin E Silverstein, *Disasters: Your Right to Survive* (Brassey's, Washington, D.C.; 1992; and Michael Silva and Terry McGann, *Overdrive* (John Wiley, New York; 1995). Valid insights can also be gained from Lawrence Susskind and Patrick Field, *Dealing with an Angry Public: The Mutual Gains Approach to Resolving Disputes* (The Free Press, New York; 1996).

27 Anthony Saponara, *Corporate Environmental Strategy*, August 1995, p48

28 Paul Shrivastava and Stuart Hart, *Business Strategy and the Environment*, July–September 1995, p159.

29 Rocky Mountain Institute, *Green Development: Integrating Ecology and Real Estate* (John Wiley & Sons, New York; 1998), p408; see also DeSimone et al, *Eco-Efficiency*, p54.

30 See, for instance, Michael A Ridley, *Lowering the Cost of Emission Reduction: Joint Implementation in the Framework Convention on Climate Change* (Kluwer Academic Publishers, The Netherlands; 1998).

31 McKinsey & Company, *Protecting the Global Environment: Funding Mechanisms* (report to the Ministerial Conference on Atmospheric Pollution and Climatic Change, Noordwijk, The Netherlands; November 1989). See also Onno Kuik, Paul Peters and Nico Schrijver, *Joint Implementation to Curb Climate Change* (Kluwer Academic Publishers, Dordrecht, The Netherlands; 1994); and MacNeill et al, *Beyond Interdependence*, p81ff.

32 *Tomorrow*, January–February 1999, p19.

33 *Tomorrow*, January–February 1999, p33.

34 *Green Futures*, September–October 1998, p7.

35 *Green Futures*, September–October 1999, p40.

36 ibid, p40.

37 *Tomorrow*, July–September 1995, p21.

38 *Harvard Business Review*, November–December 1995, p196.

39 *The McKinsey Quarterly*, 1993, Number 4, p59ff.

40 Thomas Gladwin, *Building the Sustainable Corporation* (US National Wildlife Federation, Washington, DC; 1992).

41 *The ENDS Report*, August 2000, p5.

42 *Detroit Free Press*, August 17, 1999.

43 Also see Curtis Moore and Alan Miller, *Green Gold: Japan, Germany, the United States, and the Race for Environmental Technology* (Beacon Press, Boston; 1996).

44 DeSimone et al, *Eco-Efficiency*, p58.

45 Frankel, *In Earth's Company*, p68.

46 *The McKinsey Quarterly*, 1993, Number 4, p64.

47 Also see Pieter Winsemius and Walter Hahn, *Columbia Journal of World Business*, Fall/Winter 1992, p248.

48 We'll also see this discrepancy reflected in the apprehension of what we will refer to as 'pivotal job holders' regarding corporate change in Chapter 5.

49 Helias Udo de Haes, Gjalt Huppes and Geert de Snoo, 'Analytical tools for chain management', in Pier Vellinga et al, *Managing a Material World*, p55ff.

50 Stephan Schmidheiny, Rodney Chase and Livio D DeSimone, *Signals of Change: Business Progress Towards Sustainable Development* (World Business Council for Sustainable Development, Conches-Geneva, Switzerland; 1997), p11.

51 See DeSimone et al, *Eco-Efficiency*, p174.

CHAPTER 5

1   *Green Futures*, September–October 2000, p23.
2   *Tomorrow*, March–April 1998, p19.
3   Teresa M Amabile, *Creativity in Context* (Westview Press, Boulder, Colorado; 1996), p81ff; also see Peter M Senge, *The Fifth Discipline: The Art and Practice of the Learning Organization* (Doubleday/Currency, New York; 1990), p191. For inspiring accounts of the best practices of superior creators, see also Dorris B Wallace and Howard E Gruber, *Creative People at Work* (Oxford University Press, New York; 1989); R Ochse, *Before the Gates of Excellence* (Cambridge University Press, Cambridge, UK; 1990); and Brewster Ghiselin (ed), *The Creative Process* (University of California Press, Berkeley, California; 1984).
4   For an in-depth analysis of this topic, see also Jeffrey Pfeffer and Robert I Sutton, *The Knowing–Doing Gap: How Smart Companies Turn Knowledge into Action* (Harvard Business School Press, Boston; 2000).
5   Alan M Kantrow, *The Constraints of Corporate Tradition* (Harper & Row, New York; 1987).
6   For a more detailed analysis of the so-called PC revolution and its parallels with implementing green change, see Kenneth W Ayers and Timothy T Greene, 'Bulldozing the Green Wall', in John Moxen and Peter A Strachan (eds), *Managing Green Teams*, p112.
7   Thomas J Peters and Robert Waterman, Jr, *In Search of Excellence* (Harper & Row, New York; 1982), p9ff. For other relevant reading see Terrence E Deal and Allan A Kennedy, *Corporate Cultures: The Rites and Rituals of Corporate Life* (Addison-Wesley, Reading, Massachusetts; 1982); John P Kotter and James L Heskett, *Corporate Culture and Performance* (The Free Press, New York; 1992); Geert Hofstede, *Cultures and Organizations: Software of the Mind* (McGraw-Hill, New York; 1997); and Edgar H Schein, *The Corporate Culture Survival Guide* (Jossey-Bass, San Francisco; 1999).
8   *Tomorrow*, January–February 1997, p36.
9   For further information email info@ewg.org
10 Frankel, *In Earth's Company*, p109.
11 Teresa Amabile, *Creativity in Context and The Social Psychology of Creativity* (Springer-Verlag, New York; 1983).
12 James C Collins and Jerry I Porras, *Built to Last* (HarperCollins, New York; 1994).
13 *Greenpeace Business*, August–September 1995.
14 Also see Ayers and Greene, *Bulldozing the Green Wall*, p118ff; and Michael W Morris and Steven K Su, *American Behavioral Scientist*, Vol 42, No 8, May 1999, p1334ff.
15 Pearce and Warford, *World Without End*, p65ff, and *Economic Values and the Natural World* (Earthscan, London; 1993), p54ff.
16 See, for instance, Terrence W Faulkner, *Research-Technology Management*, May–June 1996, p50ff; and Keith J Leslie and Max P Michaels, *The McKinsey Quarterly*, 1997, No 3, p4ff.
17 Neil A Chriss, *Black-Scholes and Beyond: Option Pricing Models* (Irwin, Chicago; 1997).

18 Michael E Porter and Claas Van Der Linde, *Harvard Business Review*, September–October 1995, p128.
19 *USA Today*, June 25, 1997.
20 Published annually in *The ENDS Report*.
21 Peter Senge, *The Fifth Discipline*, p174.
22 See, for instance, Makin et al, *Organizations and the Psychological Contract*, p221ff. We thank Professor Pieter Drenth of the Free University of Amsterdam for his suggestions on the subject of group behaviour.
23 See also Susskind and Field, *Dealing with an Angry Public*.
24 See, for instance, *Tomorrow*, September–October 1997, p28ff.
25 Paul Strebel, *The Change Pact: Building Commitment to Ongoing Change* (*Financial Times*/Pitman Publishing, London; 1998); see also his article in Harvard Business Review, May–June 1996, p86.
26 Actually, Strebel speaks of 'personal compacts'. In view of this term's closeness to existing psychological models, we have used more traditional terminology.
27 For a highly readable and insightful discussion of the concept of 'contracts', see also Makin et al, *Organizations and the Psychological Contract*.
28 ibid, p136.
29 *Business Week*, November 10 1997.
30 *Fortune*, July 16 1990, p27.
31 Robert A Burgelman and Leonard Sayles, *Inside Corporate Innovation* (Free Press, Macmillan, New York; 1986).

CHAPTER 6

1 We once again thank Professor Pieter Drenth of the Free University of Amsterdam for his suggestions on this topic.
2 For other workshop formats see Fussler with James, *Driving Eco-Innovation*, Chapter 22, p303ff; and Jacqueline Cramer, 'Philips Sound and Vision – Environment and Strategic Product-Planning', in *Managing a Material World*, p239ff.
3 For more detailed discussions of environmental accounting systems, see Stefan Schaltegger, Kaspar Müller and Henriette Hindrichsen, *Corporate Environmental Accounting* (John Wiley & Sons, Chichester, UK; 1996); Marc J Epstein, *Measuring Corporate Environmental Performance* (Irwin, Chicago; 1996); and Daryl Ditz and Janet Ranganathan, *Measuring Up: Toward a Common Framework for Tracking Corporate Environmental Performance* (World Resources Institute, Washington, DC; 1997).
4 DeSimone et al, *Eco-Efficiency*, p29.
5 *Business Week*, November 10, 1997, p106.
6 *Tomorrow*, January–February 1999, p64.
7 Fussler with James, *Driving Eco-Innovation*, p149ff.
8 *Managing the Global Environmental Challenge* (Business International Corporation, New York; 1992), p181ff; Willums and the World Business Council for Sustainable Development, *The Sustainable Business Challenge*, p143ff.

9   Sustainable Strategies for Value Creation (The Performance Group), p22.
10 Good overviews of the relevant management tools are provided by Richard Welford (ed), *Corporate Environmental Management 1*, and W Gary Wilson and Dennis R Sasseville, *Sustaining Environmental Management Success: Best Business Practices from Industry Leaders* (John Wiley & Sons, New York; 1999).
11 World Resources Institute and the Aspen Initiative for Social Innovation through Business, *Beyond Grey Pinstripes 2001: Preparing MBAs for Social and Environmental Stewardship* (World Resources Institute, Washington, DC; 2001). The cutting-edge schools are George Washington, Yale and the Universities of Jyväskylä (Finland), Michigan and North Carolina-Chapel Hill.
12 Ray C Anderson, *Mid-Course Correction* (The Peregrinzilla Press, Atlanta; 1998), p154.
13 Von Weizsäcker et al, *Factor Four*, p27ff; and Rocky Mountain Institute, *Green Development*, p162.
14 *Tomorrow*, November–December 2000, p20.
15 The positive effects of environmental solutions to urban problems are discussed by, amongst others, Paul A Bell, Thomas C Greene, Jeffrey D Fisher and Andrew Baum, *Environmental Psychology* (Harcourt Brace College Publishers, Fort Worth; 1996), p387ff.
16 For an overview of illustrative mission statements, see Jane Nelson, *Business as Partners in Development* (The Prince of Wales Business Leaders Forum, London; 1996), p76ff.
17 See, for instance, *Engaging Stakeholders 1998: The CEO Agenda* (SustainAbility, London; 1998).
18 Smart, *Beyond Compliance*, p188.
19 DeSimone et al, *Eco-Efficiency*, p96.
20 Frances Cairncross, *Costing the Earth: The Challenge for Governments, the Opportunities for Business* (Earthscan, London; 1991), p225.

CHAPTER 7

1   See, for instance, Frederick J Long and Matthew B Arnold, *The Power of Environmental Partnerships* (The Dryden Press, Fort Worth, Texas; 1995); Nelson, *Business as Partners in Development*; United States Agency for International Development (USAID) and World Resources Institute (WRI), *New Partnerships in the Americas: The Spirit of Rio* (December 1994).
2   DeSimone et al, *Eco-Efficiency*, p161.
3   ibid, p161.
4   For more on partnering models see Long and Arnold, *The Power of Environmental Partnerships*, p56ff; for further discussion on more generic alliance concepts see Joel Bleeke and David Ernst, *Harvard Business Review*, January–February 1995, p97.
5   Frankel, *In Earth's Company*, p90. See also DeSimone et al, *Eco-Efficiency*, p151.
6   The Conference Board, *Environmental Alliances: Critical Factors for Success* (The Conference Board, New York; 1995), p17.

7   *Scientific American*, January 1995, p32.
8   *Tomorrow*, January–February 1999, p11.
9   *Business and the Environment*, March 1998, p10.
10 Long and Arnold, *The Power of Environmental Partnerships*, p269ff.;
    USAID and WRI, *New Partnerships in the Americas*, p77ff.
11 Bradford Gentry and Lisa Fernandez, *Globalisation and the
    Environment: Perspectives from OECD and Dynamic Non-Member
    Economies* (OECD, Paris; 1998), p11.
12 Netherlands' Ministry of Economic Affairs, *Symposium on Energy
    Conservation through Multi-Year Agreements*, January 1995.
13 Long and Arnold, *The Power of Environmental Partnerships*, p291ff.
14 Tony Kingsley and Brad Whitehead, *Environment Risk*, April 1993, p12;
    USAID and WRI, *New Partnerships in the Americas*, p56ff.
15 Kingsley and Whitehead, *Environment Risk*, p42.
16 For an overview of theoretical frameworks, also see Van den Bosch and
    Van Riel, *Business Strategy and the Environment*, February 1998, p24ff.
17 For a more in-depth assessment of the progress made in different
    countries and the pros and cons of various approaches, see Pieter
    Glasbergen (ed), *Co-operative Environmental Governance:
    Public–Private Agreements as a Policy Strategy* (Kluwer Academic
    Publishers, Dordrecht, The Netherlands; 1998).
18 For a further elaboration on the boundary conditions to be met in
    setting up a partnership see Pieter Winsemius, 'Environmental Contracts
    and Covenants: New Instruments for a Realistic Environmental Policy?',
    in Jan M van Dunné (ed) *Environmental Contracts and Covenants: New
    Instruments for a Realistic Environmental Policy?* (Koninklijke
    Vermande, Lelystad, The Netherlands; 1993), p5ff.
19 The challenge of bridging culture gaps was first presented by Charles
    Percy Snow in his classic *The Two Cultures and a Second Look*
    (Cambridge University Press, Cambridge, UK; 1959/1964). Other insights
    with relevance to the present discussion may be derived from Joseph A
    Raelin, *The Clash of Cultures: Managers Managing Professionals*
    (Harvard Business School Press, Boston, Massachusetts; 1991); and
    Makin et al, *Organizations and the Psychological Contract*, p75ff.
20 See, for instance, Shabecoff, *A Fierce Green Fire*.
21 See, for instance, Pieter Winsemius and Ulrich Guntram, *Business
    Horizons*, March–April 1992, p12.
22 See, for instance, Susskind and Field, *Dealing with an Angry Public*,
    p37ff.
23 Frankel, *In Earth's Company*, p70.
24 Climate Protection Initiative, *Building a Safe Climate, Sound Business
    Future* (World Resources Institute, Washington, DC; 1998).
25 Case analyses illustrate the nature of the interactions in the environ-
    ment arena. See, for instance, on UK and Netherlands' policy
    development regarding acidification, Maarten A Hajer, *The Politics of
    Environmental Discourse* (Clarendon Press, Oxford; 1995).
26 Peter Clancy and L Anders Sandberg, *Business Strategy and the
    Environment*, October–December 1995, p210.

CHAPTER 8

1 Morris Tabaksblat, speech at Veerstichting Symposium, Leiden, The Netherlands, October 17, 1997.

2 Howard Gardner with Emma Laskin, *Leading Minds: An Anatomy of Leadership* (Basic Books, New York; 1995).

3 *Fortune*, July 16 1990, p27.

4 A proactive corporate response inevitably incorporates elements of what Joseph Schumpeter called 'creative destruction'. As colourfully illustrated by Richard N Foster and Sarah Kaplan in their book *Creative Destruction* (Currency-Doubleday, New York; 2001), especially companies that are doing well often have considerable difficulties in pursuing major transformations. For targeted application with regard to sustainability, also see: Stuart L Hall and Mark B Milstein, *Sloan Management Review*, Fall 1999, p23ff.

5 DeSimone et al, *Eco-Efficiency*, pix.

6 Interface, *Sustainability Report*, 1997.

7 *Fortune*, April 5 1993, p60.

8 For a fascinating account of charismatic leadership see Peter Makin et al, *Organizations and the Psychological Contract*, p182ff.

9 *Tomorrow*, September–October 1999, p26.

10 *Fortune*, January 25 1993, p70.

11 Senge, *The Fifth Discipline*, p224.

12 *Fortune*, December 13 1993, p41.

13 Also see Peter A French, 'Terre Gaste', in W Michael Hoffman, Robert Frederick and Edward S Petry, Jr (eds), *The Corporation, Ethics, and the Environment* (Quorum Books, Westport, Connecticut; 1990), p8ff.

14 Charles Handy, *The Hungry Spirit*, p70.

15 Christopher A Bartlett and Samantra Ghoshal, *Harvard Business Review*, November–December 1998, p19.

16 *Tomorrow*, March–April 1998, p19.

17 Bartlett and Ghoshal, *Harvard Business Review*, p84.

18 See, for instance, Gladwin, *Building the Sustainable Corporation*, and Elkington, *Cannibals With Forks*. Frequent reference also is made to 'people, planet and profit' (ie social, environmental and economic quality).

19 Also see Janet Ranganathan, *Sustainability Rulers: Measuring Corporate Environmental and Social Performance* (World Resources Institute, Washington, DC; 1998).

20 Ray C Anderson, *Mid-Course Correction*, p98.

21 Joel Makower and Business for Social Responsibility, *Beyond the Bottom Line: Putting Social Responsibility to Work for Your Business and the World* (Simon and Schuster, New York; 1994), p297.

22 *Tomorrow*, September–October 1999, p18.

23 See Pieter Winsemius, *The Emotional Revolution: A New Challenge to Leaders* (McKinsey & Company, Amsterdam; 1999).

24 Senge, *The Fifth Discipline*, p347.

25 Anderson, *Mid-Course Correction*, p97.

26 Chad Holliday and John Pepper, *Sustainability through the Market: Seven Keys to Success* (World Business Council for Sustainable Development, Conches-Geneva; 2001), p5.

27 Elkington, *Cannibals With Forks*, p141.
28 Lindahl, speech at oikos (International Student Organisation for Sustainable Economics and Management), Cologne, April 29 1999.
29 For further examples, see Makower and Business for Social Responsibility, *Beyond the Bottom Line*, and Alan Reder for the Social Venture Network, *Best 75 Business Practices for Socially Responsible Companies* (G P Putnam, New York; 1995).
30 Kathryn McPhail and Aidan Davy, *Integrating Social Concerns into Private Sector Decisionmaking* (World Bank Discussion Paper No 384, The World Bank, Washington, DC; 1998).
31 *Tomorrow*, November–December 1999, p21.
32 See, for a variety of examples, Nelson, *Business as Partners in Development*.
33 Tabaksblat, speech at Veerstichting Symposium.
34 It should be noted that, building on the thoughts of David Grayson and others, Jane Nelson presents a four-stage corporate response framework for community investment that has many parallels with the first three stages of the environmental response framework discussed in Chapter 2; see her *Business as Partners in Development*, p66.
35 Tabaksblat, speech at Veerstichting Symposium.
36 Paul Hawken, *The Ecology of Commerce: A Declaration of Sustainability* (HarperCollins, New York; 1993).
37 See, for instance, Frankel, *In Earth's Company*, p178ff.
38 Other good sources are Paul Hawken, Amory B Lovins and L Hunter Lovins, *Natural Capitalism: The Next Industrial Revolution* (Earthscan, London; 1999); John Kenneth Galbraith, *The Good Society: The Humane Agenda* (Houghton Mifflin, Boston; 1996); Handy, *The Hungry Spirit*; and Gerard Piel, *Only One World: Our Own to Make and to Keep* (WH Freeman and Company, New York; 1992).
39 See Thierry C Pauchant and Isabelle Fortier, 'Anthropocentric Ethics in Organizations: How Different Strategic Management Schools View the Environment', in Hoffman et al, *The Corporation, Ethics, and the Environment*, p194ff. For an overview of relevant schools of thought, see Gerald T Gardner and Paul C Stern, *Environmental Problems and Human Behavior* (Allyn and Bacon, Boston; 1996), Chapters 3 and 8.
40 For relevant publications on this topic, see for instance Kees Zoeteman, *Gaia-Sophia: A Framework for Ecology* (Floris Books, Edinburgh, Scotland; 1991); Stephen R Kellert and Edward O Wilson, *The Biophilia Hypothesis* (Island Press, Washington, DC; 1993); and Theodore Roszak, Mary E Gomes and Allen D Kanner, *Ecopsychology* (Sierra Club Books, San Francisco; 1995).

CHAPTER 9

1 We thank our colleague Michael Jung for his central contribution to this chapter.
2 Throughout this chapter we have benefited from the thoughts of Peter Senge expressed in his breakthrough books *The Fifth Discipline and Dance of Change: The Challenges of Sustaining Momentum in Learning*

Organizations (with Art Kleiner, Charlotte Roberts, Richard Ross, George Roth and Bryan Smith) (Doubleday/Currency, New York; 1999). For relevant textbooks on change management see, for instance, Douglas K Smith, *Taking Charge of Change* (Addison-Wesley, Reading, MA; 1996); John P Kotter, *Leading Change* (Harvard Business School Press, Boston, MA; 1996); and James O' Toole, *Leading Change* (Jossey-Bass, San Francisco; 1995).

3   Makower, *Beyond the Bottom Line*, p56ff.

4   *Fortune*, December 13 1993, p41.

5   Michael Jung, *Transforming Corporations into Innovative Communities: How to Inject the Dynamism of Start-Ups into Established Companies* (McKinsey & Company, Düsseldorf; 1997), and Jonathan D Day and Michael Jung, *The McKinsey Quarterly*, 2000, No 4, p116ff. Jung's idea is based on, but greatly extends, that of Rosabeth Moss-Kanter's 'parallel organization'; see her *The Change Masters* (Simon & Schuster, New York; 1984).

6   Jon R Katzenbach and the RCL Team, *Real Change Leaders: How You Can Create Growth and High Performance at Your Company* (Random House, New York; 1996).

7   Smart, *Beyond Compliance*, p167.

8   See, for instance, Francis Fukuyama, *Trust: The Social Virtues and the Creation of Prosperity* (Free Press Paperbacks, New York; 1996), and Handy, *The Hungry Spirit*, p181ff. For a recent theory overview see Roderick M Kramer and Tom R Tyler, *Trust in Organizations: Frontiers of Theory and Research* (Sage Publications, Thousand Oaks, CA; 1996).

9   For an insightful overview, see Jon R Katzenbach, *Peak Performance: Aligning the Hearts and Minds of Your Employees* (Harvard Business School Press, Boston; 2000).

10 *Fortune*, November 25 1996, p87.

11 Jeroen van der Veer, 'Licence to Grow?', in Rob Wolters and Laura Baguñá Hoffmann, *Globalisation, Ecology and Economy – Bridging Worlds* (The European Centre for Nature Conservation (ECNC)/Globus-Institute for Globalization and Sustainable Development of Tilburg University, Tilburg, The Netherlands; 2000), p196.

12 The required quantum leap in management thinking has been identified by others under different names, from Huibregtsen's 'emotional revolution' to a new emphasis on quality of thought (Senge's 'systems thinking'), to a focus on the individual (Ghoshal and Bartlett's 'individualized corporation'), to a stress on the quality of interaction processes (Argyris and Schön's 'double-loop learning' and Dotlich and Noel's 'action learning'). Also see Rosamund Stone Zander and Benjamin Zander, *The Art of Possibility: Transforming Professional and Personal Life* (Harvard Business School Press, Boston; 2000).

13 E Bruce Harrison, *Going Green*, p58.

14 Also see Walter Wehrmeyer and Kim T Parker, 'Identification and Relevance of Environmental Corporate Cultures as Part of a Coherent Environmental Policy', in Walter Wehrmeyer (ed), *Greening People: Human Resources and Environmental Management* (Greenleaf Publishing, Sheffield, UK; 1996), p163ff.

15 Jung, *Transforming Corporations*; also see Jonathan D Day and James C Wendler, *The McKinsey Quarterly*, 1998, No 1, p4.

16 Arthur D Little, *Prism*, p24ff.
17 Paul A Bell et al, *Environmental Psychology*, p487ff.
18 Gardner and Stern, *Environmental Problems and Human Behavior*, p85; Bell et al, *Environmental Psychology*, p538.
19 See, for instance, Rocky Mountain Institute, *Green Development*.
20 'How Do We Stand? People, Planet & Profits', *The Shell Report 2000* (Shell International, London/The Hague, 2000), p2.
21 *Fortune*, January 23 1993, p72.

REFERENCES

Amabile, Teresa M, *The Social Psychology of Creativity* (Springer-Verlag, New York; 1983).

Amabile, Teresa M, *Creativity in Context* (Westview Press, Boulder, Colorado; 1996).

Anderson, Ray C, *Mid-Course Correction* (The Peregrinzilla Press, Atlanta; 1998).

Ball, Philip, *H_2O: A Biography of Water* (Weidenfeld & Nicolson, London; 1999).

Bell, Paul A, Thomas C Greene, Jeffrey D Fisher and Andrew Baum, *Environmental Psychology* (Harcourt Brace College Publishers, Fort Worth; 1996).

Benedick, Richard E, *Ozone Diplomacy* (Harvard University Press, Cambridge, Massachusetts; 1991).

Blumberg, Jerald, Åge Korsvold and Georges Blum, *Environmental Performance and Shareholder Value* (WBCSD, Geneva; 1995).

Brenton, Tony, *The Greening of Machiavelli* (Earthscan, London; 1994).

Burgelman, Robert A and Leonard Sayles, *Inside Corporate Innovation* (Free Press, Macmillan, New York; 1986).

Business International Corporation, *Managing the Global Environmental Challenge* (Business International Corporation, New York; 1992).

Cairncross, Frances, *Costing the Earth: The Challenge for Governments, the Opportunities for Business* (Earthscan, London; 1991).

Cairncross, Frances, *Green, Inc* (Earthscan, London; 1995).

Carson, Patrick and Julia Moulden, *Green Is Gold: Business Talking to Business about the Environmental Revolution* (HarperCollins, Toronto; 1991).

Carson, Rachel, *Silent Spring* (Houghton Mifflin, Boston; 1962).

Charter, Martin, *Greener Marketing: A Responsible Approach to Business* (Greenleaf Publishing, Sheffield, UK; 1992).

Chertow, Marian R and Daniel C Esty, *Thinking Ecologically* (Yale University Press, New Haven; 1997).

Chriss, Neil A, *Black-Scholes and Beyond: Option Pricing Models* (Irwin, Chicago; 1997).

Coates, Joseph F, John B Mahaffie and Andy Hines, *2025: Scenarios of US and Global Society Reshaped by Science and Technology* (Oakhill Press, Greensboro, North Carolina; 1997).

Colborn, Theo, Dianna Dumanoski and John Peterson Myers, *Our Stolen Future: Are We Threatening Our Fertility, Intelligence and Survival?* (EP Dutton, New York; 1996).

Collins, James C and Jerry I Porras, *Built to Last* (HarperCollins, New York; 1994).

The Conference Board, *Environmental Alliances: Critical Factors for Success* (The Conference Board, New York; 1995).

Deal, Terrence E and Allan A Kennedy, *Corporate Cultures: The Rites and Rituals of Corporate Life* (Addison-Wesley, Reading, Massachusetts; 1982).

de Jongh, Paul E with Seán Captain, *Our Common Journey: A Pioneering Approach to Cooperative Environmental Management* (Zed Books, London; 1999).

de Moor, André and Peter Clamai, *Subsidizing Unsustainable Development: Undermining the Earth with Public Funds* (Institute for Research on Public Expenditure, The Hague and Earth Council, San José, Costa Rica; 1997).

DeSimone, Livio D and Frank Popoff with the World Business Council for Sustainable Development, *Eco-Efficiency: The Business Link to Sustainable Development* (MIT Press, Cambridge, Massachusetts; 1997).

Ditz, Daryl and Janet Ranganathan, *Measuring Up: Toward a Common Framework for Tracking Corporate Environmental Performance* (World Resources Institute, Washington, DC; 1997).

Druckman, Daniel, *Global Environmental Change: Understanding the Human Dimensions* (National Academy Press, Washington, DC; 1992).

Earle, Sylvia A, *Sea Change: A Message of the Oceans* (GP Putnam, New York; 1995).

Elkington, John, *Cannibals With Forks* (Capstone, Oxford; 1997).

Elkington, John and Julia Hailes, *Green Consumer Guide: From Shampoo to Champagne, High-Street Shopping for a Better Environment* (Gollancz, London; 1988).

Elkington, John and Julia Hailes, *Manual 2000: Life Choices for the Future You Want* (Hodder & Stoughton, London; 1998).

Epstein, Marc J, *Measuring Corporate Environmental Performance* (Irwin, Chicago; 1996).

Frankel, Carl, *In Earth's Company: Business, Environment and the Challenge of Sustainability* (New Society Publishers, Gabriola Island BC, Canada; 1998).

Fukuyama, Francis, *Trust: The Social Virtues and the Creation of Prosperity* (Free Press Paperbacks, New York; 1996).

Fussler, Claude, with Peter James, *Driving Eco-Innovation: A Breakthrough Discipline for Innovation and Sustainability* (Pitman Publishing, London; 1996).

Gardner, Gerald T and Paul C Stern, *Environmental Problems and Human Behavior* (Allyn and Bacon, Boston; 1996).

Gardner, Howard with Emma Laskin, *Leading Minds: An Anatomy of Leadership* (Basic Books, New York; 1995).

Ghiselin, Brewster (ed), *The Creative Process* (University of California Press, Berkeley, California; 1984).

Gladwin, Thomas, *Building the Sustainable Corporation* (US National Wildlife Federation, Washington, DC; 1992).

Glasbergen, Pieter (ed), *Co-operative Environmental Governance: Public–Private Agreements as a Policy Strategy* (Kluwer Academic Publishers, Dordrecht, The Netherlands; 1998).

Greer, Jed and Kenny Bruno, *Greenwash: The Reality Behind Corporate Environmentalism* (The Apex Press, New York; 1997).

Grünfeld, Hans, *Creating Favorable Conditions for International Environmental Change through Knowledge and Negotiation* (Delft University Press, Delft, The Netherlands; 1999).

Hammond, Allan, *Which World? Scenarios for the 21st Century* (Island Press, Washington, DC; 1998).

Handy, Charles, *The Hungry Spirit* (Broadway Books, New York; 1998).

Harrison, E Bruce, *Going Green: How to Communicate Your Company's Environmental Commitment* (Business One Irwin, Homewood, IL; 1993).

Hawken, Paul, *The Ecology of Commerce: A Declaration of Sustainability* (HarperCollins, New York; 1993).

Hawken, Paul, Amory B Lovins and L Hunter Lovins, *Natural Capitalism: The Next Industrial Revolution* (Earthscan, London; 1999).

Hoffman, W Michael, Robert Frederick and Edward S Petry Jr (eds), *The Corporation, Ethics, and the Environment* (Quorum Books, Westport, Connecticut; 1990).

Hofstede, Geert, *Cultures and Organizations: Software of the Mind* (McGraw-Hill, New York; 1997).

Holliday, Chad and John Pepper, *Sustainability through the Market: Seven Keys to Success* (World Business Council for Sustainable Development, Conches-Geneva; 2001).

IVA, McKinsey and the WWF, *Environmental Management: From Regulatory Demands to Strategic Business Opportunities* (IVA: Royal Academy of Engineering Sciences, Stockholm; 1995).

Johnson, Huey D, *Green Plans: Greenprint for Sustainability* (University of Nebraska Press, Lincoln, Nebraska; 1995).

Jung, Michael, *Transforming Corporations into Innovative Communities: How to Inject the Dynamism of Start-Ups into Established Companies* (McKinsey & Company, Düsseldorf; 1997).

Kantrow, Alan M, *The Constraints of Corporate Tradition* (Harper & Row, New York; 1987).

Katzenbach, Jon R, *Peak Performance: Aligning the Hearts and Minds of Your Employees* (Harvard Business School Press, Boston; 2000).

Katzenbach, Jon R and the RCL Team, *Real Change Leaders: How You Can Create Growth and High Performance at Your Company* (Random House, New York; 1996).

Kellert, Stephen R and Edward O Wilson, *The Biophilia Hypothesis* (Island Press, Washington, DC; 1993).

Klostermann, Judith E M, Arnold Tukker, Jacqueline M Cramer, Adrie van Dam and Bernhard L van der Ven, *Product Innovation and Eco-Efficiency* (Kluwer Academic Publishers, Dordrecht, The Netherlands; 1998).

Koechlin, Dominik and Kaspar Müller (eds), *Green Business Opportunities: The Profit Potential* (*Financial Times*/Pitman Publishing, London; 1992).

Kolk, Ans, *Economics of Environmental Management* (Pearson Education, Harlow, Essex, UK; 2000)

Kotter, John P, *Leading Change* (Harvard Business School Press, Boston, MA; 1996).

Kotter, John P and James L Heskett, *Corporate Culture and Performance* (The Free Press, New York; 1992).

Kramer, Roderick M and Tom R Tyler, *Trust in Organizations: Frontiers of Theory and Research* (Sage Publications, Thousand Oaks, CA; 1996).

Kuik, Onno, Paul Peters and Nico Schrijver, *Joint Implementation to Curb Climate Change* (Kluwer Academic Publishers, Dordrecht, The Netherlands; 1994).

Long, Frederick J and Matthew B Arnold, *The Power of Environmental Partnerships* (The Dryden Press, Fort Worth, Texas; 1995)

McIntosh, Malcolm Deborah Leipziger, Keith Jones and Gill Coleman, *Corporate Citizenship: Successful Strategies for Responsible Companies* (*Financial Times*/Pitman Publishing, London; 1998).

MacNeill, Jim, Pieter Winsemius and Tazio Yakushiji, *Beyond Interdependence* (Oxford University Press, New York; 1991).

Makin, Peter J, Cary L Cooper and Charles J Cox, *Organizations and the Psychological Contract: Managing People at Work* (Praeger, Westport, Connecticut; 1996).

Makower, Joel and Business for Social Responsibility, *Beyond the Bottom Line: Putting Social Responsibility to Work for your Business and the World* (Simon and Schuster, New York; 1994).

Maslow, Abraham H, *Motivation and Personality* (Harper and Row, New York; 1954).

Maslow, Abraham H with Deborah C Stephens and Gary Heil, *Maslow on Management* (John Wiley & Sons, New York; 1998).

Management Consultancies Association (MCA), *UK Plc on the World Stage in 2010, Book 4: Business and the Environment* (MCA, London; 2000).

McKinsey & Company, *Protecting the Global Environment: Funding Mechanisms* (report to the Ministerial Conference on Atmospheric Pollution & Climatic Change, Noordwijk, The Netherlands; November 1989).

McPhail, Kathryn and Aidan Davy, *Integrating Social Concerns into Private Sector Decisionmaking* (World Bank Discussion Paper No 384, The World Bank, Washington, DC; 1998).

Meadows, Donella H, Dennis L Meadows, Jørgen Randers and William W Behrens III, *The Limits to Growth* (Universe Books, New York; 1972).

Moore, Curtis and Alan Miller, *Green Gold: Japan, Germany, the United States, and the Race for Environmental Technology* (Beacon Press, Boston; 1996).

Moxen, John and Peter A Strachan (eds), *Managing Green Teams* (Greenleaf Publishing, Sheffield, UK; 1998).

Munn, R E, J W M la Rivière and N van Lookeren Campagne, *Policy Making in an Era of Global Environmental Change* (Kluwer Academic Publishers, Dordrecht, The Netherlands; 1996).

Myers, Norman, *Ultimate Security: The Environmental Basis of Political Stability* (WW Norton & Company, New York; 1993).

Nelson, Jane, *Business as Partners in Development* (The Prince of Wales Business Leaders Forum, London; 1996).

Ochse, R, *Before the Gates of Excellence* (Cambridge University Press, Cambridge, UK; 1990).

OECD, *Environmental Taxes and Green Tax Reform* (OECD, Paris; 1997).

O'Riordan, Tim, *Ecotaxation* (Earthscan, London; 1996).

O' Toole, James, *Leading Change* (Jossey-Bass, San Francisco; 1995).

Ottman, Jacquelyn A, *Green Marketing: Challenges and Opportunities for the New Marketing Age* (NTC Publishing, Lincolnwood, Illinois; 1992).

Pearce, David W and Jeremy J Warford, *World without End: Economics, Environment, and Sustainable Development* (Oxford University Press, New York; 1993).

Pearce, David W and Jeremy J Warford, *Economic Values and the Natural World* (Earthscan, London; 1993).

The Performance Group, *Sustainable Strategies for Value Creation: Reflections from a Learning Journey* (The Performance Group, Oslo, Norway; 1998).

Peters, Thomas J and Robert Waterman Jr, *In Search of Excellence* (Harper & Row, New York; 1982).

Pfeffer, Jeffrey and Robert I Sutton, *The Knowing–Doing Gap: How Smart Companies Turn Knowledge into Action* (Harvard Business School Press, Boston; 2000).

Piel, Gerard, *Only One World: Our Own to Make and to Keep* (WH Freeman and Company, New York; 1992).

Pleune, Ruud, *Strategies of Dutch Environmental Organizations* (International Books, Utrecht, The Netherlands; 1997).

Ponting, Clive, *A Green History of the World* (Penguin Books, London; 1992).

Porritt, Jonathon, *Playing Safe: Science and the Environment* (Thames & Hudson, New York; 2000).

The Presidential/Congressional Commission on Risk Assessment and Risk Management, *Framework for Environmental Health Risk Management* (Washington, DC; 1997).

Raelin, Joseph A, *The Clash of Cultures: Managers Managing Professionals* (Harvard Business School Press, Boston, Massachusetts; 1991).

Ranganathan, Janet, *Sustainability Rulers: Measuring Corporate Environmental and Social Performance* (World Resources Institute, Washington, DC; May 1998).

Reder, Alan for the Social Venture Network, *Best 75 Business Practices for Socially Responsible Companies* (GP Putnam, New York; 1995).

Ridley, Michael A, *Lowering the Cost of Emission Reduction: Joint Implementation in the Framework Convention on Climate Change* (Kluwer Academic Publishers, The Netherlands; 1998).

Ringland, Gill, *Scenario Planning: Managing for the Future* (John Wiley & Sons, New York; 1998).

Rocky Mountain Institute, *Green Development: Integrating Ecology and Real Estate* (John Wiley & Sons, New York; 1998).

Roszak, Theodore, Mary E Gomes and Allen D Kanner, *Ecopsychology* (Sierra Club Books, San Francisco; 1995).

Schahn, Joachim and Thomas Giesinger (eds), *Psychologie für den Umweltschutz* (Beltz Psychologie Verlags Union, Weinheim, Germany; 1993).

Schaltegger, Stefan, Kaspar Müller and Henriette Hindrichsen, *Corporate Environmental Accounting* (John Wiley & Sons, Chichester, UK; 1996).

Schein, Edgar H, *Organizational Psychology* (Prentice Hall, Englewood Cliffs; 1980).

Schein, Edgar H, *The Corporate Culture Survival Guide* (Jossey-Bass, San Francisco; 1999).

Schmidheiny, Stephan with the Business Council for Sustainable Development, *Changing Course* (MIT Press, Cambridge, Massachusetts; 1992).

Schmidheiny, Stephan, Rodney Chase and Livio D DeSimone, *Signals of Change: Business Progress Towards Sustainable Development* (World Business Council for Sustainable Development, Conches-Geneva, Switzerland; 1997).

Schmidt-Bleek, Friedrich, *Wieviel Umwelt braucht der Mensch?: MIPS – das Maß für Ökologisches Wirtschaften* (Birkhäuser Verlag, Berlin; 1994).

Schön, Donald A, *Educating the Reflective Practicioner* (Jossey-Bass, San Franciso; 1998).

Schwartz, Peter, *The Art of the Long View* (Doubleday, New York; 1991).

Senge, Peter, Art Kleiner, Charlotte Roberts, Richard Ross, George Roth and Bryan Smith, *Dance of Change: The Challenges of Sustaining Momentum in Learning Organizations* (Doubleday/Currency, New York; 1999).

Senge, Peter M, *The Fifth Discipline: The Art and Practice of the Learning Organization* (Doubleday/Currency, New York; 1990).

Shabecoff, Philip, *A Fierce Green Fire* (Hill and Wang, New York; 1993).

Silva, Michael and Terry McGann, *Overdrive* (John Wiley, New York; 1995).

Silverstein, Martin E, *Disasters: Your Right to Survive* (Brassey's, Washington, DC; 1992).

Silverstein, Michael, *The Environmental Factor: Its Impact on the Future of the World Economy and Your Investments* (Longman, Chicago; 1990).

Smart, Bruce, *Beyond Compliance: A New Industry View of the Environment* (World Resources Institute, Washington, DC; 1992).

Smith, Douglas K, *Taking Charge of Change* (Addison-Wesley, Reading, MA; 1996).

Snow, Charles Percy, *The Two Cultures and a Second Look* (Cambridge University Press, Cambridge, UK; 1959/1964).

Steger, Ulrich, *Umweltmanagement: Erfahrungen und Instrumente einer umweltorientierten Unternehmenstrategie* (Frankfurt Allgemeine Zeitung für Deutschland, Frankfurt am Main, and Gabler, Wiesbaden; 1993).

Stern, Paul C, Oran R Young and Daniel Druckman (eds), *Global Environmental Change: Understanding the Human Dimensions* (National Academy Press, Washington, DC; 1992).

Stevens, Deborah C (ed), *The Maslow Business Reader* (John Wiley & Sons, New York; 2000).

Strebel, Paul, *The Change Pact: Building Commitment to Ongoing Change* (*Financial Times*/Pitman Publishing, London; 1998).

SustainAbility, *Engaging Stakeholders 1998: The CEO Agenda* (SustainAbility, London; 1998).

Susskind, Lawrence and Patrick Field, *Dealing with an Angry Public: The Mutual Gains Approach to Resolving Disputes* (The Free Press, New York; 1996).

Szekely, Francisco, Thomas Vollman and Annette Ebbinghaus, *Environmental Benchmarking: Becoming Green and Competitive* (Stanley Thornes, Cheltenham, UK; 1996).

Thomas, Caroline, *The Environment in International Relations* (The Royal Institute of International Affairs, London; 1992).

United States Agency for International Development and World Resources Institute, *New Partnerships in the Americas: The Spirit of Rio* (December 1994).

van Dunné, Jan M (ed), *Environmental Contracts and Covenants: New Instruments for a Realistic Environmental Policy?* (Koninklijke Vermande, Lelystad, The Netherlands; 1993).

Vellinga, Pier, Frans Berkhout and Joyeeta Gupta (eds), *Managing a Material World* (Kluwer Academic Publishers, Dordrecht, The Netherlands; 1998).

von Weizsäcker, Ernst, Amory B Lovins and L Hunter Lovins, *Factor Four* (Earthscan, London; 1997).

Wallace, Dorris B and Howard E Gruber, *Creative People at Work* (Oxford University Press, New York; 1989).

Watts, Phil and Ged Davis, *A Commitment to Sustainable Development* (World Business Council for Sustainable Development, London, March 13, 1998).

Watts, Phil and Lord Holme and the World Business Council for Sustainable Development, *Corporate Social Responsibility – Meeting Changing Expectations* (WBCSD, Conches-Geneva, Switzerland; 1999).

Weaver, Paul, Leo Jansen, Geert van Grootveld, Egbert van Spiegel, and Philip Vergragt, *Sustainable Technology Development* (Greenleaf Publishing, Sheffield, UK; 2000).

Wehrmeyer, Walter (ed), *Greening People: Human Resources and Environmental Management* (Greenleaf Publishing, Sheffield, UK; 1996).

Welford, Richard (ed), *Corporate Environmental Management: Systems and Strategies* (Earthscan, London; 1996).

Willums, Jan-Olof, *The Greening of Enterprise: Business Leaders Speak Out* (International Chamber of Commerce, Paris; 1990).

Willums, Jan-Olof and Ulrich Goluke, *From Ideas to Action* (ICC Publishing and Ad Notam Gyldendal, Oslo; 1992).

Willums, Jan-Olof with the World Business Council for Sustainable Development, *The Sustainable Business Challenge: A Briefing for Tomorrow's Business Leaders* (Greenleaf Publishing, Sheffield, UK; 1998).

Winsemius, Pieter, *Guests in Our Own Home* (McKinsey & Company, Amsterdam; 1990).

Winsemius, Pieter, *The Emotional Revolution: A New Challenge to Leaders* (McKinsey & Company, Amsterdam; 1999).

Wolters, Rob and Laura Baguñá Hoffman, *Globalisation, Ecology and Economy – Bridging Worlds* (The European Centre for Nature

Conservation (ECNC)/Globus-Institute for Globalization and Sustainable Development of Tilburg University, Tilburg, The Netherlands; 2000).

World Business Council for Sustainable Development, *Exploring Sustainable Development: WBCSD Global Scenarios 2000–2050* (World Business Council for Sustainable Development, Paris; 1997).

World Resources Institute and the Aspen Institute for Social Innovation through Business, *Beyond Grey Pinstripes 2001: Preparing MBAs for Social and Environmental Stewardship* (World Resources Institute, Washington, DC; 2001)

Wilson, W Gary and Dennis R Sasseville, *Sustaining Environmental Management Success: Best Business Practices from Industry Leaders* (John Wiley & Sons, New York; 1999).

Winter, Matthias and Ulrich Steger, *Managing Outside Pressure: Strategies for Preventing Corporate Disasters* (John Wiley & Sons, Chichester, UK; 1998).

World Business Council for Sustainable Development, *Biotechnology Scenarios, 2000–2050: Using the Future to Explore the Present* (World Business Council for Sustainable Development, Conches-Geneva, Switzerland; 2000).

World Commission on Environment and Development, *Our Common Future* (Oxford University Press, Oxford; 1987).

World Resources Institute, *Frontiers of Sustainability: Environmentally Sound Agriculture, Forestry, Transportation, and Power Production* (Island Press, Washington, DC; 1997).

World Resources Institute, *World Resources Report 2000–2001: People and Ecosystems: The Fraying Web of Life* (World Resources Institute, Washington, DC; 2000).

Zander, Rosabeth Stone and Benjamin Zander, *The Art of Possibility: Transforming Professional and Personal Life* (Harvard Business School Press, Boston; 2000).

Zoeteman, Kees, *Gaia-Sophia: A Framework for Ecology* (Floris Books, Edinburgh, Scotland; 1991).

INDEX

THE CIVIL CORPORATION
The New Economy of Corporate Citizenship

Simon Zadek

'*The Civil Corporation* offers knowledge and wisdom of benefit to all types of readers – business executives, scholars, public officials, NGO leaders and citizens'
Robert H Dunn, CEO, **Business for Social Responsibility**

'In *The Civil Corporation*, Simon Zadek spotlights the enabling social, economic and political contexts for corporate citizenship. A benchmark book'
John Elkington, Chair, **SustainAbility**, author, *The Chrysalis Economy: How Citizen CEOs and Their Corporations Can Fuse Values and Value Creation*

'[A] thoughtful and thought-provoking contribution to the increasingly important and inter-related topics of corporate citizenship and global governance'
Jane Nelson, Director, Leadership and Strategy, **International Business Leaders Forum**

'*The Civil Corporation* offers not only a fascinating description of cutting-edge controversies but also a clear pathway toward the new relationships and new forms of accountability that a sustainable economy will require'
Bob Massie, Executive Director, **CERES**, Chair, Global Reporting Initiative

SIMON ZADEK is chair and co-founder of the Institute of Social and Ethical AccountAbility. He has authored, co-authored and co-edited numerous books, reports and papers, including *Building Corporate AccountAbility* (Earthscan, 1997)

Hardback £19.99 • ISBN 1 85383 813 6 • 272 pages • Figures, index

To order, visit www.earthscan.co.uk
email: earthinfo@earthscan.co.uk • tel: +44 (0)1903 828 800
• fax: +44 (0)20 7278 1142

SUSTAINABLE BANKING AND FINANCE
The Financial Sector and the Future of the Planet
Marcel Jeucken

'A most welcome contribution to the complex debate concerning the role of powerful financial institutions as they consider how best to act on the challenges and opportunities raised by the environmental, social and economic components of sustainability. This book will certainly prove to be one of the key contributions to the finance–sustainability interface'
Jacqueline Aloisi de Larderel, Director, Division of Technology, Industry and Economics (DTIE), **United Nations Environment Programme** (UNEP)

'The issues raised in this book should be in the forefront of our minds. The natural self-interest so characteristic of the financial sector will be enlightened by this book, thereby improving the chances of continuity for each and every firm'
Pieter Stek, Executive Director, **World Bank**

'[C]ombines countless examples, blueprints and analyses to provide a detailed overview of the trend towards sustainable banking... The author is the first to tackle this subject in such broad and accessible terms'
From the Foreword by **Jan Pronk, Minister of Housing, Spatial Planning and the Environment**, The Netherlands

'This book is impressive in both its scope and depth and is, to my knowledge, the first major publication which deals integrally with all aspects of sustainability and banking'
From the Foreword by **Hans Smits**, Chairman, **Rabobank Group**, The Netherlands

MARCEL JEUCKEN is a senior economist at Rabobank Group in The Netherlands, with research interests in general banking trends and sustainable banking. He has written numerous papers and is author and (co)editor of several books, including *Duurzaam Bankieren* (1998) and *Sustainable Banking: The Greening of Finance* (2001, with Jan Jaap Bouma and Leon Klinkers).

Hb £29.95 • ISBN 1 85383 766 0 • 336 pages • Figures, tables, appendices, index

---

To order, visit www.earthscan.co.uk
email: earthinfo@earthscan.co.uk • tel: +44 (0)1903 828 800
• fax: +44 (0)20 7278 1142

GREENING THE CORPORATION
Management Strategy and the Environmental Challenge
Peter Thayer Robbins

Corporate responses to environmental challenges are hotly debated, and they are often held directly or indirectly responsible for significant worldwide environmental destruction. A number of corporations are beginning to respond to environmental and social concerns and are taking these into account. This process, known as 'the greening of the corporation' is fraught with contradictions since the foremost aim of corporations is to earn profits.

In this unique book, Robbins examines traditional and social–environmental corporate cultures, green management styles, environmental regulatory systems in North America, Europe and Asia and social auditing.

He analyses the approaches of four major international companies – ARCO Chemical, Ben & Jerry's, Shell and The Body Shop – and by identifying common elements he develops a management model to resolve the dilemmas and to combine environmental and business objectives.

PETER ROBBINS is a lecturer in sociology in the Institute of Water and Environment at Cranfield University.

Pb £17.95 • ISBN 1 85383 772 5 • 216 pages • Tables, index
Hb £45.00 • ISBN 1 85383 771 7

To order, visit www.earthscan.co.uk
email: earthinfo@earthscan.co.uk • tel: +44 (0)1903 828 800
• fax: +44 (0)20 7278 1142

For Product Safety Concerns and Information please contact our EU
representative GPSR@taylorandfrancis.com Taylor & Francis Verlag GmbH,
Kaufingerstraße 24, 80331 München, Germany

Printed and bound by CPI Group (UK) Ltd, Croydon, CR0 4YY
08/05/2025
01864327-0010